The Philosophy Workbook

To Diana

The Philosophy Workbook

FRANCIS ROBERTS

EDINBURGH UNIVERSITY PRESS

© Text, Francis Roberts, 2003
© Line drawings, Joakim Dyngeland, 2003

Edinburgh University Press Ltd
22, George Square, Edinburgh

Typeset in Stempel Garamond and Officina Sans
by Pioneer Associates, Perthshire, and
printed and bound in Great Britain by
Scotprint, Haddington

A CIP record for this book is available from the British Library

ISBN 0 7486 1696 9 (paperback)

Contents

Acknowledgements

One is never too old or too young to start philosophy, as I discovered when I embarked on a course of study at Edinburgh University after completing a mathematics and theoretical physics degree. I owe a great deal to my teachers there: Professors W. H. Walsh and R. W. Hepburn, Dr George Davie, Roy Bhaskar, Dr Margaret Paton and in particular Professor Barry Barnes of the Science Studies Unit, who guided me through the final stages of my doctoral research. The debt I owe these philosophers is all the greater because they clarified ideas which were sometimes inaccessible to a novice. I realised early on that the apparent obscurity of the philosophical ideas had two sources: the first was the language as well as the vocabulary used by many philosophers, and the second was the lack of technical skills on the part of the beginner.

It was with the intention of producing a text which addressed both these issues that the first ideas for a practical book were born. They were nurtured by contacts with colleagues from whom I also learnt a great deal. Among these I wish to mention two: Dr Henry Marsh and Dr Fiona Elliott have contributed in many unseen ways to the ideas which led to the writing of this text. Dr Marsh's own research into the modes of the imagination has reinforced the belief that all philosophical ideas are accessible through practical activities, and Dr Elliott has shown me that what can count as a teaching resource is limited only by our own imaginations.

The production of a book does not, however, depend solely upon the influences on the author, significant as these might be – and this one is no exception. During each stage of production, the Edinburgh University Press has been sensitive to the need to maintain the spirit of an interactive book. I am grateful to the copy-editor, Nicola Wood, for the patience and professionalism she has shown in the difficult task of harmonising the requirements of author, production and, most of all, the reader.

Various people made contributions which helped me to produce the type-script. Joakim Dyngeland drew the cartoons of Kant, Plato and Descartes. Dilys Marsden, Sonja Hilborne-Clarke, Liz Parry and Paul Roberts all made helpful comments on various aspects of the text. Professor John Richardson helped me understand the origins and development of some of our philosophical notions in ancient Greece, and my son Thomas improved my understanding of Kant by explaining the original German – I have sometimes used his translations in preference to the nineteenth-century ones. Thomas also assisted my wife Diana during the final stages of production of the typescript, and many of their suggestions on the content as well as the style of argument have found their way into the text – where the text flows smoothly and the argument is accessible to the reader, the credit is often theirs. It is impossible to overestimate Diana's contribution to this book: she is not as passionate about philosophy as I am, but for both of us it has been a labour of love.

Grateful acknowledgement is made to Dr Barry Coddens of Northwestern University, Illinois, for permission to reproduce material from the *Introductory Bulletin* prepared by the Department of Chemistry of the Weinberg College of Arts and Sciences Office of Undergraduate Studies and Advising.

HOW TO USE THIS BOOK

This workbook has been put together with three sets of people in mind: the undergraduate embarking on a course in philosophy who is looking for a book which will continue to be used in later years; the philosophy teacher who is looking for a text which can be used as a course text or a valuable adjunct to a course; and the general reader who does not have access to help provided by academic philosophers.

A workbook achieves more than a standard textbook because it develops specific skills in tandem with an understanding of the subject matter. In physics, archaeology or psychology the understanding of theories presented in a text is supplemented with practical skills which are learnt and improved through practical activities. Philosophy tends to be taught on the assumption that the student is already able to analyse a theory and to develop an extended argument. This book makes no such assumption – on the contrary, it assumes that practical skills and theoretical understanding progress together.

With this dual target in mind the first chapter provides the reader with a brief guide on how to use the book.

Laying the Foundations – The Philosopher's Stone

1

Taking school students to performances of Oscar Wilde's *The Importance of being Earnest* does not show them how a theatre works. Obliging them to study Harold Pinter or Shakespeare's plays does not automatically turn them into playwrights. Becoming a playwright calls for more than visits to the theatre and the study of classic plays: the students need to learn the basic principles of their craft, to know how theatres work and to understand how language and the stage can be used to evoke emotive and thought-provoking responses from an audience.

Fortunately, becoming a philosopher is a good deal less complicated. Our everyday experience of living gives us a good start: it provides us with many of the basic principles and skills required to develop our craft. In this chapter we shall identify some of these basic principles and skills and lay the foundations for their development in later chapters.

The Philosopher's Stone

Some of the alchemists of the Middle Ages wanted to get rich quick. They searched in vain for the *lapis philosophorum* (the philosopher's stone), a solid substance which could turn ordinary metals into gold or silver. They were deceived. Modern physicists and chemists can demonstrate that alchemy's potential riches were illusory: they do this by relying on the success of the theories and practices of modern science which involve applying laboratory-tested knowledge in situations outside the laboratories. These activities lead the scientist to a deeper understanding of how the world works.

Some modern scientists have claimed that philosophical study does not lead to knowledge – that it too is searching for the mythical philosopher's stone. One of the most famous among these was the theoretical physicist Richard Feynman. In his biography of Feynman, James Gleick (1992) quotes him as saying that philosophers 'are always on the outside making stupid remarks' (p. 13). The irony of this remark is that Feynman himself assessed the status of the scientific theories in his subject with some highly perceptive philosophical analysis.

One of the main aims of this book is to show that not all philosophers 'are always on the outside making stupid remarks'. The riches which philosophy can bring are real, even if they are not material. They are related to changing base knowledge into golden knowledge rather than base metals into gold or silver.

Philosophical understanding can make it possible for us to look behind ordinary technical skills, leading to a deeper command of a subject. It can do this in the same way as a feeling for music can turn sequences of sounds into an inspiring concert. An inspiring musician can generate a richness of experience which goes far beyond the bare sequence of sounds he generates. But no musician can guarantee access to these riches.

Similarly, there is no set route to the riches which philosophy can bring. Indeed, if we are not careful the study of philosophy can have negative effects. Just as alchemy in the Middle Ages diverted many scientists of the day from deepening their understanding of how chemical substances behaved, so it is also possible that some forms of philosophical study may divert people today from finding the pearls which can enhance the richness of normal knowledge. It is the intention here to help us to understand this risk.

Like all subjects, philosophy requires some special training – but it is a training which can help us to get a better understanding of all other subjects as well. It achieves this by developing an understanding of specific concepts and theories concerning the nature of explanations. This enables us to put subjects like science, history, mathematics, literature and the law under the microscope. A broader understanding of knowledge can be achieved by sharpening certain specific skills which promote a critical approach to all subjects. The explanations, discussions, activities and exercises in this book are designed to train the beginner in philosophy to develop these skills and, through their development, to reach an understanding of most of the main theories in Western philosophy.

The Structure of the Chapters

Philosophical study aims at developing or improving the following three capabilities:

1. the ability to **understand** *ideas or concepts* which are specific to philosophy;
2. the ability to **understand** *theories* which are commonly used by philosophers;
3. the ability to **understand** *the relationships between sets of theories* in general.

It also aims at developing or improving the following five competences:

4. the ability to **analyse** *ideas*, especially those set out in written passages;
5. the ability to **analyse** *claims, theories* and *hypotheses*;
6. the ability to **assess** *and* **formulate** *acceptable arguments*;
7. the ability to **assess** *and* **formulate** *rigorously logical arguments and counter-arguments*;
8. the ability to **formulate, develop** *and* **assess** *definitions, claims, theories* and *hypotheses* in the various subject areas of philosophy.

The last of these is especially significant: the hallmark of a philosopher is the ability to formulate and assess his or her own theories of morals, knowledge, beauty, truth and scientific progress.

The method used is 'empirical'. The word 'empirical' is used in philosophy in two senses: it can apply both to a **method** of doing something based on experience, and to a **type of theory** whose claims are based on, and supported by, experience.

The methods employed in this book are based on experience and it will be through participation in activities that the user of the book will gain access to the riches of philosophy. Reading and passively absorbing ideas is not seen here as a fruitful way to become good at philosophy. It is through constant and gradual practice that the understanding of philosophy can best develop and deepen. Like a garden, its flowers cannot be expected to bloom immediately; the gardener needs to prepare the ground, feed it and give gentle and constant attention to the growing plants.

The user of the book does not have to do the exercises (or participate in any debate generated by the discussions) in the specific order set out in the chapters which follow. It is possible to drop in on any of the discussions. The layout is designed to give clues as to what is being done in each section and the extensive cross-referencing allows readers to find any other relevant discussion quickly.

The text is bordered differently according to what the user is doing.

> A major philosophical theory or hypothesis is given
> a three-line border.

Only the claims, theories or hypotheses which are to be discussed are highlighted in this way. They are examined and analysed in full by means of discussions and exercises.

> Exercise and Discussion Exercises designed to improve our understanding of an idea or theory are placed against a shaded background.

Most of the suggested answers to the exercises and discussions are written in a separate section; this permits readers to develop their own answers without being influenced by those offered in the book. Some are written in the text immediately after the question: on occasions this is to preserve the flow of a discussion, but mostly it is to permit the reader to see an example of an answer.

In the separate Suggested Answers section each question has been reproduced (sometimes slightly adapted) alongside the suggested answer in order to avoid constant flipping back and forth and to reinforce the notion that questions and answers form part of a unified philosophical process. Where a question includes an introductory preamble this has been reproduced or summarised in the Suggested Answer section only when it is needed for one to understand the full implications of the question.

The reader is advised to try to produce her answer to an exercise before reading the suggested answer – it is firmly believed that it is by doing, rather than just reading, that one has the best chances of getting a sound understanding of philosophy. The formulation of a claim or set of claims is perhaps the most important activity of a philosopher. While the questions do not explicitly ask for reasons, these should be given whenever possible: giving valid and convincing reasons to substantiate the claims which make up a theory is the next most important activity of a philosopher.

The newcomer to philosophy is not expected to have all the skills that are needed to practise the subject. We are not born with the ability to put an argument together: we need to acquire it. The skills are developed gradually through practice, but, on occasions, a separate section is dedicated to the development of a particular skill or method of setting out an argument. These sections are clearly indicated by the use of the word 'method' in the sub-heading.

The suggested answers are by no means intended to be definitive – philosophy is an activity which involves constant refinement of an idea. The reader is invited to give a reaction to the author's suggestions, and spaces are provided to encourage the reader to comment or react to the author's suggested answer.

Comment

_____

_____

_____

Unfortunately a book format does not permit exchanges between author and reader.

> Questions which have either prompted or generated
> philosophical inquiries are put in a shaded border.

[A few passages are written in a different typescript and have square brackets. These contain notes and enrichment material; for example, discussions of the broader aspects of a theory, such as its historical origins, or on the origins or meanings of words. The continuity of the discussions will not be affected by the omission of these passages.]

The Order of the Chapters

If this were a book on mathematics or physics then it would be advisable to work through it, chapter by chapter, in the order set out in the book. Mathematics and physics are subjects which we learn in ways similar to building a house: we start with the foundations, then we build the walls, then the roof and finally we put together its beautiful interiors. On occasions we may need to build an extension on the side, add a window or maybe build upwards. Philosophy is very different: it is more like getting to know a person. When we first meet someone at a party or the person who teaches us art at school, we do not need to know their dates of birth in order to get to know them. We learn about people in bits and pieces and, by gradually building up more knowledge about people, we come to appreciate their strengths and weaknesses.

Something similar happens in philosophy: we do not have to start with any particular aspect of philosophy or with the ideas of any particular philosopher. This feature of philosophy as a subject is reflected in the possible uses which can be made of this book: for example, the reader is advised to work through Part I first, but thereafter can choose to read Part IV before Part II, or work through Part III before attempting anything else. Some chapters include advanced sections containing some difficult material that may require a more considered approach.

[Note: In an introduction to philosophy it is inevitable that personal pronouns will be used. When these refer to the specific properties of a general individual who could be either male or female, a single female or male pronoun has been used to denote the general person. The use of 's/he', of 'her or him', or of plural pronouns to indicate a singular subject, has all been avoided.]

PART I

WHAT IS PHILOSOPHY?

There are three aims of the first part of this book: to give an overview of philosophy as a subject, to develop some of the basic skills philosophers need to ply their trade but most of all to give a taste of what it is like to be involved in doing philosophy – and it is with philosophy as an activity that we begin in Chapter 2. The approach is gradual and graded, starting with descriptions and examinations of everyday experiences and the ways in which we describe and explain them. It is by asking questions about these descriptions and explanations that we begin our involvement in philosophy as an activity and begin to understand what makes the subject unique and absorbing. We then round off the chapter by answering the question, 'What is philosophy?'

In Chapter 3 we look at the beginnings of the subject, only to realise how modern most of the philosophers in ancient Greece were: without the advantages provided by particle accelerators and the benefit of two millennia of accumulated learning, they developed a deep understanding of the nature of the human condition, of knowledge in general and of science in particular. This gives us a basis for a brief introduction in Chapter 4 of the two main interrelated concerns of philosophers in ancient Greece: the nature of reality and the nature of values.

Philosophy as an Activity

2

This chapter is concerned with understanding the question, 'What is philosophy?' It focuses on philosophy as an activity rather than a set of beliefs. We assume that one of the best ways to understand the nature of any activity is to do it.

IN THIS CHAPTER

Concepts discussed

- Philosophy
- Consequentialism
- Analytic philosophy
- Empiricism
- Essentialism
- Continental philosophy

Skills developed

- Analysis of text
- Assessment of theories

References made to the following philosophers

- Immanuel Kant

'Philosophy'– Two Meanings

Usually the word 'philosophy' has one of two meanings. We either talk about '*a* philosophy' or simply about 'philosophy'. The *Oxford English Dictionary* (*OED*) tells us that '*a* philosophy' is 'a system which a person forms for the conduct of life'; it is a system of beliefs. '*A* philosophy' is a way of life, not an academic discipline, so it is not what we are looking for in this book.

In the second sense, 'philosophy' is an academic activity or discipline. Like all academic disciplines, it is characterised by particular types of problems and questions. Analysing the problems and answering the questions requires the philosopher to use certain methods and deploy particular skills.

We shall now try to understand what sort of activity philosophy is and what sort of problems and questions characterise it. To do this, we shall assess the following claim:

Taking part in a human activity is the best way to understand what it is (Claim 1). In order to investigate the strength of this claim about activities, we shall do an activity and assess the acceptability of Claim 1. Assessing the acceptability of a claim is a philosophical activity.

We shall try to see if experience can help us decide how good the claim is. This method of assessing how we can learn something also gives us an insight into a philosophical tradition. Obtaining knowledge through experience is a central principle of 'empiricist practice' in all forms of learning, including philosophy.

Exercise 2.1

1. Describe two human activities which can be understood well by doing them and without having thought about how the activity works.

_____

_____

2. Describe a human activity which can be understood well even without ever having done the activity.

_____

_____

3. Assess Claim 1 by giving it a grade A to F, with A being excellent and F being a failure. If it needs to be changed, amend Claim 1.

_____

_____

Suggested answers are on p. 241.

Understanding philosophy as an activity is, in some ways, similar to understanding acting. Everyone can do a bit of acting; we can all put ourselves in someone else's shoes, so we can all get a feel for what acting is. But you need to do it on a stage, in front of an unknown audience, to gain a fuller appreciation of the activity. The actors in a school play will have learned to recognise the magic of the stage. They will often carry that feeling of magic with them into adulthood. The professional actor, however, reaches a deeper understanding which comes with appropriate training and experience. The deeper understanding also enables the professional actor to generate experiences and emotions which are beyond the reach of the normal amateur actor.

Getting a feel for the magic of philosophy also comes with doing it. Like the amateur actor, the amateur philosopher can taste some of the excitement of a deeply rewarding activity. There is, however, a danger: an inadequately trained philosopher can become disillusioned and miss out on the rewards completely. Some amateur philosophers might not even know that the rewards exist. Fortunately, appropriate training, which also makes the trainee mentally fit, can guard against this disillusionment. We shall see that mental fitness is not difficult to achieve, and with it both illusion and disillusion can be avoided.

As with all training, we shall start with an exercise. The eventual aim of the exercise is to get a feel for what philosophy is by doing some of it. (The eventual aim that something is intended to reach is sometimes referred to as its 'final cause'.) The more immediate reason for doing the exercise is to develop some skills of analysis and we shall try to answer three types of question.

(i)   What are the consequences, for the person involved, of pursuing an activity?
(ii)   What exactly is the activity?
(iii)   How, if at all, are Questions (i) and (ii) related to each other?

Question (i) is a **consequentialist** question. It asks about the consequences, or results, of doing something. It focuses on what lies beyond the activity.
Question (ii) is an **essentialist** question. It asks about the internal structure, or form, of the activity. It focuses on what is internal to the activity.
Question (iii) is a **philosophical** question. It asks about the relationships between human activities by focusing on the principles which link them together. An example of this type of question is [Q2], on page 140, when we ask:

> What is the nature of the pressure which a person feels, to act in
>
> a moral manner? [Q1]
>
> How is this pressure related to moral value? [Q2]

Knowing how the pressure to behave morally is related to moral value enriches our understanding of moral theories. In a similar way, answering Question (iii) enriches our answers to Questions (i) and (ii) – it is the sort of question that someone seeking a deeper understanding of the world tends to ask. Understanding the relationship between 'consequentialist' and 'essentialist' issues is a typical concern of a philosopher: several 'consequentialist' and 'essentialist' moral theories have been developed and debated. Knowing how these are related helps us to improve our understanding of moral theories, as we shall see in Chapter 11. This, in turn, will help us to form better laws or enable us to lead better and more fulfilling lives.

As these are our first steps in the subject, we shall delay answering questions of type (iii) until we attempt Discussion Exercise 2.8 on page 20 below.

We shall, instead, start by using the distinction between 'consequentialist' and 'essentialist' issues in order to do some philosophy and familiar, everyday situations will be used to help us reach our aim. The eventual aim of our present exercises is to give us an insight into the nature of philosophy. Our first Discussion Exercise illustrates that both consequentialist and essentialist answers are often given to ordinary questions.

Discussion Exercise 2.2

A restaurant's kitchen assistant is asked why he washed the dishes after dinner.

1. Give three **consequentialist** reasons why he might have washed the dishes.

_____

_____

2. Give three **essentialist** reasons why he might have washed them.

_____

_____

Suggested answers

We could say that the dishes were washed to ensure that vermin would be discouraged from coming into the kitchen. Another reason might be to ensure that the restaurant manager paid the kitchen assistant at the end of the evening. It may also have been done to make room for the arrival of the dirty plates from the tables. These would all be 'consequentialist' reasons – they depend upon what someone believes the consequences or **outcomes** of washing the dishes might be. 'I washed the dishes to make sure the manager would subsequently pay me.' Alternatively: 'I washed the dishes to make sure that when the dirty plates subsequently arrived from the tables, there would be somewhere to put them.'

We could say that the dishes were washed because washing them is a kitchen assistant's duty; or because a kitchen assistant automatically washes dishes; or because this particular kitchen assistant enjoys having clean dishes. These would all be 'essentialist' reasons – they depend upon the nature of the action of washing the dishes or upon the nature of the kitchen assistant. 'I washed the dishes because it was my duty as a kitchen assistant.' Alternatively: 'I washed the dishes because I can't stand seeing dirty pans in a kitchen.'

Comment

_____

_____

_____

_____

Exercise 2.3

1. Give three **consequentialist** and three **essentialist** reasons for studying history.

_____

_____

2. Give one **consequentialist** and one **essentialist** reason why a car driver might stop at a red traffic light.

_____

_____

3. Formulate a question which can have only an **essentialist** answer.

_____

_____

4. Are there any human activities which have no **consequentialist** aspects?

_____

_____

Suggested answers are on p. 242.

We are nearly ready to shift our attention from cooking and history to philosophy. Let us first ask similar questions about other activities; for example, we can ask Questions (i) and (ii) about studying physics and gardening.

Discussion Exercise 2.4

1. What are the consequences, for the person involved, of studying physics?

_____

_____

. . .

2. What exactly is physics?

_____

_____

Suggested answers

In answering Question 1, we might say that the students of physics increase their understanding of the world, improve their ability to cope with some dangerous situations, learn how to exploit some favourable situations and develop techniques to control how objects change. In particular, they will increase their understanding of how physical bodies and fluids move, how they change shape and how their temperatures alter. They will also learn at least two things about how these changes operate. Firstly, they will learn how to isolate the mechanisms which bring about these changes and alterations – in other words, they will learn the techniques of laboratory investigation. Secondly, they will learn how to apply the knowledge gained in the special conditions of laboratories in uncontrolled, non-laboratory environments.

In answering Question 2, we might say that physics is the science which deals with the properties of matter and energy and the effects of different forms of energy on matter.

Comment

_____

_____

_____

Exercise 2.5

1. What are the consequences, for the person involved, of learning about gardening?

_____

_____

. . .

2. What exactly is gardening?

_____

_____

Suggested answers are on p. 244.

Discussion Exercise 2.6

1. What are the consequences, for the person involved, of studying subject X?

_____

_____

2. What exactly is subject X?
   (Where subject X is a subject of your choice, but not philosophy – not yet!)

_____

_____

No suggested answers are provided.

Before moving on to the first proper philosophical question, it is worth sharpening our analytical skills a little further. In order to take part in philosophical activities, we often need to be able to analyse what other people have said. This is a skill which is needed for us to cope with normal social activities (such as understanding normal conversation), but in an academic discipline it needs to be sharper: for example, a sociologist needs to be aware that the conclusions drawn from the results of a social survey must be compatible with the meanings of the terms used in the questionnaire used for the survey – a degree of awareness which is unnecessary and cumbersome in ordinary conversation.

Exercise 2.7

Read the following three paragraphs of text and then answer the questions asked about it. The text is taken from the Introductory Bulletin prepared by the Department of Chemistry of the Weinberg College of Arts and Sciences Office of Undergraduate Studies and Advising, Northwestern University, Evanston, Illinois.

Chemistry is the study of matter and its transformations. Chemists synthesize new compositions for many uses, such as medicines, superconductors, and structural and electronic materials. They determine the structure of compositions and explain their properties in terms of basic principles. Chemists seek to understand the processes that transform substances so that they may control their course and outcome. Because such transformations occur everywhere, in the earth and living systems and in the stars, chemistry is essential to understanding many other sciences. Chemistry is contributing to the solution of many pressing problems, not only acid rain and the disappearance of the ozone layer but also the revitalization of American industries and the exploration of space.

WHY STUDY CHEMISTRY?

There are many reasons for studying chemistry. Some students study chemistry because they find the subject interesting and challenging. There is great appeal in both the scientific rigor and the usefulness of chemistry. Some study chemistry because it provides the language and the conceptual framework for a deeper understanding of other subject areas – geology, biology, physiology, astronomy, environmental science, and energy studies.

The majority of students study chemistry because it is an essential part of the preparation for their professions, as chemists, engineers, physicians, dentists, consultants, etc. In recent years about one half of our chemistry majors have continued their studies in graduate school, primarily, but not exclusively, in chemistry doctoral programs. Most of these eventually find positions in research and development in the chemical industry, government, or academic institutions. Typically thirty to forty percent of our majors enter medical school after graduation, with a small number going into dentistry or law. About fifteen percent of recent graduates have taken positions as chemists in industrial or governmental laboratories without further study.

1. According to the text (line 1), what processes are studied in chemistry? And why do chemists seek to understand these processes (lines 4–7)?

•••

2. According to the text, what are the **consequentialist** reasons which should encourage someone to study chemistry?

_____

_____

3. According to the text, what are the **essentialist** reasons which lead some people to study chemistry?

_____

_____

4. Give some reasons why someone might **not** want to study chemistry. Contrast these negative reasons with the positive reasons given in the text. Can each negative reason be paired with a positive one?

_____

_____

Suggested answers are on p. 244.

Understanding Philosophy as an Activity – A First Step

On page 13 above three types of question were asked:

(i)   What are the consequences, for the person involved, of pursuing an activity?
(ii)   What exactly is the activity?
(iii) How, if at all, are Questions (i) and (ii) related to each other?

Having answered questions of type (i) and (ii), we now tackle questions of type (iii).

Discussion Exercise 2.8   A one-way or a two-way street?

(iii) How, if at all, are Questions (i) and (ii) related to each other?
In other words, how are the consequences of studying a subject or learning how to do an activity related to what the subject or activity is?

_____

_____

[Note: Understanding what is involved in answering a question is an important skill in philosophy. Breaking up the requirements of a question is known as 'deconstructing' the question (see Exercise 6.1, p. 67).]

Suggested answer (a beginner is not expected to go into such depth!)

This question requires us to carry out two investigations: firstly, we need to look at how studying a subject might change the subject itself. If the consequences of studying it change, does this mean that the subject has changed? Secondly, we need to look at how a change in the nature of the subject might change what happens to us when we study it. If a subject has changed, will the consequences of studying the subject also change?

These seem to be complicated, perhaps knotty, questions, but loosening and untying knotty questions is one of the skills a philosopher develops – it is a skill which is developed by working through this book. When answering a question, we need to know what the question is about. Question (iii) is about how we study a subject like physics or learn the principles of good gardening. It asks a question **about** the study of the general principles of some particular branch of knowledge, experience or activity. This is the type of question which many modern philosophers ask both in the 'analytic' and the 'Continental' traditions in philosophy.

Comment

_____

_____

_____

[Note: A strand of modern philosophy in the English-speaking world, which has developed from 'analytic philosophy' of the twentieth century, operates within a distinctly different framework from 'Continental philosophy'. This strand of philosophy sees the process of analysis as determining the acceptability of any claim.

'Continental philosophy', widespread in continental Europe, tends to focus on an examination of the forces which condition our knowledge. The word examination, rather than analysis, may be significant here.

'Analysis' is the process by which we resolve a complex thing into its simple elements; it comes from the Greek word αναλυσις (analysis), which means 'an unloosening or a release'. This unloosening is contrasted with 'synthesis', which is a process by which we construct a complex thing from its simple elements. The Continental tradition tends to look for a synthesis in philosophy rather than an analysis. Further, the 'Continental' philosopher is likely to argue that the processes of analysis may themselves be conditioned and so are not the bedrock on which philosophy is founded. The social conditions which fashion human knowledge form that bedrock.

Both traditions consider that: philosophy is 'the study of the general principles of some particular branch of knowledge, experience or activity.' (*OED*)]

In asking Question (iii) about gardening and physics we are asking a philosophical question. Our answers help us to understand more about the nature of gardening and physics. They help us understand something about the general principles of these particular activities or branches of knowledge.

In the cases of gardening and physics Question (iii) can be given a general answer as follows. In both cases, we can say that **the answer to the essentialist Question (ii) would affect the answer to the consequentialist Question (i)**. However, the reverse is not true: **the answer to (i) would not affect the answer to (ii)**.

We can now expand on this general answer and give some details. Suppose that apples were no longer to fall vertically from trees, but were to start seeking out people's heads as if they had homing devices. In these new circumstances it is possible that students might react differently to studying physics. What physics is influences any consequences which result from studying physics. If the behaviour of energy, gravity and physical objects changes then I am likely to react differently to studying them: Question (i), 'How am I affected by physics?' is **not independent of Question (ii)**, 'What is physics?'

By contrast, if my prospects of finding a job were suddenly to improve if I studied how apples fell out of trees, then it is highly unlikely that nature would change its ways and cause apples to behave differently. The consequences which result from studying physics do not influence what physics is. The way energy, gravity and physical objects behave does not change if I react differently to studying them: the question 'How am I affected by learning physics?' **is independent of the question** 'What is physics?'

Similarly, the way plants in general grow in soils of particular types does not change if I react differently to studying them: the question 'How am I affected by learning about gardening?' **is independent of the question** 'What is gardening?' We need to be precise about stating 'plants in general' here as it is possible that my own plants will grow better if I have green fingers! The way I react to learning about gardening can have an effect on the specific plants I look after.

The principles governing physics and gardening are somehow **independent** of how people react to physics and gardening.

Comment

_____

_____

A Philosophical Question about Philosophy

When it comes to philosophy, however, things are different. The way I react to studying philosophy is part of the subject matter of philosophy. This is because any explanation of my behaviour can be examined and criticised. Criticising explanations is an important form of philosophical activity. This means that Question (iii) (formulated above on page 13 and reproduced here) may have a different type of answer when we ask it of philosophy from when we ask it of physics and gardening.

(i)   What are the consequences, for the person involved, of pursuing an activity?
(ii)   What exactly is the activity?
(iii) How, if at all, are Questions (i) and (ii) related to each other?

1. Understanding **that the answer is different** is an important aspect of philosophy.
2. Understanding **why the answer is different** is also part of philosophy.
3. Understanding **whether the difference is important** is also part of philosophy.
4. Understanding **in what way different subjects differ** is also part of philosophy.

Gaining the understanding is philosophy in action. We began this in Discussion Exercise 2.8, which is the first thoroughly philosophical activity we have done.

Philosophy is one of the subjects which turns in on itself. The activity of doing physics is not one of the things that physicists study, but the activity of philosophy is one of the things, but not the only one, that philosophers study.

As we did in the cases of gardening and physics, we shall now ask Questions (i), (ii) and (iii) of philosophy.

Exercise 2.9

(i) What are the consequences, for the person involved, of studying philosophy?

_____

_____

Suggested answers are on p. 246.

Discussion Exercise 2.10

(ii) What is philosophy?

_____

_____

Suggested answer

One possible answer to Question (ii) emerged when asking how the consequences of studying gardening and physics were related to the natures of gardening and physics; in other words, asking Question (iii) of other subjects gives an indication of what the nature of philosophy is. This can be seen by referring back to the dictionary definition of philosophy given on page 21 above: philosophy is 'the study of the general principles of some particular branch of knowledge, experience or activity'. This definition looks at philosophy from a particular viewpoint: it sees philosophy from the viewpoint of human beings and their perception of reality. If we look at this definition from a different perspective, and perhaps even invert the viewpoint, we reach another dictionary definition of 'philosophy'. The different perspective consists of starting from what is perceived or experienced by humans, that is, a world they see as being 'out there'.

Let us now look at knowledge and experience from this position. The reality or imaginary nature of what is thought to exist becomes the framework within which philosophy is set. This framework of 'reality' generates another widely accepted definition of philosophy. Evidence for the wide acceptance of this definition is found in the *OED*, where one of the definitions is given as follows: philosophy is 'that department of knowledge or study which deals with ultimate reality, or with the most general causes and principles of things'. This definition has its origins in ancient Greece, where the subject has its roots. The first philosophers were concerned with what really exists, that is, with 'ultimate reality'.

Comment

_____

_____

_____

In order to understand this second definition of philosophy, we shall use the same strategy as before: we shall do some philosophy. This time, however, it is better to follow the historical path the ancient Greeks took, asking some of the same questions they asked.

The analysis involved in answering Question (iii) is more involved than one expects to find in an introduction. Only readers who feel reasonably comfortable about going more deeply into philosophical analysis at this stage should attempt Discussion Exercise 2.11; others should move directly to Chapter 3 and return to the exercise at a later date.

Discussion Exercise 2.11

Having answered Question (i) 'What are the consequences, for the person involved, of studying philosophy?' and (ii) 'What is philosophy?' we now turn our attention to:

(iii) How, if at all, are Questions (i) and (ii) related to each other?

Suggested answer

Question (iii) requires a little more attention than it did before.

We saw above (p. 21) that, in the cases of gardening and physics, the consequences on the student did not affect the nature of the subject: what gardening is remains unaffected by what I do or how I change by way of knowing more about gardening. The reverse is not, however, true: a change in what gardening is can alter the ways in which learning about it affect me. For example, if gardening suddenly were to become a cult activity mostly associated with a mystical religious order, then it is clear that this change would affect the ways in which I could learn to garden. The learning might become necessarily associated with certain rituals and oblige me to wear specific clothes and chant prescribed incantations at particular times of day.

The same applies to physics: the way I respond to learning physics (i) does not affect what physics is (ii), but what physics is (ii) affects (i) the way I respond to learning it. In both gardening and physics (i) does not affect (ii), but (ii) affects (i).

In the case of philosophy, however, Question (iii) is given a two-way answer. This is because my reactions to learning something form part of the very subject-matter of philosophy. Philosophy is concerned with, among other things, the nature of theories which explain human behaviour. If a new form of human behaviour emerges, then the explanations of human behaviour will alter. This, in turn, will alter any assessment of that explanation.

This means that philosophy **changes** if I react differently to studying it. How I might be affected by philosophy could significantly affect what philosophy is.

Comment

The Origins of European Philosophy in Ancient Greece   3

This chapter is concerned with understanding what has driven people in the past to become philosophers, and how this has led them to seek and provide answers to questions which still concern us today.

IN THIS CHAPTER

Concepts discussed

- Validity
- Justice
- Ethics
- Harmony
- Ontology
- Aesthetics
- Virtue
- Metaphysics

Skills developed

- Analysis of arguments
- Assessment of theories

Types of argument examined

- Deductions from premises
- *Reductio ad absurdum*

Philosophers whose ideas are discussed

- Thales
- Anaximander

References made to the following philosophers

- Anaximenes
- George Berkeley
- Thomas Kuhn
- Immanuel Kant
- Karl Popper

Setting the Scene

The first philosopher that we know about from the Greek period is Thales of Miletus whose date of birth was certainly before 600 BC; he is known to have predicted the eclipse of 585 BC, which suggests he was a 'cosmologist'.

[Note: A 'cosmologist' was someone who studied the 'cosmos', which is defined in the *OED* as 'the world or universe as an ordered system'. Liddell and Scott (1863), give four definitions of the word cosmos (κοσμος). The first is *'order, in order, duly'* while the fourth is *'the world or universe*, from its *perfect arrangement'*. This indicates that the cosmologist was someone who studied all aspects of the universe, but started with an assumption that it is ordered.]

In Thales' times there were no distinctions between specialists in different subjects or disciplines: someone who wanted to understand the world would study every aspect of it – the Greeks did not, for example, distinguish between politics, physics, poetry and theology. We know little of Thales' life and work from primary sources; much of our knowledge stems from what was written later by writers such as Aristotle. The main reference work in the English language is by John Burnet (Oxford 1920) who cites not only Aristotle as a secondary source, but also Theophrastus' book Φυσικων Δοχων (*Phusikôn doxôn*).

What seems to have singled Thales out was that he wanted to know *why* something happened as well as *how* it happened. From the theories he produced, we can deduce that he wanted to *understand* why things happened; he would not have been willing to accept a religious myth just because others had accepted it. He needed to be able to justify his knowledge by appealing to his ability to think.

The desire for explanations based on reasons, rather than on myths, made people like Thales different. They were literally lovers of knowledge, or 'philosophers'. The original Greek meaning of φιλοσοφια (*philosophia*) is the love of knowledge or wisdom, a meaning which is still used today. One of the *OED* definitions states philosophy is 'the love, study, or pursuit of wisdom, or knowledge of things and their causes, whether theoretical or practical'.

Exercise 3.1

1. Describe a situation in which someone has **wisdom** without **knowledge**.

_____

_____

2. Describe a situation in which someone has **knowledge** without **wisdom**.

_____

_____

Suggested answers are on p. 247.

Discussion Exercise 3.2

What is the relationship between **wisdom** and **knowledge**?

_____

_____

No suggested answers to Discussion Exercise 3.2 are provided at present. The question will be discussed after Chapter 12.

The modern academic definition of philosophy tends to lean in the direction of knowledge rather than wisdom. This constitutes a return to the original Milesian concept of philosophy and a shift away from the Athenian one of Socrates and Plato. The Platonic concept considered wisdom to be one of the four virtues, (see p. 36 below) and an essential feature of knowledge.

What Exists (1) Thales' Problem

As a scientist Thales wanted to know why things change. His aim was to discover why things decay, decompose, grow, mutate, melt or evaporate. If everything is always changing, is there then anything stable which determines or controls the changes? The answer Thales suggested rested on a basic idea, which we can call Thales' Hypothesis 1.

Thales' Hypothesis 1:

Everything is made of one fundamental, or primary, substance. Each thing we see is a mutation of the fundamental substance. This principle indicates that Thales wanted the explanation of why things change to be as simple as possible.

[Note: Modern physicists have had a similar desire to find explanations for the phenomena we experience based on the changes of a single type of substance: a century ago it was the atom, then it became the component part of the atom. Each time someone discovers subdivisions of these 'fundamental' particles, scientists start the search for theories which explain the subdivisions in terms of a single type of more fundamental particle.

Notice also the definition of chemistry given by the Department of Chemistry of the Weinberg College of Arts and Sciences: 'Chemistry is the study of matter and its transformations' (p. 19 above). This definition of chemistry assumes that Thales' Hypothesis 1 is valid. The search for simplicity seems to be what drives scientists. It has also driven philosophers through the ages. One of the most famous was William of Ockham (c. 1287–1347) who gave us 'Ockham's Razor' (see Glossary).]

Thales also proposed a solution to the problem of why things change, a solution which seems slightly ridiculous to us today. We can describe it as Thales' Hypothesis 2.

Thales' Hypothesis 2:

The one fundamental, or primary, substance is water. Everything we see, touch, smell, taste or hear is a mutation of water.

[Note: I have no evidence that Thales ever proposed what I have called Thales' Hypothesis 1. There is evidence, however, that he formulated the hypothesis which I have called Thales' Hypothesis 2 – Bertrand Russell tells us that 'According to Aristotle, he (Thales) thought that water is the original substance out of which all other substances are formed; and he maintained that the Earth rests on water.' (1946, p. 45) Russell's own source is John Burnet.

My claim here is that Thales' Hypothesis 1 is needed if Thales' Hypothesis 2 is to make sense. I also admit that one reason for splitting Thales' theory into two units is to show how modern his ideas were: they can be compared with the work of elementary particle physicists who tend to look for a single substance/particle which forms the basis of all physical matter.]

Exercise 3.3

1. Assess Thales' Hypothesis 2 by giving it a grade A to F, with A being excellent and F being a failure.

_____

_____

2. Give the reasons for your mark.

_____

_____

Suggested answers are on p. 248.

The assessment of Thales' Hypothesis 2 is based on the acceptability of his Hypothesis 1, so we ought to assess this as well.

Exercise 3.4

1. Assess Thales' Hypothesis 1 (p. 28) by giving it a grade A to F, with A being excellent and F being a failure.

_____

_____

2. Give the reasons for your mark.

_____

_____

Suggested answers are on p. 249.

What Exists (2) The Primary Substance and its Transformation

Thales was trying to understand the world around him. He wanted to understand why things change. The main question he asked himself was:

How do things change?

This is a question which modern scientists, rather than modern philosophers, ask.

[Note: This last statement needs to be qualified. Modern philosophers are very concerned about how concepts and conceptual systems change, especially in science. Descriptions of scientific revolutions and theories explaining how these occur have been commonplace among philosophers of the twentieth century – notably Thomas Kuhn and Karl Popper. These descriptions and theories will be discussed in Part IV, Chapter 13.]

Thales only partly answered the question: he suggested that changes were mutations of one single substance, namely water. He did not go on to say how water changed from a liquid we drink to the corn we eat or the linen we wear as clothing. Others were dissatisfied with his theory and proposed rival theories as to what makes up basic substances. In particular, Anaximander expanded Thales' theorem into what turned out to be a three-pronged claim: Anaximander, who was about 64 years old in 546 BC, also lived in Miletus – he is the second philosopher of the

Milesian School. More details of Anaximander's life and work are described by John Burnet (1920).

Anaximander's Three-pronged Claim

Claim (1): There is an infinite, eternal, ageless 'primary', or 'fundamental', 'substance'. The 'primary substance' is transformed into the subsidiary substances we know such as 'Earth', 'Fire', 'Air' and 'Water'.*

Claim (2): Each 'subsidiary substance' tries to establish itself as the dominant substance.

Claim (3): The primary substance maintains the balance between these 'subsidiary substances'. It does not favour any of them. It operates according to a principle of 'justice'.

[Note: The term 'Anaximander's Three-pronged Claim' is one which I have coined. It is used here in order to help the reader understand Anaximander's theory.

*The notions of Earth, Fire, Air and Water were not as specific as our modern ones. The Greeks' notion of 'fire' would be nearer to our modern notion of 'energy', and 'earth' would include a variety of substances such as 'ashes'. Anaximenes, the third philosopher of the Milesian School, developed a theory which is not all that different from the theories of modern physics. Russell, writing about Anaximenes in the *History of Western Philosophy*, states on p. 47:

> The fundamental substance, he said, is air. The soul is air; fire is rarefied air; when condensed, air becomes water, then, if further condensed, earth, and finally stone. This theory has the merit of making all the differences between different substances quantitative, depending entirely upon the degree of condensation.

Anaximenes' theory is similar to an obsolete theory of some modern physicists. In the early part of the twentieth century many scientist believed that hydrogen was the fundamental element and all other elements developed by the repeated fusing of hydrogen atoms.]

Anaximander's second and third claims suggest that there are purposes which determine the changes we experience. These purposes, ends or aims provide answers to another question philosophers and scientists have asked themselves:

Why do things change?

Anaximander provides us with two 'principles' which guide us in our search for any specific explanation of how things change. These principles are Claims (1) and (2) above. Here we have the real beginnings of philosophy. Philosophy can be seen as a process in which we search for, and assess, a set of principles which govern the explanations of the phenomena we experience. This brings us to a more modern definition of philosophy: philosophy is the search for, and assessment of, the principles which sustain and govern the explanations of the phenomena we experience.

Let us now get involved in some philosophical activity of the type described in this definition. We shall assess how Anaximander justified his claim that the 'primary substance' is neutral in its dealings with the subsidiary substances.

Exercise 3.5

It is believed that Anaximander developed an argument which he claimed established that water, or any other element, cannot be the **primary substance**. The argument appears in Aristotle's book *Physics* (1024b), which is believed to be a rewriting of Anaximander's argument.

α (*alpha*) Suppose that one of the known elements, such as earth, fire, air or water, is the **primary substance**.

β (*beta*) The elements are in opposition to each other: air is cold, water is moist, and fire is hot.

γ (*gamma*) If one element were the **primary substance**, it would conquer the others. The **primary substance** would become infinite; the rest would have ceased to exist by now.

δ (*delta*) Elements which are in opposition to each other have not ceased to exist.

ε (*epsilon*) We can conclude that (α) is false. The **primary substance** is neutral and cannot be one of the elements which is in opposition to the others.

[Note: The argument was taken from Russell (1946), who does not tell us whether earth was in opposition to the other elements.]

> **1. Is Anaximander's argument a valid one? Justify your answer.**

General advice: Firstly, you will need to determine which statements are the premises. Secondly, you will also need to say whether there are any premises which have not been stated. Are there any unstated assumptions being made in the argument? Finally, you will need to say whether the final conclusion has been validly deduced from the premise(s).

> **2. Determine whether Anaximander's argument is an acceptable one.**

You will need to discuss the acceptability of the premises as well as of the deduction.

• • •

[Note: If an argument is **invalid**, then it **cannot be acceptable**. If all its premises are acceptable and it is valid, then the argument is acceptable. If not all its premises are acceptable and it is valid, then the argument is not acceptable. This means that a **valid** argument might, or might not, be an **acceptable** one.]

Suggested answers are on p. 250.

What Exists (3) The Search for Reality

Just as Thales had done before him, Anaximander addressed the question

How do things change?

This scientific question concerns what happens in nature. The answer Anaximander gave it, in what was described above as his second claim (p. 31), was: Each 'subsidiary substance' tries to establish itself as the dominant substance.

This is similar to some of the principles to be found in modern science. Not only does it address the question of **how** things change it also looks at **why** they change. There are many parallels in modern science: for example, the principle of Natural Selection provides the logical and theoretical basis on which the Theory of Evolution stands – developed by Charles Darwin in Chapter 4 of *The Origin of Species*. This principle gives us a framework within which we can understand why evolution occurs, and in doing this we are practising science.

The point at which scientific and philosophical activities merge is when they come to the question of how one validates a scientific claim such as the one incorporated in the principle of Natural Selection and this is important when we assess the Theory of Evolution's acceptability. The assessment of the validity of theories and the validation processes themselves are both activities which form part of modern philosophy of science.

In a similar way, assessing the validity of Anaximander's second claim is an activity which we would today describe as a philosophical activity. The processes of questioning theories such as Thales' hypothesis and Anaximander's three-pronged claim marked the real beginnings of European philosophy. By assessing Thales' hypothesis and Anaximander's Claim 1 we inquire into the nature of existence.

The modern branch of philosophy in which theories about what exists are developed is known as 'ontology'. A broader branch of philosophy known as 'metaphysics' deals with the examination and validation of those theories, as well as with their development.

By assessing Anaximander's Claim 2 we inquire into the nature of explanations of what happens in the physical world.

[The branch of philosophy which inquires into the nature of knowledge in general is known as 'epistemology'; the one which inquires into the nature of explanations of natural phenomena is known as the 'philosophy of science'. Inquiries into the nature of explanations of social phenomena come under the umbrella of the 'philosophy of the social sciences'.]

By assessing Anaximander's Claim 3 we inquire into the nature of values and of explanations of what distinguishes good human behaviour from bad.

[Note: There are several branches of philosophy which inquire into the nature of values and of explanations of how values affect behaviour. Among the most frequently studied we find: 'moral philosophy' or 'ethics'; 'aesthetics'; the 'philosophy of religion'; and 'political philosophy'.]

The assessment and criticisms of Thales', Anaximander's and Anaximenes' theorems led scholars in ancient Greece to try to find answers to two fundamental questions. The most famous among these scholars are probably Parmenides, Socrates, Plato and Aristotle. These questions are now universally recognised as belonging to formal philosophical activity:

What really brings about the changes we experience?

or

What is **ultimately real**? [Q1]

---

and

What gives value to the changes we experience?

or

What is **ultimately valuable**? [Q2]

Thales' hypothesis and Anaximander's first principle provide us with starting points for the construction of an answer to [Q1]. In doing Exercises 3.3 and 3.4 we assessed Thales' hypotheses. We shall now assess Anaximander's.

Exercise 3.6

1. Assess Anaximander's first principle (p. 31) by giving it a grade A to F, with A being excellent and F being a failure.

· · ·

2. Assess Anaximander's second principle by giving it a grade A to F, with A being excellent, and F being a failure.

3. Describe something which can be seen yet is usually accepted as being **unreal**.

4. Describe something which cannot be seen yet is normally thought to be **real**.

Suggested answers are on p. 252.

Discussion Exercise 3.7

Consider the following:
Only our perceptions are real. Things like tables, chairs and dogs do not exist. We believe they exist because we perceive them with our senses. We build them in our imaginations, and they exist only in our imaginations.

5. Give one reason why this claim might not be acceptable to a reasonable person.

This is the sort of claim which 'idealist' philosophers such as George Berkeley make. No suggested answers are given at present as this is a topic which will be discussed in the suggested answer to Discussion Exercise 8.2, p. 282.

What Exists (4) 'Justice' and the Search for Values

As we have seen, Anaximander was not only searching for an answer to the question concerning how things change, he also wanted to discover why things change. We indicated above, on page 31, that the second part of his three-pronged claim indicates that there is a purpose behind the operations of nature.

The third part indicates that he believed that there is a **value** associated with the purpose. Claim (3): The primary substance maintains the balance between these 'subsidiary substances'. It does not favour any of them. It operates according to a principle of 'justice'.

This answer gives a sense of purpose to the operations of the 'primary substance'. There is value associated with the work of nature; it attempts to establish harmony in the world. This idea was natural to the ancient Greeks. There was not the same division between religion and science as we find in modern European culture. The Greeks believed that the notion of justice or 'harmony' applied to anything that changes, whether natural or social. Indeed, it is unlikely that they would have made the same distinction as we do between 'natural' and 'social' – a distinction which will be briefly discussed when we meet the concept of a social construct. In view of this, it is likely that our modern word 'justice' is probably not an entirely accurate translation of the Greek word.

[Note: Francis Cornford, whose translation of Plato's *Republic* is perhaps the most widely used one in the English language, writes:

> The Greek word for 'just' has as many senses as the English 'right'. It can mean: observant of custom, righteous; fair, honest; legally right, lawful; what is due to or from a person, deserts, rights; what one ought to do. Thus it covers the whole field of the individual's conduct in so far as it affects others – all that they have a 'right' to expect from him or he has a right to expect from them, whatever is right as opposed to wrong. A proverbial saying declared that **justice is the sum of all virtue.** (emphasis added)

Cornford is here referring to 'the four cardinal virtues' which were widely accepted as the basis of morality in Greek culture. These virtues were: 'wisdom', 'moderation' (or 'temperance'), 'fortitude' (or 'courage') and 'justice'.

In *The Laws*, Bk. I, 631, Plato emphasises this division of virtues: '**Wisdom** is the chief and leader: next follows **temperance**; and from the union of these two with **courage** springs **justice**. These four virtues take precedence in the class of divine goods' (emphasis added).

Plato sees 'justice' as a union or harmony between the other virtues; the notion of maintaining a balance is deeply imbedded in the Greek concept of 'justice'. This is why it would make sense for a Greek scholar like Anaximander to talk about the primary substance operating according to a principle of justice.

It is interesting to note that there was more than one expression which is now translated as 'justice' in Greek: Plato used the term δικαιοσυνη (*dikaiosunê*) in *The Republic*, but elsewhere also used το δικαιον (*to dikaion*). The word αδιοκια (*adikia*) meant wrongdoing and δικη (*dike*) meant 'penalty', but could also mean justice in the more abstract sense of *dikaiosunê*.]

Philosophy as a Subject

4

This chapter is concerned with understanding the question, 'What is philosophy?' It focuses on what is of concern to philosophers; namely, the study of reality and the study of values associated with reality. To gain a better understanding of what these two broad areas of philosophy are, we briefly examine the way modern philosophy has split into branches concerned with facts and values, with what exists and the values associated with what exists.

IN THIS CHAPTER

Concepts discussed

- Ontology
- Fact/value distinction
- Epistemology
- Value and values

Skills developed

- Analysis of arguments
- Assessment of theories

Types of argument examined

- *Reductio ad absurdum*

Philosophers whose ideas are discussed

- David Hume

References made to the following philosophers

- Karl Popper
- Thomas Kuhn

The Study of What Really Exists

The discussions and exercises in Chapters 2 and 3 have enabled us to determine two general, but inter-linked, areas of philosophical activity: the study of reality and the study of values associated with reality. This directed our attention to what marked the beginnings of European philosophy in ancient Greece. We have already noted (on p. 24), that one of the principal philosophical activities in ancient Greece dealt with reality, or what really exists, and how it is known to us. This remains, to this day, one of the main areas of philosophical activity.

In modern philosophy what we term 'metaphysics' and 'ontology' cover the areas of inquiry which examine the nature of reality and what exists.

The discussions of the origins of European philosophy have led to the identification of various definitions of philosophy as an academic study. Among these we have found a modern definition in which we consider that 'philosophy' is the search for, and assessment of, the principles which sustain and govern the explanations of the phenomena we experience. The second part of this definition captures the essence of a particular branch of philosophy, one which inquires into the nature of knowledge. 'Epistemology' is the branch of philosophy which inquires into the nature and scope of knowledge and into the reliability of claims to knowledge.

There are two sub-domains of epistemology which have developed into specialist subjects in modern philosophy. They both inquire into the nature of explanations of natural and social phenomena: the 'philosophy of science' is the branch of epistemology which inquires into the nature of our knowledge of the physical world; and the 'philosophy of the social sciences' is the branch of epistemology which inquires into the nature of our knowledge of the social world.

[Note: The phenomenon of scientific change and progress is a social phenomenon, so technically it ought to be a concern of the philosophy of the social sciences; however, philosophers such as Karl Popper and Thomas Kuhn inquiring into the nature of science and of scientific knowledge have also addressed the issue of scientific change and progress. This has led to its incorporation into the philosophy of science.]

Exercise 4.1

1. State, on a scale of 0 to 10, how confident you are that the book you are reading really exists and is not just a figment of your imagination. Describe an event which would (1) increase, (2) decrease the confidence. (10 = certain that it exists, 0 = certain that it does not exist).

_____

_____

. . .

2. State, on the same scale of 0 to 10, how confident you are that books in general exist, irrespective of whether or not they are being read. Describe an event which would (1) decrease the confidence, (2) increase the confidence.

_____

_____

Physicists tell us that electrons cannot be seen, as they are smaller than the wavelength of visible light. The eye cannot pick them out; it is restricted to detecting the effects electrons have on special equipment, usually involving oscilloscopes. They tell us that a television set works by firing electrons against a screen.

3. State, on the same scale of 0 to 10, how confident you are electrons exist. Describe an event which would (1) decrease the confidence, (2) increase the confidence.

_____

_____

No suggested answers are given to Exercise 4.1 as this is a topic which will be discussed in the answers to Exercise 7.6, p. 275.

Discussion Exercise 4.2

Is the knowledge of the existence of books, which depends on our direct perception, more certain than the knowledge of the existence of electrons, which we cannot perceive directly?

_____

_____

No suggested answers are given as this topic is discussed in some detail in Chapters 5 and 6.

• • •

One area of epistemology is the 'philosophy of the social sciences', which has itself generated further branches of philosophy which straddle the fact/value divide. Among these we find 'political philosophy' and the 'philosophy of psychology' along with its sister subject, the 'philosophy of mind'.

The 'philosophy of mind' is the branch of philosophy in which we 'formulate, develop and assess' the principles governing theories which explain the relationships between mind and matter.

[Note: Cognitive functions are those functions which determine how we understand concepts as well as the way things work. These will be discussed throughout the remaining chapters, and also in some detail in Part V.]

It is here that the many subdivisions of philosophy tend to break down. When inquiring into the nature of the theories which explain the cognitive functions of humans, it may be impossible to ignore questions about moral and/or aesthetic values. Naturally, the question of whether it is possible to ignore these is itself a question which interests philosophers. A brief examination of the definition of political philosophy will show us that when epistemology is concerned with explanations of human behaviour, it is either very difficult, or maybe even impossible, to avoid discussing the values associated with that behaviour.

'Political philosophy' is the branch of philosophy in which we formulate, develop and assess the principles governing the theories which explain the relationships between individuals, social groups and the government.

While political philosophy has aspects which are epistemological, its main focus of attention is on the values associated with human behaviour and the operations of institutions created by humans. It is concerned with more than just the interactions between the individual and government. Political philosophy is also concerned with the nature of the set of 'values' which enable and constrain the formation and development of those relationships. It questions whether these values are natural and somehow inherent in human beings or whether humans create them. In political philosophy there is an overlap between 'descriptive' questions about what happens and 'normative' questions about what ought to happen.

The overlap would not have surprised philosophers in ancient Greece, as they did not have any of our modern formal distinctions between various areas of philosophy. They merely got on with trying to understand the world and the principles which governed their understanding of it. This meant that they inevitably wanted to know how well they understood something; *de facto* they were automatically involved in what we call 'epistemology'. However, they found that inquiring into how well they understood something naturally led to inquiries into the nature of values and to explanations about how values affect behaviour. As we saw on page 27, Greek 'cosmologists' studied 'The world or universe, from its perfect arrangement.' Justice for them was to be found everywhere in the universe. What is the case could not be separated from what ought to be the case – facts and values were inevitably intertwined. It is not surprising that the search for what constitutes the 'just' or 'good' life became an important, perhaps the most important, aspect of their activities. This may be why, even today, we still use the term 'philosophy' to mean 'a system which a person forms for the conduct of life'.

[Note: In the modern 'analytic' tradition in philosophy, the separation between facts and values has been virtually taken for granted. This probably has its origins in David Hume's discussion in his famous passage on the imperceptible, and in his opinion, illicit, move from 'is' to 'ought' in moral discourse (see p. 163 below). More recent developments in this tradition have begun to question the rigid separation – see, for example, 'Beyond the Fact/Value Dichotomy' Hilary Putnam (1990, Ch. 9).

In the 'Continental' tradition the impossibility of such a separation is hardly ever questioned. All philosophical traditions, however, consider it important to inquire into explanations of how values are associated with what happens in the world.

It should be emphasised that in no philosophical tradition do we find a mix up between fact and value; the two concepts are distinct. The difference between the 'Continental' and the 'analytic' traditions can be understood using an analogy of a triangle. The Continentals would argue that fact and value inhere in every statement just as area and perimeter inhere in every triangle; they are different but both equally necessary, aspects of being a triangle. Philosophers in the analytic tradition would argue that fact and value are more like the length and colour of the perimeter of a triangle: a perimeter can be either red or not red without affecting its length. Similarly, a statement can have, or not have, value without affecting its factual content.]

The Study of the Values Associated with Reality

The study of the nature of values in human behaviour has led to the development of various branches of philosophy. These branches are concerned with the values associated with the things and structures humans perceive as real and the appearance and behaviour of those things and structures. The areas of study which focus on value and values today include two major branches of philosophy: ethics and aesthetics.

'Ethics' (or 'moral philosophy') and 'aesthetics' are the branches of philosophy which deal with the values associated with what really exists.

Moral Values and their Associated Fields of Study

Specifically, ethics is concerned with moral value (the worth or usefulness of human actions) and moral values (the principles which determine codes of human behaviour).

'Ethics' (or 'moral philosophy') is the branch of philosophy which inquires into the nature of right, wrong, good, evil, duties and responsibilities and into the nature of theories about right, wrong, good, evil, duties and responsibilities.

The importance of this branch of philosophy is found mostly in how it affects our rules of human behaviour. This can be seen by attempting a brief exercise.

Exercise 4.3

Consider the following actions:

(i)   I pour some ice cold water on a rock. As a result the rock cracks.
(ii) I pour some ice cold water on a vine which normally produces poor grapes. As a result the vine produces even poorer grapes.
(iii) I pour some ice cold water on a cat. As a result the cat lets out a wild screech.
(iv) I pour some ice cold water on a 90-year-old man. As a result the man catches a cold.

Let us assume that, in each case, pouring some ice cold water is not part of a ceremony or a ritual – there is no special meaning associated with the act. Nothing and no one else other than the recipient of the ice cold water is directly affected.

1. In each case (i) to (iv), state whether you believe that the act has a moral value.

_____

_____

2. In each of the cases (i) to (iv) it is possible to claim that the action is a moral act. Give a possible reason in each case and state whether it is a **consequentialist** reason, an **essentialist** reason or neither consequentialist nor essentialist.

_____

_____

3. In each case (i) to (iv), state whether I have a duty to refrain from pouring the ice cold water.

_____

_____

• • •

4. Are duty and moral value necessarily inter-linked?

_____

_____

5. How, if at all, is the result of an action related to whether it has moral value?

_____

_____

No suggested answers are given to Exercise 4.3. We shall discuss the issues raised in this exercise in Chapter 11.

Questions concerning the moral values of actions and/or rules underpin the ways in which we assess legal, social, political and religious systems. The philosophy of law is not discussed directly in this introductory book, but, as has been indicated above, the other areas which touch on human moral values are studied. One aspect of the philosophy of religion, the existence of God, is discussed in Chapter 14. A preliminary definition of the subject could be stated as: 'The philosophy of religion' is the branch of modern philosophy which inquires into the nature of theories about the existence of God and the values associated with beliefs in God or in a supernatural being.

Aesthetic values

Aesthetics is the other branch of modern philosophy which inquires into theories about the nature of the values associated with the things and structures humans perceive as real, and the appearance and behaviour of those things and structures.

'Aesthetics' is the branch of modern philosophy which inquires into the nature of beauty and theories about beauty. To the extent that art is concerned with beauty, aesthetics also concerns itself with theories about the nature of art.

The nature of the theories of aesthetics will be briefly investigated in Chapter 10. The branches of philosophy identified in this chapter form the basis of the discussions and exercises found in the succeeding chapters.

Part I: A Summary

We have used empirical methods to develop an understanding of modern philosophy. It was pointed out on page 12 that the word 'empirical' is often used in different ways in philosophy. It can apply to a method of doing something as well as to a theory. The methods used in the book are overtly empirical. However, the philosophical principles being promoted in it will view the empirical traditions of the English-speaking world with a critical eye. It is important to distinguish between the use of the term to describe a **method** and its use to describe a **theory**.

By experiencing what it is like to get directly involved in philosophical activity, we are likely to understand what philosophy is. In philosophy we often ask questions and analyse possible answers. This approach is used extensively in this book.

The discussions in Part I have mostly involved responses to questions. The first question, which was asked in Chapter 1, was: '**What does philosophical study aim at?**'

[Note: This question itself prompts and generates philosophical inquiries.]

Philosophical study aims at developing or improving the following three capabilities:

1. the ability to **understand** a set of *ideas or concepts* which are specific to philosophy;
2. the ability to **understand** a set of *theories* which are commonly used by philosophers;
3. the ability to **understand** *the relationships between sets of theories* in general.

It also aims at developing or improving the following five competences:

4. the ability to **analyse** *ideas*, especially those set out in written passages;
5. the ability to **analyse** *claims, theories* and *hypotheses*;
6. the ability to **assess** *and* **formulate** *acceptable arguments*;
7. the ability to **assess** *and* **formulate** *rigorously logical arguments and counterarguments*;
8. the ability to **formulate, develop** *and* **assess** *definitions, claims, theories* and *hypotheses* in the various subject areas of philosophy.

The second question, which was asked in Chapter 2, was: '**What is philosophy?**'

'Philosophy' as an academic discipline was distinguished from '*a* philosophy', 'a system which a person forms for the conduct of life'. Four slightly different, but related, definitions of philosophy as an academic discipline were discussed.

1. The study of the general principles of some particular branch of knowledge, experience or activity.
2. That field of knowledge or study which deals with ultimate reality, or with the most general causes and principles of things.
3. The love, study, or pursuit of wisdom, or knowledge of things and their causes, whether theoretical or practical.
4. The search for, and assessment of, the principles which sustain and govern the explanations of the phenomena we experience.

In doing the activities and exercises in this book, the reader will be developing the concept of philosophy specified in definition (4).

The third question, which was asked in Chapter 3, was: '**Where did philosophy begin?**'

The answer given was: 'As far as we know, in Miletus in Ancient Greece.'
    An examination of what was happening in Miletus indicated that the philosophers of the time were asking themselves some fundamental questions.
    This led to our asking the fourth question:

> How do things change?

This led naturally to the fifth, and more significant, question:

> Why do things change?

The members of the Milesian School, Thales, Anaximander and Anaximenes gave scientific answers to these scientific questions. In Chapter 13 the nature of scientific answers to questions will be discussed. Thales, Anaximander and Anaximenes also attempted to assess the validity of their answers; we begin our own discussion of what constitutes 'validity' in Chapter 5, and continue it throughout the remainder of the book. This search for validity led to the search for answers to two fundamental questions, [Q1] and [Q2]:

> What really brings about the changes we experience?
>
> or
>
> What is **ultimately real**? [Q1]

> What gives value to the changes we experience?
>
> or
>
> What is **ultimately valuable**? [Q2]

The search for answers to these two questions has led, over the centuries, to the development of specialist areas of philosophy. Many of these were identified in Chapter 4. The discussions in Parts II to VI will guide the reader through most of the obstacles which lie in the way of deepening our understanding of how we humans interact with the complex world we live in.

Revision Exercises

Revision Exercise 2.1

At dawn one morning an early bird leaves its nest in search for food. It catches a worm. An ornithologist is watching and records the following events.

(i)   A small hole is found in the earth at the point where the bird caught the worm.
(ii) The bird flies back to its nest carrying the worm.
(iii) The bird feeds the worm to its chicks.
(iv) The bird's chicks are no longer making as much noise as they were before being fed.
(v)   Having fed its chicks, the bird is standing on the edge of its nest. It is casting a shadow on a squirrel which is at the foot of the tree.

1. Specify which of the events (i) to (v) are accidental consequences of the bird's successful foraging expedition and which are not accidental. Explain your answers.

. . .

2. Are the accidental consequences of foraging related to the essential features of foraging?

_____

_____

Suggested answers are on p. 253.

Revision Exercise 2.2

The following two dictionary definitions of philosophy were given above:

(i) 'the study of the general principles of some particular branch of knowledge, experience or activity' (p. 21)
(ii) 'that department of knowledge or study which deals with ultimate reality, or with the most general causes and principles of things' (p. 24).

Decide whether each of the following claims is a philosophical claim. If it is, state whether it comes under definition (i), (ii) or both (i) and (ii). Give a justification for your decision. State why you believe it is an example of (i) and/or (ii). State also why you believe it is not an example of (i) or (ii).

1. The methods an ornithologist uses to gather data can affect the accuracy of the results.

_____

_____

Suggested answer

This claim seems clearly to be of definition type (i) as the gathering of data is done in science. Such a claim about how this might affect the accuracy of results will apply to all scientific activity. This means that it falls under the category of a 'study of the general principles of some particular branch of knowledge'.

The claim is not of definition type (ii). The question is about the methods in science and methods are not related directly to 'ultimate reality'; at best, the methods might restrict the scientist to certain parts of 'ultimate reality'.

Comment

_____

_____

_____

2. The existence of God can be neither proved nor disproved.

_____

_____

3. Modern physicists are near to finding the fundamental building blocks of matter.

_____

_____

4. 'Do not commit murder' is a fundamental law which applies to all human beings.

_____

_____

Suggested answers are on p. 254.

Revision Exercise 2.3

Are Claims 1 and 2 in Revision Exercise 2.2 **valid** claims?

_____

_____

Suggested answers are on p. 255.

[Note: It may be interesting to try this exercise immediately after working through Part I, and then again after finishing the whole book. The differences in approach to the answers should give an indication of the effect of having taken the first steps in philosophy.]

Revision Exercise 2.4

The cartoonist on p. 14 suggests that Kant's reason for writing the *Critique of Pure Reason* was to avoid washing the dishes. Kant is giving a negative reason for doing something.

> 1. Is Kant giving an **essentialist** or a **consequentialist** reason for writing the *Critique of Pure Reason*?

> 2. Give an example of a negative reason for doing something which is **essentialist**.

Suggested answers are on p. 256.

Revision Exercise 3.1

The ancient Greeks asked the question: 'How do things change?' Anaximander claimed that when something changes, its change is brought about by something else; only the primary substance does not change.

> 1. Is it possible for something to change completely on its own without outside influences? In other words, does Anaximander's claim hold true for all changes?

[Note: In order to give a **negative** answer to a question about **all** changes, we need only find one example of a change which occurs without any outside influences. Giving a **positive** answer involves giving reasons why no object can transform itself on its own.]

. . .

2. When you change your mind, is it always because of an outside influences?

_____

_____

Suggested answers are on p. 257.

Revision Exercise 3.2

The ancient Greeks asked the question: 'Why do things change?' In answering this question, Anaximander suggested that nature operates according to a principle of **justice**. He claimed that when something changes, the changes are brought about for a reason; to **maintain order,** or to ensure that a principle of justice is upheld.

1. Is a partial absence of order in the world possible? In other words, could the world still function with just a little bit of disorder?

_____

_____

2. Can a bit of disorder be thought of as a good thing? In other words, does **justice** always have to involve total order?

_____

_____

3. Let us suppose that nature operates according to a principle of **justice**. Does this mean that there must be something, or some being, beyond nature which generates or maintains the justice?

_____

_____

Suggested answers are on p. 257.

Revision Exercise 3.3

The ancient Greeks asked questions about what is real, that is, about what exists.

> Are ideas just as real, more real, or less real than mountains, trees and houses?

Suggested answers are on p. 259.

Further Reading

Kenny, Anthony (ed.): *The Oxford Illustrated History of Western Philosophy* (Oxford University Press, 2001). This is less extensive but more up-to-date than Russell's history. It includes sections on Continental philosophy, but there is not much there for a reader who believes that aesthetics is part of philosophy.

Russell, Bertrand: *History of Western Philosophy* (George Allen & Unwin, 1946). This is a veritable tour de force covering the history of Western philosophy from its birth in ancient Greece through to the beginning of the twentieth century. Its one drawback is the total absence of any discussion of aesthetics.

PART II

REALITY, PERCEPTION and BELIEF

In Part II we take a journey through reality. We have already seen in Chapter 2 (p. 26) that Greek philosophers were concerned with what really exists – with 'ultimate reality'. Our concern is more modest: we restrict ourselves to what exists without being concerned with whether this existence is ultimate. In the last chapter of Part II, however, we examined a reaction to the conviction that the 'ultimate reality' consists of the phenomena we experience using our senses. The first part of our present journey, in Chapter 5, takes us through the relationship between reality and our sensations and actions. We take a detour in Chapter 6, without leaving the topic of reality, by focusing more on the skills we need to develop our theories. Chapter 7 takes up the theme of how the development of our thoughts, theories and beliefs is related to reality.

When considering how our senses and reality are related, we rarely question our assumption that the phenomena we experience are real; we accept that what we experience exists. In Chapter 5 we examine the relationships between these real phenomena and the things we assume exist in the world. This will be done by an introduction to the methods philosophers, scientists and ordinary people who sit on juries use to accept or reject an argument that something has happened or that something exists.

Chapter 6 consists of two sections dedicated to the development of philosophical skills. It has a dual aim: firstly, to extend our examination of how reality is related to our experience; secondly, to enhance the development of our skills as philosophers. In the first part of the chapter we take a look at a structured method for constructing an extended philosophical argument, considering how the method can also be applied to arguments in other subjects. In the second part, we look at how a particular type of philosophical argument is used – a type which is closely associated with Immanuel Kant. In both the skills sections, we explore the possibility of there being a link between reality and the methods we use to understand reality. This theme partly drives the discussion in Chapter 7, where we look at the relationships between reality and our thoughts and beliefs.

The discussions in Chapters 5, 6 and 7 all accept the assumption that the phenomena we experience are real. Some philosophers make a further assumption that these phenomena are the fundamental entities, or fundamental building blocks, from which we are to construct reality. We shall use the term 'fundamental entity' to denote something which has separate existence or whose existence cannot be determined by referring to other entities.

[Note: The notion of a fundamental entity is similar to the Greek notion of a primary substance, which we examined when discussing Anaximander's three claims on p. 31. Here, however, we avoid the use of the word 'substance'. This has two advantages: the first is that in philosophy it is a rather overworked word which has several meanings; the second is that the word 'entity' means an existing thing, so the term 'fundamental entity' already contains the ontological (existential) aspect of the meaning of the term 'substance'.]

In Chapter 8 we examine some of the arguments which question this second assumption; in doing so, we consider some of the arguments that have led to the development of existentialist philosophy and one of the most enduring arguments in philosophy, Plato's 'Theory of Forms'.

The Senses, Action and Reality

5

In this chapter we tackle metaphysics – the subject which deals with what really exists and its relationship with our knowledge of its existence. Here we focus on how our perception is related to reality; we examine the information provided by our sense organs and assess how trustworthy it is in informing us about what exists. The exercises prepare some of the ground for later discussions in 'epistemology', to be covered in Chapter 12. We examine claims that our senses can give us incontrovertible evidence that things we see, touch, smell, hear and taste, really exist.

The reader will develop an understanding of why some empiricist philosophers believe that our senses can never give us such incontrovertible evidence. At the same time the basis of the non-empiricist philosophers' reply is given by examining some arguments which are not often discussed in modern philosophy, in particular those formulated by Henri Poincaré. These not only provide a basis for criticising the writings of some empiricist philosophers, but they also introduce the reader to a type of philosophical argument associated with Immanuel Kant. In Chapter 6 the reader will be encouraged to construct and criticise arguments of this type.

IN THIS CHAPTER

Concepts discussed

- Logical possibility
- Incontrovertibility
- Proof
- Beyond reasonable doubt

Skills developed

- Assessment of theories
- Analysis of text

Types of argument examined

- Deductions from premises
- *Reductio ad absurdum*

Philosophers whose ideas are discussed

- George Berkeley
- Henri Poincaré
- René Descartes

References made to the following philosophers

- David Hume
- Thomas Reid

Real Things

There are two separate questions contained in the question

How real are physical things?

One is a general one and one is specific. We can get an understanding of this difference by examining a short extract from Lewis Carroll's famous story *Alice's Adventures in Wonderland* (1865). The story is a fantasy about a young girl who finds herself in Wonderland, a place where strange things happen.

In the extract, we are in Chapter 1. Alice had previously followed a rabbit down a rabbit hole and fallen downwards until she landed 'upon a heap of sticks and dry leaves, and the fall was over'. She found herself in a hall – there were doors all round the hall. Finding a golden key on a little three-legged table, she tried to open the doors. One of them was very small . . .

Exercise 5.1

Read the following extract and then answer the questions.

Alice opened the door and found that it led into a small passage, not much larger than a rat-hole: she knelt down and looked along the passage into the loveliest garden you ever saw. How she longed to get out of that dark hall, and wander about among those beds of bright flowers and those cool fountains, but she could not even get her head through the doorway; 'and even if my head would go through,' thought poor Alice, 'it would be of very little use without my shoulders. Oh, how I wish I could shut up like a telescope! I think I could, if I only knew how to begin.' For, you see, so many out-of-the-way things had happened lately, that Alice had begun to think that very few things indeed were really impossible.

There seemed to be no use in waiting by the little door, so she went back to the table, half hoping she might find another key on it, or at any rate a book of rules for shutting people up like telescopes: this time she found a little bottle on it, ('which certainly was not here before,' said Alice,) and round the neck of the bottle was a paper label, with the words 'DRINK ME' beautifully printed on it in large letters.

. . .

It was all very well to say 'Drink me', but the wise little Alice was not going to do THAT in a hurry. 'No, I'll look firstly,' she said, 'and see whether it's marked "poison" or not'; for she had read several nice little histories about children who had got burnt, and eaten up by wild beasts and other unpleasant things, all because they WOULD not remember the simple rules their friends had taught them: such as, that a red-hot poker will burn you if you hold it too long; and that if you cut your finger *VERY* deeply with a knife, it usually bleeds; and she had never forgotten that, if you drink much from a bottle marked 'poison', it is almost certain to disagree with you, sooner or later.

However, this bottle was *NOT* marked 'poison' so Alice ventured to taste it, and finding it very nice, (it had, in fact, a sort of mixed flavour of cherry-tart, custard, pine-apple, roast turkey, toffee, and hot buttered toast,) she very soon finished it off.

1. (i) Identify the statement in the first paragraph which connects some of Alice's specific experiences to the general properties of her environment.
   (ii) State why she believes the claim to be true.

2. (i) Identify the statement in the last paragraph which makes a claim about the appearance of a specific object.
   (ii) Why do you think Alice believed the claim to be true.

3. (i) Identify three claims Alice makes in the third paragraph about the general properties of some types of object or occurrence.
   (ii) State why she believes the claims to be true.

Suggested answers are on p. 260.

Like all normal children, Alice had reasons for doing some things whilst holding back from doing other things. Her reasons were based on two categories of belief: her belief in the existence of specific things and her beliefs about the properties which things of a particular type have. In this chapter we shall be looking at how we justify our beliefs about what exists. Like Alice's, the beliefs are of two types: those about the existence of specific things (like bottles marked 'poison') and those about things of particular types (like red-hot pokers). We shall be examining how we justify our beliefs about the **properties** of things in Chapter 12, which deals with the philosophy of science; in this chapter we concentrate on the justification of belief in the **existence** of things.

Alice's reasons for believing that 'this bottle was *NOT* marked "poison"' are based on the reliability of her senses in providing her with evidence. We shall now examine how trustworthy the senses are in enabling us to distinguish what is real from what is not: the senses will be examined first individually, and then in combination. At this point it is worth being reminded about what led some of the earliest philosophers to search for an understanding of the nature of reality.

We saw in Part I that the ancient Greek philosophers wanted to understand the world they lived in. This led them to ask questions about the nature of the everyday things we see, touch, hear, smell, taste and maybe just sense: they wanted to understand their own experiences. Their other concern was whether they might be mistaken about what their experiences led them to understand: to this end, they wanted to be able to distinguish between the things that really exist and those which we merely believe to exist.

One approach to the question of deciding whether something really exists is to consider some things whose existence we hardly ever question (outside philosophy classes!). We can also examine the reasons we give for justifying why we accept that these things exist. The most common reason we give for claiming that a thing like a chair, an apple, a flower, a lake or a dog exists, is that we can **see, hear, smell, taste** or **touch** it.

To this list of faculties, some people may even add the possibility that somehow we **sense** the thing in a different way. For example, some scientists have discovered that not all living things are restricted to the use of the five senses: they have observed that some sharks feed off small sea creatures that hide in the sand on the seabed. In their article, 'Detection of weak electric fields by sharks, rays, and skates' (1998), R. K. Adair, R. D. Astumian and J. C. Weaver show that a shark is able to find these hidden sea creatures by sensing the very weak electromagnetic field generated by their nervous system.

[Note: It is certainly possible that humans might develop means to sense the world which are different from those used by our five senses. After all, in order to find out that sharks could detect electromagnetic fields, Adair, Astumian and Weaver needed to use scientific equipment which could detect electromagnetic fields, so it is imaginable that other means of sensing may evolve naturally.]

Before investigating the relationship between the use of our senses and our claims that things really exist, we shall briefly discuss the ways in which we assess the acceptability of the results of our investigations.

Methods (1) Assessing Claims About What Really Exists

When philosophers examine the reasons we give for making any claim, they submit the reasons to detailed scrutiny. We shall do this by testing claims based on each of our senses against three specific, and increasingly rigorous, standards of acceptability.

1. The minimum standard of acceptability we shall use will be 'logical possibility'. If a claim does not contradict itself, then it meets this standard of acceptability.

   [Note: Claims based on reasons provided by the sense organs are logically possible if the organs are able to function in such ways as to provide the desired evidence. For example, the sense of sight can gather information if the lights are on, but it is logically impossible for it to gather information in the dark. It is also logically impossible for the sense of hearing to determine whether or not an object is blue.]

2. The general standard of acceptability we shall use is the legal criterion of 'beyond reasonable doubt', which is the one used, for example, in criminal courts in the USA, the United Kingdom, Canada, Australia and New Zealand. We shall also use the weaker legal criterion of the 'preponderance of evidence', which is used in the civil courts in the USA. In order to meet either of these two standards of acceptability, a claim has at least to convince an ordinary person.

   [Note: We shall not use this last criterion in this chapter, but will discuss its use when we consider the nature of scientific theories in Chapter 13. What we mean by an 'ordinary person' will be discussed in Chapter 15, which is on Personal Identity.]

3. The highest standard of acceptability we shall use is 'proof'. In order to meet this standard of acceptability, a claim has to be 'incontrovertible': in other words, there should be no available means to show that the claim is false. Even if no contrary evidence against a claim has been found but it is nevertheless still possible, then the claim has not been proved; to prove the claim, we have to show that it is 'impossible to find evidence against it'.

   [Note: We can see that proving something depends upon the means we have available to us: for example, if we have no way of examining the side of the moon which looks away from the earth, we cannot even attempt to prove, or disprove, any statement about what exists on the other side of the moon. This means that it is possible that what is not (dis)provable today might become (dis)provable tomorrow. Two hundred years ago scientists did not have the means to test out any theory about the ability of sharks to detect apparently hidden prey; they do now. What constitutes proof in science will be discussed in Chapter 13, The Philosophy of Science.]

We shall use these three standards – logical possibility, beyond reasonable doubt, and proof – in order to investigate how effective the senses are in backing up claims about the nature of reality and about what exists in that reality.

Seeing, Hearing, Smelling and Tasting Real Things

Exercise 5.2

Information acquired by seeing and hearing real things
Sheepdogs, roses and bananas are all objects whose existence we detect using our various senses in different ways.

   1. Can **seeing** or **hearing** a sheepdog provide us with:
     (i) **logically possible** reasons that the sheepdog exists?

_____

_____

     (ii) reasons that put the sheepdog's existence **beyond reasonable doubt?**

_____

_____

     (iii) reasons that **prove** that the sheepdog exists?

_____

_____

Suggested answers are on p. 262.

Information acquired by smelling and tasting real things

   2. Can **smelling** a rose provide us with reasons that put the rose's existence **beyond reasonable doubt.**

_____

_____

· · ·

3. Can **tasting** a banana provide us with reasons that put the banana's existence **beyond reasonable doubt?**

_____

_____

Suggested answer

The answer to Question 1 (i) also applies to both Questions 2 and 3: in normal circumstances the senses of smell and taste can provide evidence which puts the rose's and the banana's existence beyond reasonable doubt – although even the smell of a rose is now being simulated by commercial companies interested in creating the impression that roses are present.

There is, however, a difference between these four senses: the sense of taste is more immediate than sight, hearing and smell. In tasting the banana we are in direct contact with it; whereas when we see the image of the sheepdog, we hear it bark or we smell the perfume of the rose, we are at a distance. The directness or immediacy seems to give the sense of taste more reliability than the less direct senses – something that becomes even more striking when we examine the sense of touch.

Comment

_____

_____

[Note: This difference gives us an insight into a distinction made by some philosophers between the sensation and the thing sensed. Philosophers like David Hume claim that we are not directly aware of a sheepdog, but rather of our mind's representation of a sheepdog; we do not smell a rose, but rather our mind's representation of a rose. The sheepdog and rose are 'out there', while our sensations are 'in here'. The distinction between 'out there' and 'in here' seems reasonable in the cases of sight, hearing and smell: the sensation arrives and is processed, sometimes to the extent of generating illusions and hallucinations. Illusions and hallucinations can only occur if what is 'out there' is distinct from what is 'in here'. The less reasonable aspect of accepting the distinction is that it is at odds with our everyday use of language: when I say that I see a sheepdog, I do not mean that I have seen a representation of a dog, I mean that I can see the dog itself. When I say that I see a representation of a sheepdog, I normally mean that I can see a picture or drawing of a sheepdog, I do not mean that I can see a sheepdog. Thomas Reid uses this argument to reject David Hume's unusual use of the words 'impression' and 'idea' (Brodie, 1997, e.g. p. 87).]

The investigation of the use of our senses has not, so far, included the possibility that we may have other sources of information which can help us distinguish what is real from what only appears to be real. A shark's abilities, cited above on page 62, seem to go beyond these five senses. We ought therefore to leave ourselves open to the possibility that we might also have some shark-like capabilities.

Sensing Real Things

Exercise 5.3

Information acquired by 'sensing' real things
Water dowsers are sure that they can 'sense' the presence of springs or other underground sources of water.

1. Should we reject the water dowsers' claim to possess another form of sensing, different from the five senses, because it is not logically possible for them to 'sense' water?

_____

_____

2. Can any form of 'sensing', different from the five senses, provide us with **proof** that a particular underground source of water exists?

_____

_____

Suggested answers

1. No. There is no logical contradiction in suggesting that 'sensing' an underground source of water provides grounds for claiming that the underground source of water exists. There could be people with a special sense, similar to that of a shark, which detects some form of emission from underground sources of water.
2. No. The answer to this question is the same as the answer to Exercise 5.2 1(iii).

Comment

_____

_____

[Note: In Exercise 4.1 we noted that: 'Physicists tell us that 'electrons' cannot be seen, as they are smaller than the wavelength of visible light. The eye cannot pick them out; it is restricted to detecting the effects electrons have on special equipment, usually involving oscilloscopes.' Our sense organs are not designed to detect single electrons, so they give us no direct means by which we can gather evidence that electrons exist.]

The discussions so far in Chapter 5 have indicated that our perception of the world does not give us incontrovertible arguments on which to base a claim that something exists. This may be due to the restriction of our discussion to the passive reception of information from our senses. We shall now extend the discussion to include an evaluation of the role action plays in backing up claims about what really exists in the physical world.

Touching Real Things

The suggested answers to Exercise 5.2 (p. 262) indicate that the senses of taste and touch may be qualitatively different from the other senses. We have not yet discussed the sense of touch. We can do this by examining a famous example found in Boswell's biography of Samuel Johnson, in which Johnson is behaving as would any self-respecting direct realist.

Exercise 5.4

Information acquired by touching real things
Dr Samuel Johnson famously 'refuted' George Berkeley's claim that physical objects exist only in our, and God's, minds by kicking a rock.

After we came out of the church, we stood talking for some time together of Bishop Berkeley's ingenious sophistry to prove the non-existence of matter, and that every thing in the universe is merely ideal. I observed, that though we are satisfied his doctrine is not true, it is impossible to refute it. I never shall forget the alacrity with which Johnson answered, striking his foot with mighty force against a large stone, till he rebounded from it – 'I refute it thus.' James Boswell (1791, Book 3).

1. Can **touching**, or **kicking**, a rock provide us with reasons that put the rock's existence beyond reasonable doubt?

---

2. Did Dr Johnson succeed in refuting Berkeley's theory that physical things exist only as ideas in people's and God's minds?

_____

_____

Suggested answers are on p. 264.

3. Is the fact that he kicked the stone, rather than just felt it hit him, significant?

_____

_____

Suggested answer to Question 3

The significance of the individual's activity in perception is often ignored. Philosophy in the English-speaking world tends to accept David Hume's passive analysis of perception which describes the perceiver purely as a receiver of information. We need to question the notion that our experience is one which is purely receptive. I can choose to look in a particular direction to see what was barking, or stretch out to touch the quadruped I can see and smell. I can also adjust my position in order to determine a more precise position for the dog or to gather more precise information about its colour or size. Therefore each of these activities of muscular movement adds further and more precise information to the information gathered by the receptive sense organs.

It is reasonable to argue that this further information is essential for someone to be able to build up a picture of a stone as well as a picture of the world in which the stone is found. The argument which identifies the central role played by the action of the individual in building up a picture of the world will be developed in the answer to Exercise 6.1 (p. 68). The argument there indicates that the fact that Dr Johnson kicked the stone, rather than just felt it hit him, is very significant.

Comment

_____

_____

_____

[Note: **Extension – A transcendental deduction using Henri Poincaré's muscles**
The French physicist, mathematician and philosopher of science, Henri Poincaré also pointed out that an important part of the jumble of information from the senses comes from the movement of our muscles. He argued that we cannot build up a concept of physical space by merely receiving signals, we have to participate in the generation of the signals.

> *None of our sensations, if isolated, could have brought us to the concept of space; we are brought to it solely by studying the laws by which those sensations succeed one another.*
> (Poincaré's italics)
>
> If, for example, it were a question of the sight, and if an object were displaced before our eyes, we can 'follow it with the eye', and retain its image on the same point of the retina by appropriate movements of the eyeball. These movements we are conscious of because they are voluntary, and because they are accompanied by muscular sensations.
>
> Given this, what characterises change of position, what distinguishes it from change of state, is that it can always be *corrected* by this means. It may therefore happen that we pass from an aggregate of impressions A to the aggregate B in two different ways. Firstly, involuntarily and without experiencing muscular sensations . . . secondly, voluntarily, and with muscular sensation . . .
>
> It follows that sight and touch could not have given us the idea of space without 'muscular sense'. Not only could this concept not be derived from a single sensation, or even from *a series of sensations*, but a *motionless* being could never have acquired it (1952, pp. 58–9).

The reason Poincaré gives for a purely passive being's inability to develop a concept of space is that, in order to distinguish objects in space, we need to be able to 'correct by our movements the effects of the change of position of external objects'. He emphasises that the movements must be voluntary and accompanied by sensations. The implication of all this is that it is likely that Poincaré would have approved of Dr Johnson's refutation of Berkeley!]

In this chapter we have examined how we use the senses individually to determine what justifies claims about the physical reality we live in. In practice, we do not use the senses one at a time; rather, we normally combine them to see how, in combination with each other, they tell us what might be real. In Exercises 5.2, 5.3 and 5.4 we examined how the use of a particular sense organ might provide evidence justifying a claim about the existence of particular objects. We shall now test the supposition that the combined use of our senses may give us a firmer hold on reality than the use of any single sense in isolation.

Philosophical Analysis and Reality

6

In this chapter we continue the discussion about what really exists. In Chapter 5 we focused on how our perception is related to reality: we were concerned with the ways our sense organs give us information about what exists. Here we concentrate on how we interpret the information our sense organs give us.

Our analysis will not, however, restrict itself to describing how we interpret information from our sense organs; in Exercise 6.2 we shall also examine some of the conditions which permit us to interpret that information – a type of examination which is characteristic of non-empiricist philosophers. In carrying out the examination, we shall come to appreciate that the methods philosophers use are often as important as the conclusions they reach. The aim of the chapter is to develop an understanding of the approach of non-empirical philosophers, and to criticise and assess their work.

IN THIS CHAPTER

Skills developed

- Analysis of a question
- Construction of an extended answer

Types of argument examined

- Transcendental proof

Philosophers whose ideas are discussed

- Immanuel Kant
- Henri Poincaré

References made to the following philosophers

- David Hume

Methods (2) Answering Real Questions

In the previous three exercises, we investigated the way we use the senses indi-vidually to determine the reality of sheepdogs, roses, bananas and the question of whether senses can detect underground sources of water. We shall now turn our attention to the way we use the senses in combination with each other. In doing so, we shall focus our attention on a racing pigeon, which is a pigeon that can be trained to fly to particular locations.

There are three reasons for focusing our analysis on a racing pigeon: firstly, it is a physical object which does not make any conscious contributions to the development of our language; secondly, it responds to, and generates, stimuli which can be detected by all of the sense organs; thirdly, there are some individuals who have significantly greater knowledge than others about their nature and habits. These factors permit us to carry out an analysis which covers several aspects of the ways in which we become aware of a physical thing's existence.

Let us now examine the possibility of the senses combining to provide grounds which put the existence of the racing pigeon **beyond reasonable doubt**. We can use the results of our analysis of the individual senses, which we developed in the previous chapter, in order to avoid repeating the arguments. We noted there that the senses individually can provide us with **logically possible** reasons that a particular racing pigeon exists. Since it is logically possible for each of the senses to provide grounds for claiming that the pigeon exists, it is also logically possible for all the senses together to provide such grounds.

Up to this point, most of the questions we have answered have already been broken up into sub-questions, and we have proceeded to provide answers to these sub-questions. The analysis of a question so as to form a set of sub-questions is itself a process which philosophers utilise regularly – the term 'analysis' means the resolution of anything complex into its basic elements. The process provides the basis for the construction of a comprehensive and coherent answer to a philosophical question. The analysis is not done in a haphazard way; each question will have its own framework to guide our analysis. In answering a question in philosophy, we often intuitively know the general answer we wish to give, but find it difficult to formulate a structured answer. One way of doing this is to go through the following five processes:

(a)   specify the framework which guides the analysis of the question;
(b)   decompose (or 'deconstruct') the question into sub-questions;
(c)   form the answers to the sub-questions;
(d)   place the sub-answers into the framework;
(e)   form the answer to the question.

[Note: This list is not prescriptive: it does not set out a law which must be followed in order to compose an answer to a question. It offers a method rather than **the** method of analysing a question and composing an answer.]

These processes are not carried out in a random manner; they are all guided by the intention of examining the intuitive general answer. It is possible that the examination will demonstrate that this intuitive answer is unacceptable; be that as it may, it most importantly gives us a starting point for our analysis. Let us now return to the question of the combined use of our senses and go through these five processes.

Exercise 6.1 Combining the senses to experience real things

Suppose we are trying to establish the existence of a particular racing pigeon **beyond reasonable doubt.**

1. Can the combined use of the senses provide us with better reasons than the use of an individual sense?

_____

_____

2. If so, in what ways does it do so?

_____

_____

The framework which guides the analysis of the question

An answer to a question always consists of some form of reasoned argument which needs to be presented within a structured setting. The design of the structure is determined by the assumptions contained in the argument, together with the types of method it employs.

In order that our readers can understand our answer, we need to tell them what type of argument we are going to employ; for example whether we are going to use a logical deduction from an accepted starting point or whether we shall be appealing to an analogy to support our claims. The methods we use will often depend upon our aims, on whether we wish to prove something or to establish it beyond reasonable doubt. The readers also need to know what assumptions are being made – these could include theories or definitions which we accept as valid.

(a)(i) Indicate what method or type of argument you will be employing in order to answer the question. For example, is your argument one which deduces your conclusion from an accepted theory together with some supporting empirical evidence?

· · ·

(ii) Specify the assumptions you will be making in order to answer the question.

Decomposition into sub-questions

Breaking up the question into smaller component questions is helpful in two respects. For example, in Discussion Exercise 2.8 (p. 20) we were concerned with how the consequences of doing an activity were related to what the activity is. We formulated two sub-questions to help us answer the main question. There is another advantage to breaking up the question: as well as making it easier to formulate an answer; breaking a question up into sub-questions makes it easier for the reader to follow the argument. It is also a valuable thing to do as it focuses our own attention, and eventually the reader's, on the steps to be taken in constructing the answer to the original question.

(b) List any sub-questions you will be making which you believe need to be answered before you formulate your final answer.

(c) Formulate answers to your sub-questions.

The process of formulating answers to the sub-questions may generate other sub-questions, so there will often be cross-fertilisation between processes (c) and (d).

• • •

> (d) Ensure that the sub-answers conform with the assumptions specified in (a).
>
> _____
>
> _____
>
> (e) Formulate the answer to the original question.
>
> We should now be in a position to bring together the sub-answers and formulate an argument which will convince our readers. This process involves us in identifying the most significant elements of our answers to the sub-questions.
>
> _____
>
> _____
>
> _____

Suggested answer

[Note: The aim in providing this particular suggested answer is to show **one** method of carrying out philosophical analysis and to introduce the reader to some non-empirical approaches to philosophy. The beginner whose experience in philosophy is restricted to this book is not expected to develop such a detailed answer. The more experienced philosopher is likely to choose a different strategy to answer the question, but it will be a strategy which develops similar points to the ones in the suggested answer.]

The basic answer to the first question is 'yes': it is **logically possible** for two or more pieces of information to provide better grounds for believing something than one piece. This can occur when each of the pieces of information corroborates what the others say. In answer to Question (2), the combined use of the senses is more likely than a single sense to convince someone of the existence of a racing pigeon **beyond reasonable doubt**. With these general answers in mind, let us go through processes (a) to (e) and construct a philosophical argument which supports them.

(a) The framework which guides the analysis of the question – assumptions and methods

We make at least three assumptions in constructing an answer to the questions. The first is that it is possible for one set of reasons to be better than another.

Anyone who answers the second question is implicitly accepting this assumption: a refusal to accept it would necessitate a refusal to answer the second question. Implicit in this first assumption is another: an argument which tries to persuade us that a certain set of information provides better evidence that another set cannot be a proof, since the aim of proof is to convince, rather than persuade.

The third assumption concerns the starting point of the answer to the second question, 'If so, in what ways does the combined use of the senses provide us with better reasons than the use of an individual sense?' Our starting point assumes that none of the senses contradicts the other senses in providing evidence about the existence of the racing pigeon in question. It is clearly the case that a single sense, whose evidence has not been contradicted, is a better source of support for the claim that something exists than two senses which contradict each other. It is possible to develop an argument that demonstrates the validity of this assumption, but this would not be worthwhile, as it would add nothing to our ability to answer either of the questions.

The decision to accept an assumption may carry some consequences with it. In this case, it obliges us to adopt certain methods: the assumption that it is possible for one set of reasons to be better than another obliges us to demonstrate that one set of reasons is, in the specific case in question, better than another set. We need to construct an incontrovertible argument, or a proof, that combining the senses can be better than using them singly. This is not a difficult task: the arguments in the suggested answers to Exercise 5.2 (p. 262) can be used to develop a proof. They demonstrate that either seeing or hearing an object can provide the basis for claiming that a particular sheepdog exists; this leaves open the possibility that any combination of seeing and hearing can also provide the basis for claiming that a particular sheepdog exists. Substituting a racing pigeon for the sheepdog in the proof does not alter its validity. This brief proof answers the first question and tells us that the combined use of the senses **can** provide us with better reasons than the uses of an individual sense. It answers the first question, but it does not answer the second; it does not tell us whether the combined use of the senses **does** provide us with better reasons; and in the cases where it does provide better reasons we are not told the ways in which this is done.

Our second assumption springs from accepting the challenge of answering the second question, which requires us to describe a process or a procedure rather than argue a case. We are asked for a comparison of the support given to a claim by the combined use of the senses on one hand with the use of an individual sense on the other. In following this instruction, we try to persuade the readers that our comparison of the two processes demonstrates the superiority of the combination of senses over the use of a single sense. We do this with the use of an analogy, but it has to be an appropriate analogy – one that invites them to compare the persuasiveness of combining the evidence from different witnesses in a court of law with the persuasiveness of combining the information from the different senses.

Comment

_____

_____

We acknowledged in the last paragraph that the discussion about our assumptions led us to specify the methods which are to be used to determine whether, and in what way, combinations of the senses give better access to reality than single senses. We now move to the stage where we analyse the question by decomposing it into sub-questions. This gives us the opportunity to introduce the analogy of a court of law.

(b) Decomposition into sub-questions

The question requires us to compare the combined use of the senses with the use of a single sense. Let us break this requirement down into component parts: firstly, we need to determine how good a single sense can be in supporting a claim that a particular racing pigeon exists. Having done this, we ask ourselves whether combining the use of more than one sense contaminates, enhances or leaves unaltered the information each individual sense provides. Let us state these questions in a formal way:

Suppose that a trainer of racing pigeons cannot hear, smell, touch or taste a racing pigeon, but she can see one flying above her.

> (i) In what circumstances is the information from the use of a single sense so reliable that it puts the existence of the pigeon **beyond reasonable doubt?**

In answering this question we introduce our analogy. For example, in some circumstances the evidence from a single witness in a court case may be acceptable: if the witness is an expert, or if forensic evidence corroborates what the witness says. We can ask whether the individual sense can be an expert witness and whether its evidence can be corroborated by something other than the other senses. The trainer is gathering information from the use of a single sense, in this case sight.

> (ii) Does she have to use a faculty, other than one of the other senses, in order for her to put the existence of the pigeon **beyond reasonable doubt?**
> (iii) In establishing the pigeon's existence, what is the significance of the use of faculties other than the senses?

When addressing the original question, the answers to these three questions need to be set against the reliability of the combined use of the senses. We can formulate a question which addresses this issue. Suppose that the evidence of the trainer's sight is deemed good enough to establish, beyond reasonable doubt, that a racing pigeon is flying above her; she cannot smell, touch or taste it, but can hear its cry and the noise it has made while flying. We note that hearing and sight combine to convince her that there is a racing pigeon in the sky.

> (iv) Does the combination of sight and hearing weaken the evidence from the individual senses, strengthen it or leave it unaltered?

Comment

_____

_____

_____

(c) Suggested answers to the sub-questions

> (i) In what circumstances is the information from the use of a single sense so reliable that it puts the existence of the pigeon **beyond reasonable doubt**?

In most legal jurisdictions, the uncorroborated evidence of a single witness is considered to be a shaky basis for determining the guilt of a defendant beyond reasonable doubt. Nonetheless, it is possible that a highly reliable expert witness might be instrumental in leading a court to the conclusion that a person was guilty beyond reasonable doubt. In the same way, if one of the trainer's senses is an expert sense, she may be able to use that sense to establish beyond reasonable doubt that a racing pigeon exists; for example, she may be hawk-eyed.

Courts of law often accept even a single non-expert witness when there is additional forensic evidence to support the witness's evidence. In a similar way, a trainer's normal eyesight, along with some corroborating evidence, could establish beyond reasonable doubt that a racing pigeon exists. Should the movement of the bird in the air be a racing pigeon-like flight, then this extra corroborative evidence could be enough to establish the existence of the pigeon beyond reasonable doubt.

Comment

_____

_____

_____

The trainer is gathering information from the use of a single sense, in this case sight.

(ii) Does she have to use a faculty, other than one of the other senses, in order for her to put the existence of the pigeon **beyond reasonable doubt**?

The information a single sense organ supplies needs to be coherent: each piece it supplies has to corroborate what the previous pieces supplied. Something similar happens in court cases when a single witness gives evidence: if he is to be believed, each piece of evidence he gives must endorse and sustain the evidence he has previously given. The single witness and the single sense organ must operate coherently.

In both situations there are three forms of endorsement taking place. One of these involves the application of expertise to the information gathered by the single witness; another involves an activity in which further information is gathered; and finally there is the cross-examination of the witness. The skill of the expert witness is mirrored by the skill of the trainer's hawk-eyed vision. The extra evidence gathered by using muscular movements to follow the bird's flight mirrors the extra forensic evidence presented in a court. The cross-examination of the witness in a court case is mirrored by the constant adjustment and read-justment of the sense organ so as to check and countercheck the information it provides.

These forms of endorsement cannot be carried out by the sense organ functioning independently of other faculties. Without the trainer's use of her intellect, and her 'muscular sense', she has no means of determining whether the sequences of information from her sense of sight are consistent with the notion that a racing pigeon is flying overhead.

[Note: The term 'muscular sense' is one which Henri Poincaré used to describe the sensation a person has when moving a muscle. He explained it in the following words quoted above (p. 65):

> If, for example, it were a question of the sight, and if an object were displaced before our eyes, we can 'follow it with the eye,' and retain its image on the same point of the retina by appropriate movements of the eyeball. These movements we are conscious of because they are voluntary, and because they are accompanied by muscular sensations.]

Both her intellect and her 'muscular sense' must be employed actively in two ways: on the one hand, they probe and test the evidence from her other 'witnesses', the senses; and on the other, they act as witnesses themselves by corroborating what her senses say. She uses her intellect to question each image she gets by using her sight in order to see whether it confirms what all the other previous images have told her.

The trainer's 'muscular sense' has a dual function when she is attempting to determine whether a racing pigeon exists. The focusing and refocusing of the eye, the movement of her head and the positioning of her body in order to follow the pigeon's flight only make sense if she is gathering a series of connected images which are consistent with the flight of a racing pigeon. The series of images have a meaning. The sense of sight needs to be directed by something which understands the meaning of the series, otherwise it cannot gather the appropriate images. This means that directing the muscles to build up a series of images needs some input from the intellect. When the intellect's powers of reasoning are limited or it has inadequate theories at its disposal about the nature of racing pigeons, it is not able to help direct 'muscular sense' to ensure that sight provides the appropriate images.

The second function of 'muscular sense' is to check that any rival conceptualisation of the series of images is excluded. The object in the sky could be another bird of prey which is of a different size or colour and whose flight is characteristically different. 'Muscular sense' is needed in order to cross-examine the evidence from sight to ensure that the images it supplies are neither faulty nor open to alternative interpretations. This checking operation also needs some input from the intellect.

[Note: Kant pointed out the role the intellect plays in directing the attention of the senses, 'Thoughts without intuitions are empty, intuitions without concepts are blind' (A51/B75). Henri Poincaré pointed out the role of 'muscular sense' in enabling the intellect to develop a concept of physical space (see above, p. 65).]

Without the use of her intellect and 'muscular sense' the trainer would not be able to gather the information needed to judge whether the single sense has provided appropriate evidence. It is necessary for her to use these other faculties, apart from her other senses, in order for her to put the existence of the pigeon **beyond reasonable doubt**.

Comment

_____

_____

_____

> (iii) In establishing the pigeon's existence, what is the significance of the use of faculties other than the senses?

The use of faculties other than the senses is significant in at least two respects. The use of the mental faculty of the intellect, with its component faculty of reason, is significant because of the fact that it limits the scope for scepticism. The use of the faculty of 'muscular sense' is significant because it highlights the fact that real things exist which are independent of our senses.

The fact that the trainer's reason tells her to continue asking for further evidence from her sight before she commits herself to asserting that the flying object is indeed a racing pigeon, means that it has to be possible to reduce her doubt. She has to be able to differentiate between different levels of confidence, so criteria for discriminating between acceptable and unacceptable claims about reality have to exist. This becomes even clearer when we consider the use of sight by persons who know little about racing pigeons; such people would require more evidence than a trainer in order to be convinced, and even then they may be mistaken because their intellects have inferior capacities when it comes to assessing visual information about racing pigeons.

[Note: The argument responding to (iii) is philosophically significant because of the impact it has on scepticism. If we can differentiate between the acceptability of two sets of evidence about the existence of an object, it is clear that not all experience makes the existence of objects equally doubtful. It becomes possible for us to criticise extreme scepticism such as that proposed by David Hume.]

There is a philosophical by-product of the necessary role of the intellect in gathering information from the senses to assess whether something exists. The intellect limits the possible claims about existence which we can make using our senses. The trainer's expertise enables her to use her intellect to make claims about birds which those of us without her knowledge cannot make. Similarly scientists with knowledge of, and access to, some types of scientific equipment can make claims about the existence of elementary particles which are beyond the reach of non-scientists. Our faculty of reason may impose bounds on our senses. The fact that we can expand the limits means that limits exist!

[Note: The bounds that reason imposes on sense is one of the central themes of Kant's argument in his *Critique of Pure Reason*. This gave rise to the title of Peter Strawson's commentary on Kant (1966).]

The argument above has established that 'muscular sense' is needed in order to cross-examine the evidence from sight with the aim of ensuring that the images it supplies are neither faulty nor open to alternative interpretations. This checking operation also needs some input from the intellect. In making judgements about what exists, we have to try to give meaning to how the intellect informs our 'muscular sense' to 'cross-examine' a sense organ in a particular way. This attempt to give meaning to the combined use of our 'muscular sense' and our intellect is at odds with the assumption that nothing exists independently of the information provided by the senses. The actions of directing and correcting a single sense organ are only comprehensible if the sense organ is independent of the information it receives; in other words, if real things exist which are independent of our senses.

Comment

_____

_____

_____

(iv) Does the combination of sight and hearing weaken the evidence from the individual senses, strengthen it or leave it unaltered?

We note that hearing and sight combine to convince the trainer that there is a racing pigeon in the sky.

The question seems a little naïve. If the trainer herself has used each of her senses to confirm what the other is telling her, it is natural to say that the combination of sight and hearing strengthens the evidence from the individual senses. The possibility remains, however, that she might be deluding herself and, in reality, the information from one of the senses is continually polluting the information from the others.

We can deal with this point quickly. It is certainly possible that, in some circumstances, the information coming from one of the senses creates expectations which provoke misinterpretations of the information coming from the others. Indeed, illusions are likely to be related to the perceiver's expectations, some of which are caused by information received from the senses.

This is, however, a long way from establishing that the senses pollute each other. If they did, there would be no sense in a person crosschecking to see whether what he sees and what he hears both correspond to a single racing pigeon. We now invoke the answers to (ii) and (iii); in analysing the conditions which make the crosschecking processes intelligible, they provide all the arguments we need to answer this question. Crosschecking the evidence provided by the various witnesses is a procedure which makes sense if it is capable of strengthening the evidence from the individual witnesses.

Comment

_____

_____

_____

_____

(d) and (e) We now ensure that our sub-answers conform with the assumptions described in (a) and formulate the answer to the question (Exercise 6.1 p. 68)

1. Can the combined use of the senses provide us with better reasons than the use of an individual sense?
2. If so, in what ways does it do so?

We have not attempted to **prove** that the combined use of the senses provides us with better reasons that something exists than the use of an individual sense. We have, however, supplied a few mini-proofs in answering the sub-questions: the arguments used were incontrovertible in the sense that any attempt to controvert them would involve us in accepting something which is unacceptable, such as making the operations of our own reason unintelligible.

[Note: An argument which cites unacceptable sacrifices which have to be made by anyone denying its conclusions is known as a 'transcendental argument'. We first met this sort of argument in the suggested answer to Exercise 5.1 (p. 265) when giving the reason why Alice believed something was true: 'Alice looked at the bottle; in order to make sense of the world, she has to have basic faith in the reliability of her sense experience.' This means that Alice would have to sacrifice her faith in the reliability of her sense experience if she were to reject her belief that there was a bottle with 'a paper label, with the words "DRINK ME" beautifully printed on it in large letters'.]

Inasmuch as the first question asks a strictly logical question, we answered it above, on page 71, by referring to the answers to Exercise 5.2. Given that it was possible for them to provide us with better reasons than a single sense alone, we made the assumption that the combined senses did not contradict each other. Using the analogy of a court case we went on to argue that the procedure of cross-examining the witnesses gave us a basis for claiming that the combined use was a means for providing better reasons. Our intellect and our 'muscular sense' conduct the cross-examinations of the senses and are able to ensure that the combined use of the senses provides us with better reasons than the use of an individual sense that a racing pigeon, or indeed any other object, exists.

[Note: All analogies break down at some point precisely because they are analogies; the court-case analogy is no exception. It breaks down in at least one respect: advocates who cross-examine witnesses do not necessarily have the same perspective or motives as the court whereas the intellect cross-examines the senses with the same motives – they both operate in order to understand reality. The analogy is, however, representative of sense perception in one further respect: cross-examining advocates invoke perspectives and knowledge not directly relevant to the case in their cross-examination. Similarly, the intellect utilises perspectives and knowledge not directly relevant to the perception of the moment when it uses 'muscular sense' to cross-examine sight, smell or hearing.]

Comment

_____

_____

_____

Methods (3) Transcendental Analysis: A First Step

(Advanced section)

Throughout Chapters 5 and 6 we have been discussing some aspects of the relationships between sense experience and reality. In such discussions, philosophers often use an indirect form of argument; for example, the transcendental arguments used in the answers to Exercise 6.1 (pp. 70–8). The strength of transcendental arguments is that they enable philosophers to draw conclusions that take them beyond the information gathered by the senses. We can get a feeling for this type of argument by considering an everyday event: the selling of goods for money. The result of the exchange is the substitution of ownership of an object with the ownership of some money. So far, we have considered the relationship between our senses and specific types of physical objects such as bananas, underground sources of water and racing pigeons. Money is also a specific type of thing which has specific characteristics. Let us investigate these characteristics and the relationships between them.

The two necessary qualities or characteristics, which something must have in order for it to be money, are that it is universally accepted as a means of exchange and that it acts as a store of value. My gold ingot is undoubtedly valuable; if, however, it is not acceptable as a means of buying a cup of coffee, bus ride or refrigerator, then the ingot is not money. If my banknote stops having a reliable value compared with a cup of coffee, bus ride or refrigerator, then my banknote ceases to function as money.

Exercise 6.2 (Advanced exercise)

Money is defined as something which is universally accepted as a means of exchange.

1. (i) What physical or other characteristics must money have in order for it to be **practically possible** for it to be used as a means of exchange?

· · ·

(ii) Which of these characteristics, if any, are needed in order for it to be **logically possible** for money to be used as a means of exchange?

Only those things which act as a store of value can be universally accepted as a means of exchange. We can deduce that money must also act as a store of value.

2. (i) What physical or other characteristics does money have to have in order for it to be **practically possible** for it to be used as a store of value?

(ii) Which of these characteristics, if any, are needed in order for it to be **logically possible** for money to be used as a store of value?

Suggested answers are on p. 265.

The analysis just carried out in Exercise 6.2 focuses on the characteristics money itself must have in order for it to function properly. A 'transcendental analysis' can also look at the conditions in the environment which may be needed in order for money to function properly. Let us now carry out a deeper analysis of the conditions which must hold in order for buying and selling to take place. We can also examine the conditions which must hold in order for buying and selling to make sense to us.

Discussion Exercise 6.3 (Advanced exercise)

1. A physical object is bought. What relationship must the object have with the seller before the sale?

2. Describe a society in which trading is **logically impossible**.

3. A more general (advanced) question

A society is an environment in which human beings interact with each other. In order for something to be a society it must possess certain characteristics: for example, there must be rules which determine what is acceptable and unacceptable behaviour between people.

What characteristics or processes does a society have to have in order for it to be able to function as a society?

Suggested answers are on p. 267.

We can now look back at what we have done in the last two chapters. We started by investigating the basis of some claims that things really exist; the first investigations centred on the use of the senses either individually, or in combination with each other. We then proceeded to an examination of the significance of the way in which we direct our muscular movements; in particular, we looked at how we integrate these actions with the use of our senses. In all the examinations, we concentrated our attention on the trustworthiness of the information provided by the sense organs.

We also found that the trustworthiness of the sense organs is not the only question which can have a bearing on arguments about whether things really exist. Commenting on the extract from *Alice in Wonderland*, we noted in the suggested answers to Exercise 5.1, Question 4 that, 'Alice looked at the bottle; in order to make sense of the world, she has to have basic faith in the reliability of her sense experience.' Alice was trying to make sense of the world; one of the factors which was needed to facilitate this activity was her faith in the reliability of her sense experience. This reliability was necessary in order for the world into which she had plunged to be intelligible to her.

Then, in Exercise 6.2, we discussed the conditions associated with the activities of buying and selling. Analyses such as these do not examine a process or activity directly; instead they look at the factors which either condition or enable the process or activity to occur. They are generally known as 'transcendental analyses' or 'arguments'.

[Note: Examples of these arguments are to be found in some of the extended analyses in earlier discussions. For example, we noted in our 'transcendental deduction using Henri Poincaré's muscles' (p. 65) that our ability to develop a concept of space depends on our being able to use our 'muscular sense' and move solid objects. Poincaré's is a transcendental argument.]

We could also attempt an in-depth analysis of the conditions which must hold in order for sense experience to function properly. For example, we might ask the question: 'What conditions must hold in order for us to be able to see, touch, hear, taste, smell or move something?' We might also ask the question: 'What conditions must hold in order for touching, hearing, tasting, smelling or moving something to make sense to us?'

[Note: Both these questions are typical of philosophers who produce transcendental arguments; they look, for example, for the conditions which must hold if we are to be able to communicate with each other. The question concerning what conditions must hold in order for us to be able to have sense experience is one which Kant asks himself in the 'Transcendental Aesthetic' in the *Critique of Pure Reason*.]

Both Chapters 5 and 6 have been concerned with answering the question 'How real are physical things?' At the beginning of the discussion, we distinguished between the question of the reality of things in general and the reality of a particular thing. We have focused on the ways in which our senses might contribute towards justifying a claim that a particular thing forms part of reality. We now extend the analysis to considering the ways in which other aspects of our conscious experience might contribute towards justifying a claim that a particular thing forms part of reality.

Thought, Belief and Reality

7

In Chapters 5 and 6 we examined the interplay between the information gathered by our senses and physical reality. We noted that the information does not just appear via each sense organ, but is purposely sought out through the activities of our muscular movements. In short, we are not merely robots passively receiving information and reacting to it: our active participation is necessary if we are to obtain an understanding of physical reality. Information-gathering processes must be continuously directed in order for us to crosscheck that each sense organ is confirming what the others are telling us. We need constantly to be carrying out mini experiments to confirm that sight is telling us the same story as, for example, hearing and touch.

In this chapter we analyse the relationship between the processing of the information gathered by our senses and physical reality. This processing involves the organisation of the information in accordance with concepts of physical and other objects. Since the processing has to be carried out according to rules, we investigate the relationships between the rules and the nature of observable reality. In doing this we ask three questions:

> When are we entitled to call something a 'thing'?

> Can thought generate real 'things'?

> How are knowledge, belief and/or faith related to real 'things'?

Addressing these questions introduces us to one of the most significant distinctions that is made in philosophy – that between *a priori* and *a posteriori* knowledge. This dates back to the seventeenth century and the work of philosophers such as Leibniz and Descartes. *A priori* knowledge is acquired independently of the operation of the senses, while *a posteriori* knowledge is dependent upon them.

Our concern in this chapter is with 'ontological issues', which focus on the nature of reality. This is closely related to the nature of our knowledge of reality, which is one of the central concerns of epistemology. Our work here also acts as a preparation for the examination of the nature of knowledge, which we undertake in Chapter 12.

IN THIS CHAPTER

Concepts discussed

- *A priori*
- *A posteriori*
- Natural kind
- Social kind
- Ontology

Types of argument examined

- Transcendental proof
- *Reductio ad absurdum*

Philosophers whose ideas are discussed

- Immanuel Kant
- W. V. Quine

References made to the following philosophers

- David Hume
- Thomas Reid

'You are a metaphysician. Bah!'

In Exercise 6.1 we carried out an extended analysis of how combining the senses might give us a better understanding of reality than using them individually. The argument indicated that sense experience is not a passive process: we use muscular movements to check and countercheck the information provided by sense organs. We also use muscular movements to help confirm that the various pieces of information from the different sense organs corroborate each other. We move our head to direct our eyes and ears to the best positions to receive information, constantly readjusting it to crosscheck that the information from each sense organ corroborates that which the others are supplying. If we were to detect an unanticipated noise we would move our eyes in order to gather information which would help explain the unexpected addition to the information our senses are supplying. This suggests that, in order to use my sense organs, I have to organise my body in such a away that my sense organs can gather the information I need in order to make sense of the world.

Two further provisional conclusions can be drawn from the argument.

[Note: These were not explicitly stated in Exercise 6.1, as the argument there was directed towards another specific question: How, if at all, does the combined use of the senses provide us with better reasons for believing that something exists than the use of an individual sense?]

- We gather only the information which our sense organs are capable of gathering.
- We need to process the information from the senses in order to understand something of the world.

[Note: The analysis of both the above conclusions forms the core of what occupied Immanuel Kant in the *Critique of Pure Reason*. In his 'Transcendental Aesthetic' he claimed that there are rules which govern what sort of information the senses are able to gather; and in the 'Transcendental Analytic' he claimed that there are rules which govern the ways we process that information. He wanted to see whether the ways these two sets of rules operate can tell us something about the world we live in.]

An introductory book is not the place to examine the arguments of the *Critique of Pure Reason* in detail. However, a fishy story, told by Sir Arthur Eddington (1939), may help us understand the sort of arguments Kant was using. Eddington tells the tale of an ichthyologist – someone who studies the natural history of fish.

Exercise 7.1

An extract from Sir Arthur Eddington's Tarner Lectures of 1938

Let us suppose that an ichthyologist is exploring the life of the ocean. He casts a net into the water and brings up a fishy assortment. Surveying his catch, he proceeds in the usual manner of a scientist to systematise what it reveals. He arrives at two generalisations:

1. No sea-creature is less than two inches long.
2. All sea-creatures have gills.

These are both true of his catch, and he assumes tentatively that they will remain true however often he repeats it.

1. Are both, either or neither Statements 1 and 2 true?

_____

_____

Eddington tells us that the ichthyologist has a net with a two-inch mesh, and it cannot catch sea-creatures which are less than two inches long.

. . .

---

2. Does the nature of the net affect what type of creatures there are in the sea?

_____

_____

3. How, if at all, does the nature of the net affect what type of creatures the ichthyologist can determine there are in the sea?

_____

_____

4. How, if at all, does the nature of the net affect the truth of the statements?

_____

_____

Suggested answers are on p. 268.

Eddington's concerns are wider than ours are in this chapter. He uses the analogy of the icthyologist to identify some of the limitations facing scientists: for example, scientific theories and equipment restrict the scientist. He makes this clear in the paragraph which follows the one quoted in Exercise 7.1, referring to the sensory and intellectual equipment which we use in obtaining knowledge.

In applying this analogy, **the catch** stands for **the body of knowledge** which constitutes physical science, and the **net** for the **sensory and intellectual equipment which we use in obtaining it**. The casting of the net corresponds to observation; for knowledge which has not been or could not be obtained by observation is not admitted into physical science.

An onlooker may object that the first generalisation is wrong. 'There are plenty of sea-creatures under two inches long, only your net is not adapted to catch them.'

The icthyologist dismisses this objection contemptuously. 'Anything uncatchable by my net is ipso facto outside the scope of icthyological knowledge.' In short, '**What my net can't catch isn't fish**.'

Or – to translate the analogy – 'If you are not simply guessing, you are claiming a knowledge of the physical universe discovered in some other way than by the methods of physical science, and admittedly unverifiable by such methods. You are a metaphysician. Bah!' Sir Arthur Eddington (1939).

[Notes: This extract from Eddington's original was a single paragraph – the emphasis and italics have been added; Eddington is using the term 'metaphysician' with its derogatory meaning, which associates it with the supernatural. These negative meanings are based on the third definition of 'metaphysical' given in the *OED*: 'Applied to what is immaterial, incorporeal or supersensible'. This gives rise to other definitions: 'addicted to witty conceits and far-fetched imagery' and 'fantastic'.]

In the paragraph Eddington makes some indirect remarks about the nature of science by referring to 'icthyological knowledge'. We shall return to a discussion of the ichthyologist's scientific methods in Chapter 13 on The Philosophy of Science. At present, our interests are focused on the nature of reality and of what exists in that reality; in particular, we shall inquire into the validity of the ichthyologist's claim that '**what his net can't catch isn't fish.**'

Exercise 7.2

Let us coin an Eddingtonian phrase: 'What my five sense organs can't detect isn't real.'

1. Describe something **physical** that my sense five organs can't detect.

_____

_____

2. Describe an **emotion** that my five sense organs can't detect.

_____

_____

3. Describe a **social entity** that my five sense organs can't detect **directly**.

_____

_____

• • •

4. Describe something whose existence is **independent** of what my sense organs **can** detect.

_____

_____

5. Is the statement 'What my five sense organs can't detect isn't real' true or false?

_____

_____

Suggested answers are on p. 270.

An alternative strategy which we can use to show that the statement Exercise 7.2, Question 5 is false would be to examine the ways in which we understand and talk about our social lives: we can argue that social 'objects' such as banks, governments and universities are real because they have the properties we ascribe to real tangible objects such as trees and rivers in our everyday speech. The social 'objects' are not directly experienced by our five senses, yet we talk about them in the same way as we talk about the real objects we can directly experience with our five senses. We would be disregarding the meaning of the word 'real' if we denied that social objects such as banks, governments and universities are real. This issue became contentious for a short period after the British Prime Minister, Margaret Thatcher, made the following statement in an interview in *Woman's Own* magazine in 1987:

> I think we've been through a period where too many people have been given to understand that if they have a problem, it's the government's job to cope with it. 'I have a problem, I'll get a grant.' 'I'm homeless, the government must house me.' They're casting their problem on society. And, you know, there is no such **thing** as society. There are individual men and women, and there are families. And no government can do anything except through people, and people must look to themselves first. It's our duty to look after ourselves and then, also, to look after our neighbour. People have got the entitlements too much in mind, without the obligations. There's no such thing as entitlement, unless someone has first met an obligation (emphasis added).

Here Thatcher claims that the term 'society' does not refer to something real; she does not claim that no real social objects exist. Indeed, she refers to social objects such as families, jobs, and grants. She implicitly accepts that a government is a 'thing': it has the ability to do things, even though 'no government can do anything except through people.' A government exists and is real. We can conclude that some social things that my five sense organs cannot directly detect are real. Denying their reality would seem to make nonsense of the way we use our language.

[Note: This is a variant of the argument Thomas Reid used in his criticism of David Hume – see p. 61, above.]

Comment

_____

_____

In her interview Thatcher was also concerned with moral issues. She was making a reasonable assumption that moral responsibility cannot be ascribed to an entity which is not a 'thing': it can be ascribed to people, and by implication to families, but not to society. In Chapter 16 we shall consider the questions of moral responsibility raised in the Thatcher interview; here we are concerned with the relationship between reality and how we obtain information about reality.

Thought and Reality

(Advanced section)

In the suggested answer to Exercise 7.2, Question 5, we noted that when we can detect the effects of something's behaviour, we are justified in claiming that it exists. Our senses can no more detect radio waves than they can detect a government; they seem, however, to be capable of detecting the effects of the behaviour of radio waves and governments. Detecting these effects justifies the claim that radio waves and governments exist. We conclude that using the operations of our senses to detect the effects of radio waves or a government's actions is not an activity which operates independently of the operations of our faculties of thought and reasoning.

The question of whether the senses can detect the effects of radio waves or of a government seems to depend upon how we interpret the information we get from the senses: Does what I can hear come from the impact of a radio wave on this little box with dials on it? Could I improve my senses so that they might detect the effect of the radio waves without using the box? Am I properly interpreting the noises I hear from the box when I say they are generated by radio waves?

These questions inquire into the nature of our knowledge about what our senses are able to detect. Questions about the nature of knowledge are referred to as 'epistemological questions'; these will be examined in Part IV. At present, we are concerned with questions of 'ontology' (that is, the nature of being and/or of reality). The analogy of the icthyologist has made us realise that our sense organs and the ways in which we reason may restrict what we can know about reality. Margaret Thatcher's assertions now induce us to ask two questions. She was saying that something which has a name, that is society, is not a 'thing'. This induces us to ask:

> When are we entitled to call something a 'thing'?

[Note: The contrast between a 'thing' and something which could be a thing was made by C. D. Broad (1925, p. 141) when he distinguished between 'epistemological objects' and 'ontological objects'. He defines an 'epistemological object' as an object which is 'envisaged by an act of knowledge' irrespective of whether the knowledge corresponds to real events, is illusory or hallucinatory. He defines an 'ontological object' as 'a real thing that is envisaged by an act of knowledge where knowledge corresponds to real events'. Thatcher seems to be saying that society is not even an epistemological object, because it is not an object.]

Thatcher contrasted the non-thing, society, with individual men and women, and families. This seems to indicate that individual men and women, and families, are 'things'. This induces us to ask ourselves the questions: When does a group of people become a 'thing'? Can we create a thing like a family by the ways in which we think about social relationships? In other words,

> Can thought generate real 'things'?

Let us look at the first question: 'When are we entitled to call something a "thing"?' In Exercise 7.2 we noted that we can justifiably call a radio wave a 'thing' for the same reasons that we can call a golf ball a 'thing'. In both cases we base our justification on the need to make sense of our actions of striking a golf ball or of tuning a radio. The first action has a direct effect on the thing we assume exists by changing its position: the golf ball moves through the air towards the green where the hole is located. The second action has an indirect effect on the thing we assume exists by altering its effect on the radio's speakers: by tuning the radio, we alter its internal configuration so that a radio wave of a different wavelength has priority in determining how the speakers react. In both cases, we act on something in order to bring about some effects which we can detect. If we did not call the golf ball and the radio wave 'things', we could not make sense of our actions.

We now examine the social events which might indicate that society as a 'thing' has detectable properties similar to those which radio waves possess; the aim is to determine whether society behaves like a 'thing'. Can we tune a sort of social radio so that society reacts and generates effects which we can detect?

Exercise 7.3 (Advanced exercise)

Various events can change the nature of an organisation or a person. When police officers were first issued with portable telephones/communicators, the police force could be said to have undergone a change. Every member of the public has a restricted citizen's power of arrest; when British police cadets are sworn in, they are given powers of arrest which exceed those they had as ordinary citizens.

1. Describe how a police force might change without any of the force's equipment or buildings changing.

   _____

   _____

2. Describe an effect of the change identified in Question 1.

   _____

   _____

3. Is the police force a 'thing'? If so, how do we know?

   _____

   _____

Suggested answers to Questions 1 and 2 are on p. 272.

Suggested answer to Question 3

The answer is 'yes'. We are justified in calling the police force a 'thing' because it has properties which satisfy the criteria of 'thinghood'. These are the criteria which are used to identify 'natural' and 'social kinds', and to differentiate them from each other. If it were to be a 'thing', the police force would be a social kind.

[Note: In philosophy the term 'kind' is used to denote a class of entities whose members have a common characteristic that differentiates them from non-members. A 'social kind' would be a class of objects whose differentiating characteristics included some which depended upon the cognitive interactions between people, and a 'natural kind' would be a class of objects whose differentiating characteristics were independent of the cognitive interactions between people.]

There are essentially two criteria which something has to satisfy if we are to be justified in calling it a thing. The first criterion is that the candidate for 'thinghood' must be capable of interacting with people, other social entities and/or with physical objects. Every interaction involves a change of some sort, so the candidate for 'thinghood' must be able to alter while retaining the characteristics which differentiate it from other 'things'. The alteration could be as minor as a change of position relative to something else or a change of colour (unless its position or colour are defining characteristics); but at the end of the alteration, it is still possible to detect the identifying characteristics. The second criterion is that such interactions have to be detectable by more than one individual. This seems to indicate that the alteration must measure up to acceptable objective standards; for example, it is insufficient for it to be detected by a single individual. If Elwood Dowd (a character in the Mary Chase play *Harvey*) is the only person who could ever detect the behaviour of Harvey, a six foot three and a half inch (1.94m) white rabbit, then what he is detecting is not a 'thing'.

Clearly the police force satisfies both these criteria. Like the army, the government and multinational corporations, a police force can acquire property, its personnel can change and it can bring about changes in the behaviour of many people. This means that it satisfies the first criterion. It satisfies the second since police forces are also detectable by more than one person. We can conclude that the police force is a 'thing'; if we were to deny it our use of language would be unintelligible.

Comment

_____

_____

_____

We shall now address the Thatcher question.

Discussion Exercise 7.4 (Advanced exercise)

Is there such a thing as society?

_____

_____

Suggested answers are on p. 273.

Belief and Reality

(Advanced section)

At the beginning of the chapter we set out to answer three questions. The first of these

> When are we entitled to call something a 'thing'?

deals with what we know as well as what exists; it straddles the topics of epistemology and ontology. The overlap emerged, in the suggested answer to Exercise 7.3, Question 3, when we looked for the criteria of 'thinghood'. When we apply criteria which justify the use of a concept, we concern ourselves with how we know something; in other words, with an epistemological issue. In Part IV below, the epistemological aspects of this question will be discussed.

Our discussions in this chapter have been concerned with the existence of 'things', with what distinguishes possible from actual entities. We have reached the conclusion that an entity's ability to affect our perceptions, even if only indirectly, is a quality something needs to possess if it is to be considered a real 'thing'. Margaret Thatcher claimed that 'society' fails this test. The counterclaim that society is a 'thing' is based on the affirmation that it passes the test. The suggested answer to Exercise 7.4 rejected the counterclaim on the grounds that society provides the context in which social things operate, but it is not itself a social thing. In making the claim, Thatcher was not merely making a political point, she was disputing the belief that anything which is defined by conscious beings becomes, de facto, a 'thing'.

The notion that redefinition of virtually any social thing is possible is associated with some branches of post-modernism.

[Note: Post-modernism is itself subject to constant redefinition. A working definition of 'modernism' can be found in Hall and Gieben (1992, p.6). Stuart Hall identifies four characteristics of modern societies: the dominance of secular forms of political power, a monetarised exchange economy, the decline of the traditional social order, and the decline of the religious world view. Post-modernism consists of the overthrow of modernism, consisting of 'a style and school of thought that rejects the dogma and practices of modernism'. (Collins English Dictionary)]

We do not need to go into the details of the discussions between post-modern social theorists; instead, we shall ask ourselves a question which their discussions generate:

> Can thought generate real 'things'?

Let us examine the case of thought generating a rabbit who would have been bemused by post-modernism.

Exercise 7.5 (Advanced exercise)

Elwood Dowd lived in a small town in the Mid-West of the USA in the 1940s. He had a constant companion, Harvey, a six foot three and a half inch (1.94m) white rabbit.

1. Does the fact that Elwood could interact with Harvey provide us with sufficient grounds for saying that Harvey really existed?

Both Harvey and Elwood were created by Mary Chase for her theatre play *Harvey*. No one else apart from Elwood could see Harvey. A film of the play was made by Universal in 1950; the part of Elwood was played by James Stewart and Josephine Hull played the part of his sister Veta, who wanted to have him committed to an asylum. Eventually Veta admits to having seen Harvey, so she is committed instead of Elwood.

2. If Elwood and Veta had been real people, rather than characters in a play and a film, would we be justified in saying that Harvey was also real?

Suppose a group of James Stewart fans were to form a Harvey Society. Suppose they were to hold annual dinners at which Harvey was the guest of honour with a special reserved seat at the top table.

3. Would we now be justified in saying that Harvey existed?

· · ·

Mickey Mouse was the product of Walt Disney's imagination. He seems to meet many of the conditions needed to be real: real things are imitated and so is 'he', 'he' gives children's parties and 'he' is registered as a trademark.

> 4. Is it possible to create a real thing just by using the imagination?

_____

_____

Suggested answers are on p. 273.

The Story So Far: A Brief Review

In Chapter 7 we are concerned with the relationships between thought, belief and reality. Up to this point, our attention has been occupied with the ways in which our thought processes are related to how we perceive 'real' things. We have examined some of the methods we use to gather and interpret information about real things; our attention has been focused on the processes which control the flow of information from a real object to our conscious experience. We have not considered how our conscious experience might condition the nature of 'real' objects. In the last section, however, the story of Harvey made us examine how conscious experience might influence the nature of 'real' objects; it obliged us to question the processes by which we determine whether what our senses detect is real.

In all the discussions we have used the fact that processes such as gathering and interpreting information are necessarily governed by rules. When we discussed Eddington's fishy story, we asked ourselves the typically Kantian question of how these rules govern the relationship between 'real' entities and conscious experience. The rules act as filters which control and restrict the information we can process: for example, they prevent us from experiencing anything physical except for three-dimensional objects. The discussions sprang from two observations made in the previous two chapters. We identified these on page 85.

- We gather only the information which our sense organs are capable of gathering.
- We need to process the information from the senses in order to understand something of the world.

[Note: We noted that these two form the basis of Kant's arguments in the 'Transcendental Aesthetic' and the 'Transcendental Analytic' sections of the *Critique of Pure Reason*.]

We have also noted that the gathering and processing of information does not operate independently of our own mental and physical activities. We seek out particular types of information for various reasons, but in particular to confirm that our picture of reality is consistent with all the possible information that we have gathered, and that we could gather. In other words, our activities are not random; they are set within a context which makes some sort of sense. This now leads us to a third observation:

- When we gather and process information we do so on the basis of the acceptance of a theory or a creed. In accepting a theory or a creed, we commit ourselves to accepting all the assumptions about reality contained in that theory or creed. These assumptions are often speculations.

[Note: The speculations come under the broad umbrella of 'speculative metaphysics'. They form the basis of the third part of the *Critique of Pure Reason* – the 'Transcendental Dialectic'. In this, Kant formulates a strong attack on speculative metaphysics, concluding that reason cannot justify any speculation which postulates things that exist beyond the reach of our senses.]

In the last section of this chapter we shall examine the analysis of speculative metaphysics by 'analytic philosophers'. In doing this, we are addressing the third, and more general question of this chapter:

> How are knowledge, belief and/or faith related
> to real 'things'?

Ontological Commitment

(Advanced section)

Some people believe in ghosts. Their beliefs are sometimes linked to their behaviour: for example, they may search for evidence of ghosts in ruined castles. This leads us to the examination of the suggestion that a set of beliefs and/or a particular type of behaviour commits someone to accepting that certain types of things exist.

Exercise 7.6 (Advanced exercise)

Some theories and some beliefs postulate the existence of real entities which the senses have never directly detected.

• • •

1. Make a list of five things which some people believe are real, or have been real, yet which their senses have never directly detected.

_____

_____

2. Consider two of the things you have described in Question 1. Describe a theory, belief or form of behaviour which implicitly commits people to accepting that these things exist.

_____

_____

Suggested answers are on p. 275.

In Exercise 7.6 we examined some unusual or limiting cases where behaviour commits a person to an acceptance that something exists. This leads us to the formation of a formal definition of 'ontological commitment' – a term coined by W. V. Quine (1948).

'Ontological commitment' is an implicit endorsement of the existence of an entity resulting from a person's behaviour and/or beliefs. If a person's behaviour cannot be intelligible without an assumption that some 'thing', let us call it X, exists, then the person is said to have made an implicit ontological commitment to the existence of X.

This means that, by behaving in a particular way, the person is endorsing the claim that X exists. For example, a person's participation in a religious ceremony may implicitly commit that person to accepting that a deity exists; alternatively, a person's use of a particle accelerator implicitly commits that person to accepting that a particular type of elementary particle exists.

The Reality of People and Ideas 8

Our discussions in Chapters 5, 6 and 7 have been based on an assumption that the internal elements of our conscious experience are the fundamental building blocks from which we construct reality. This assumption creates two gulfs between the subject of experience and reality: the first is the gulf between these known 'internal experiences' and an unknown 'world out there', which we have addressed in the last three chapters; the second is the gulf between these known 'internal experiences' and the unknown subject of the experience, me.

[Note: David Hume, in a famous passage in the Appendix to his *Treatise of Human Nature* (1888, p. 633), recognised that there was an inadequacy in his theory. The assumption that mental impressions received from the sense were the fundamental building blocks of knowledge of reality prevented him from having any knowledge of the subject of his own experiences.]

We are now going to see whether we can intelligibly assert that something other than our internal experience is a fundamental building block of reality. We shall examine the two 'gaps' again in Chapter 12, when we discuss the nature of our knowledge, and Chapter 15, when we discuss the nature of a person. Philosophers in the past have asserted that various things, other than our mental images, are fundamental building blocks of reality. In this chapter we discuss two of the best known of such claims: the first is that people, or perhaps the subjects of experience, are fundamental building blocks. It suggests a specific answer to the question:

> How real are people?

The second claims that universal ideas, sometimes also referred to as forms, are fundamental building blocks. It suggests a specific answer to the question:

> How real are ideas?

The first claim is associated with philosophers classified as 'existentialists' and the second with the Greek philosophers Socrates and Plato.

[Note: These categories are not rigid. There have been philosophers in other traditions whose position was close to that of the modern existentialists. The medieval scholastic philosopher Duns Scotus argued that the mind, consisting of intellect and will, is a fundamental entity, as did Thomas Reid in the eighteenth century.]

We start by examining some of the claims made by 'existentialists', and we move on to a brief examination of Plato's 'Theory of Forms'. The two sections are self-contained and can be tackled independently of each other. The first is an introduction to some of the ideas which have influenced much of Continental philosophy during the last two centuries – although, as we shall see they have earlier roots. The arguments are not easy to grasp and might require more than one reading. In addition, even if we end up by rejecting them, we can nonetheless find them rewarding, as they give us an insight into the human condition. In the second section, which starts on page 105, we analyse a thumbnail sketch of the 'Theory of Forms'.

IN THIS CHAPTER

Concepts discussed

- Intentionality
- Platonic 'idea' or 'form'

Theories discussed

- Existentialism
- Platonic 'Theory of Forms'

Skills developed

- Analysis of a theory
- Construction of an extended answer

Philosophers whose ideas are discussed

- Duns Scotus
- Plato

References made to the following philosophers

- David Hume
- Søren Kierkegaard

Real People – Introducing Existentialism

(Advanced section)

We noted in the previous chapter that the principle of ontological commitment states that behaving in a particular way or accepting a particular faith or set of beliefs commits us to acknowledge that particular things exist. The approach of the existentialists is similar, but distinctly different. Existentialist philosophers argue that cognitive experience is not a passive phenomenon; it actively involves the assent of the subject of the experience. This assent involves acts of will.

> Experience, therefore, presupposes the existence of a subject
> who has a will and an intellect; in other words, an individual.

In the *Oxford English Dictionary* existentialism is described as, 'A doctrine that concentrates on the individual, who, being free and responsible, is held to be what he makes himself by the self development of his essence through acts of the will.' It goes on to state that existentialism 'is a philosophy of will that stems from that unhappy Danish philosopher Søren Kierkegaard'.

Our interest, for the present, is the nature of reality; we shall concern ourselves with the question of the nature of the individual in Part IV. In concerning ourselves with the nature of reality, we shall discuss only part of what is commonly accepted to be the existentialist approach to philosophical issues. We shall leave out discussions of some key existentialist themes such as the individual and systems, being and absurdity, and the nature of communication, but examine the theme of freedom, and the nature and significance of choice, when we discuss moral value in Part III.

We shall not assess existentialist philosophy using a direct approach; instead, our reactions to certain human experiences will be examined. Our attention will be directed towards the way in which we react to repeated occurrences of similar experiences, which we do because the recognition that they are repeated means that we are aware that they are experiences of a particular type – in other words, we react because there is an element of self-monitoring in the experience.

We shall then ask ourselves whether we can use our will to modify our reactions to an experience, even where the experience is not a repeated one. Finally, we shall ask ourselves whether the use of the will provides us with grounds for asserting that the individual is a fundamental entity; we shall ask ourselves whether the will is something which has separate existence – an existence which cannot be completely determined by reference to other entities.

Exercise 8.1 (Advanced exercise)

Suppose you have experienced something for the first time. The experience is either positive or negative or neutral. A second or subsequent experience will also be either positive or negative or neutral.

1. Indicate whether this subsequent experience would be more or less positive than the first, more or less negative, or of equal value to the first experience.

· · ·

	First experience	Subsequently more/less positive/negative?

(i)   Eating an ice cream   _____

(ii)   Hearing a particular joke   _____

(iii)   Re-reading a particular thriller   _____

(iv)   Seeing a multi-coloured sunset   _____

(v)   Proving Pythagoras' Theorem   _____

(vi)   Responding to questioning after   _____
        being arrested

(vii)   Riding a bicycle in a straight line   _____

(viii) Acting a particular part in a play   _____

2. Specify which of the above repeated experiences can become more positive or less negative through your own mental effort? Describe how one of these experiences can be made more positive.

_____

_____

_____

3. If you claim that one experience cannot be enhanced, explain why it is impossible in that particular instance.

_____

_____

_____

4. Does the fact that we can modify an experience mean that we are more fundamental entities than the experience?

_____

_____

Suggested answers are on p. 277.

The suggested answers to Exercise 8.1 demonstrate the plausibility of existentialism: they indicate that there is a prima facie case supporting the claim that the individual is a fundamental entity. If the mental image which we experience can be modified, then there is something, other than the image itself, doing the modifying; this means that there is something, other than the image itself, which is a fundamental entity. The individual who believes that he is doing the modifying is a candidate for being such an additional fundamental entity. At minimum, we can state that individuals as existing entities are no less fundamental than the phenomena which are present in their consciousness.

We shall now move on to considering the possibility that there is more than just a prima facie case. For this purpose some preparatory work is necessary. If we are to understand and assess existentialism, we need to discover what arguments are relevant to supporting or refuting its claims. Such a task, however, requires an in-depth study which is beyond the scope of this book. We shall, therefore, restrict ourselves to an examination of two aspects of existentialism: in the first, conducted in this chapter, we look at the fundamental nature of the mind as a single entity with a will and an intellect; in the second, to be carried out in Part V, we shall discuss the idea of the individual as a free and responsible being who, by the self development of her essence through acts of the will, contributes to the creation and maintenance of her identity and is responsible for her own actions.

We would, however, be doing existentialism an injustice if we were not to concede that our emphasis on analysis is at odds with its principles, which are driven by a desire for synthesis rather than analysis. An analysis is a process in which component parts are separated in order to understand their function, whereas synthesis involves putting component parts together to see how the unified organism works. If a theory claims that a unified entity is a fundamental one, then the process of analysing it contradicts the claim ab initio, so any analysis of the fundamental entity cannot validly test the theory.

With this proviso in mind, let us proceed with the first of our examinations of existentialism. In our answers to Exercise 8.1 we noted that the mind can modify an experience. We also noted above (p. 65) that Henri Poincaré argued that an immobile individual could not formulate a concept of physical space: without directing his attention to his movements and moving his body using his 'muscular sense', the individual is unable to formulate the concept of three-dimensional space. We now broaden the question and ask whether every form of experience, and not just experience which helps us understand physical space, must be directed. We ask whether, in cognitive experience, the mind always directs its attention towards an object (in other words, whether the mind is a fundamental single entity with a will and an intellect).

The answer to this question forms the core of the argument of this section. The reader, especially one who is relatively new to philosophical analysis, is not expected to produce a detailed answer to Discussion Exercise 8.2. However, the effort involved in attempting to produce an answer proves to be rewarding. It is also possible to leave working through the suggested answer to a second reading of the text, as its central argument is stated below.

Discussion Exercise 8.2 (Advanced exercise)

1. Is it possible for an individual to have an experience which he does not direct towards some object?

_____

_____

Outline an answer using a scheme for developing an extended answer similar to the one set out on p. 67 above, and then reproduce a complete answer.

[Note: An answer to a question ought not to follow one particular scheme too rigidly: it needs to be sensitive to the specific requirements imposed by the particular question which is being addressed. Every scheme, however, must have a basic structure similar to the one given on p. 67.]

(a) Indicate what method or type of argument you will be employing in order to answer the question, that is, specify the parameters which guide the analysis of the question.

_____

_____

(b) Simplify (or 'deconstruct') the questions into sub-questions.

_____

_____

. . .

(c) Form the answers to the sub-questions.

_____

_____

(d) Ensure the sub-answers conform to the parameters which guide the analysis of the question.

_____

_____

(e) Form the answer to the question.

_____

_____

2. What impact does the answer to Question 1 have on the question of whether the individual is a fundamental entity?

_____

_____

Suggested answers are on p. 279.

We started this chapter with the intention of examining two claims that contest the notion that the only fundamental things from which reality is constructed are the phenomena we experience. Discussion Exercise 8.2 suggests that the subject of experience has a strong claim to be considered to be another fundamental element from which reality is constructed. The argument used in the suggested answer is a form of 'transcendental argument': the kernel of the argument is given on page 283.

Duns Scotus uses two transcendental arguments. In the first he states that a condition of the continued presence of a thought is the operation of the will; in the second he states that a condition of the possibility that the intellect can work on the content of consciousness is that it does so in conjunction with the will. In other words the mind, consisting at minimum of intellect and will, is a single unified entity.

In the answer to Discussion Exercise 8.2 we have established a prima facie case which gives some credence to one of the existentialist contentions, that the subject of experience is a fundamental entity.

[Note: This may go some way towards explaining the problem David Hume faced in his passage in the Appendix of his *Treatise of Human Nature* (p. 633), where he tried, but failed to find, the subject of his experiences amongst the images he found in consciousness.]

Our discussion in the present chapter has not thrown much light on some of the central concerns of existentialist philosophers. We have touched on a small aspect of the question of the individual as a free and responsible being who, by the self-development of his essence through acts of the will, somehow creates himself through acts of the will; we have not touched on other issues such as the nature and significance of choice, the individual and systems, being and absurdity, and the nature of communication. We shall now turn our attention to the second of the two challenges to the notion that the phenomena we experience are the most fundamental existing things.

Real Ideas and Plato's 'Theory of Forms'

In the previous section we discussed the existentialist refusal to accept the assumption that the internal elements of our conscious experience are the fundamental building blocks from which we are obliged to construct reality. Existentialist philosophers do not in general dispute the claim that inner sense experience provides us with one of the building blocks; rather, they challenge the claim that it provides us with the fundamental building blocks. We shall now examine a 2,400-year-old theory whose challenge to 'the theory of the primacy of inner sense experience' is total and complete.

[Note: The expression 'the theory of the primacy of inner sense experience' is not a standard philosophical expression. It is being used here to describe those philosophical positions which take the images presented to us by our senses as the fundamental building blocks of existence. In such theories, all other existing things are referred to as derivatives of these images.]

In the fifth and fourth centuries BC, Socrates and Plato developed a theory which rejected the possibility that sense experience could provide the basis of any claim concerning the nature of reality. Their theory is elaborated in various sections of Plato's writing, especially in *The Phaedo*, but the most famous exposition is to be found in *The Republic*. We touched on the theory in Revision Exercise 3.3 (p. 52) where we compared the reality of ideas with that of mountains, trees and houses.

It is not possible to do justice to Plato's exposition of the 'Theory of Forms' in a general introduction to philosophy. The theory covers virtually all areas of philosophy from the nature of reality and the basis of moral values to the nature of knowledge. In Exercise 8.3 we examined a synopsis of one of the arguments

Plato uses to support his theory. It is not the only argument Plato employs: in *The Republic*, he also makes use of an analogy between the state and the individual to convince his readers of the acceptability of some aspects of the theory. The exercise asked us to identify which aspects of the theory deal with ontology (theories about what exists) and which aspects deal with epistemology (theories about the nature of knowledge).

In this chapter the discussion of Plato's theory is restricted to what it tells us about fundamental real entities. In Exercise 8.3, where it is set out in a series of nine statements, this is done by analysing a synopsis of one of the arguments Plato uses to support his theory. As the statements are intended to represent Plato's argument, they are labelled with Greek letters.

[Note: We should be aware of the possible inaccuracies resulting from criticising a theory by using a synopsis. Firstly, someone who is interpreting the original work from English translations, some 2,400 years after the original was written, is unlikely to have picked up the nuances of Plato's Greek. Secondly, condensing an argument must diminish it in some way – had it been possible to capture all its essential features in such condensed form, it is likely that Plato would have done so himself! Ideally the reader should read, or even study, the arguments in *The Republic* or *The Phaedo* before tackling this exercise. Further, a post-modern critique would claim that the very process of drawing up a synopsis imposes modern notions onto Plato's theory, thus very probably ignoring the classical Greek mind-set. The exercise is nonetheless useful in that it gives us further experience of analysing a 'rationalist' argument.]

Exercise 8.3 (Advanced exercise)

Study the following synopsis of one of the arguments which Plato uses to support the 'Theory of Forms'.

α (*alpha*) Our sense experience always provides us with imprecise and ever-changing images of the world.

β (*beta*) Imprecise and ever-changing images cannot provide us with knowledge of reality – knowledge must be certain.

Some of our ideas are of perfectly formed abstract objects which are never-changing; for example, mathematical ideas of the perfect circle and the perfectly equilateral triangle, aesthetic ideas of absolute beauty and the moral notion of absolute goodness.

γ (*gamma*) Perfect, unchanging, abstract ideas, or 'forms' exist.

· · ·

The idea of absolute beauty enables us to explain why things are beautiful (*The Phaedo*, 99D–101A) and the idea of the perfect circle enables to us to explain circular motion.

δ (*delta*) The perfect 'forms' enable us to understand and explain the properties of the things we perceive in our inexact and ever-changing experiences.

We notice that there is a relationship between the way we get to know reality and the nature of reality.

ε (*epsilon*) An explanation of the presence of a property in an object or event is given on the basis of something more fundamental than the object or event.

ζ (*zeta*) The perfect, unchanging, abstract 'forms' are more fundamental entities than those provided by our concrete, inexact and ever-changing experiences.

η (*eta*) The entities which our ever-changing experience perceive obtain each of their properties from the corresponding 'form' of that property.

θ (*theta*) Reason alone, unpolluted by interference from the other faculties, can provide us with knowledge of the nature of these fundamentally real entities.

ι (*iota*) The unchanging, perfect forms are related to each other in perfect harmony. The harmony is provided and sustained by a supreme 'form', the 'Form of the Good'. It is the primary, or fundamental, 'form'.

Plato goes on to make a value judgement about the purpose of philosophy.

κ (*kappa*) The aim of philosophical study is to train the faculty of reason so that it can gain access to this primary, or fundamental, 'form'.

. . .

1. Indicate whether each statement makes a claim about our experiences, the nature of reality and/or our knowledge of reality. Where possible, indicate also whether you believe the statement to be true or false.

Statement	Experience	Reality	Knowledge	True or false
α (*alpha*)	_____	_____	_____	_____
β (*beta*)	_____	_____	_____	_____
γ (*gamma*)	_____	_____	_____	_____
δ (*delta*)	_____	_____	_____	_____
ε (*epsilon*)	_____	_____	_____	_____
ζ (*zeta*)	_____	_____	_____	_____
η (*eta*)	_____	_____	_____	_____
θ (*theta*)	_____	_____	_____	_____
ι (*iota*)	_____	_____	_____	_____
κ (*kappa*)	_____	_____	_____	_____

2. Basing your answer on what you have learnt so far of Plato's 'Theory of Forms', how do you think Plato himself would have answered the question in the cartoon? Do you think he would have accepted that the book is real?

_____

_____

_____

_____

_____

. . .

Suggested answers are on p. 285.

In this chapter we have examined two philosophical positions which question the notion that inner sense experience provides us with the fundamental building blocks of reality. We started by discussing the work of some relatively recent philosophers and finished with one from ancient Greece; in the latter we discussed a theory which philosophers throughout the world still discuss today. We shall return to question the relevance of Plato's theory in the Revision Exercises and ask why philosophers are still concerned with a theory written at a time when much of our knowledge of science was still in embryonic form. In order to do this profitably, we must develop our understanding of two of the main themes of Plato's 'Theory of Forms': ethics and epistemology. These are the topics discussed in Parts III and IV.

Part II: A Summary

We embarked on our quest into the nature of reality in Part II with a discussion of some of the extraordinary events which befell Alice at the beginning of her journey to Wonderland. We were addressing the question

> How real are physical things?

In answering this question, we embarked on a journey, which, like Alice's, also involved us in some detours.

The detours
The detours took us through some of the paces which are necessary in order to learn the skills philosophers frequently use to ply their trade. In the second section of Chapter 5 we discussed the criteria used when assessing the acceptability of claims about what really exists. These are general criteria, not restricted to the assessment of claims about reality. The minimum level of acceptability was that the claim should be **logically possible**; the next level was that the **preponderance of evidence** should convince us that the claim is valid, although we did not use this criterion in assessing any of the claims set out in the exercises; our most frequently used criterion was that the claim should be established as valid **beyond reasonable doubt**; the criterion which left no doubt as to the validity of the claim was that **proof** can be provided, in other words, that the claim was **incontrovertible**. Similar distinctions between levels of acceptability are used in courts of law. The purpose of taking this detour was to achieve some of the aims of philosophical study set out on page 4 above, with particular emphasis on the sixth, seventh and eighth skills listed concerning the assessment of arguments:

6. the ability to assess and formulate acceptable arguments;
7. the ability to assess and formulate rigorously logical arguments;
8. the ability to formulate, develop and assess definitions, claims, theories and hypotheses which are specific to the subject.

In our second detour, conducted in Chapter 6, we developed two skills, one in each section of the chapter. In each of these we focused on the ability to formulate arguments rather than assess them. The first of the two skills was a general one about how to structure an argument in order to answer a question. The question we answered involved an explanation of how the combined use of the senses might provide us with better reasons for accepting that something exists than the use of one individual sense alone. In Exercise 6.1 (p. 68) we followed five stages in formulating an argument and suggested that these stages provide a structure which can be a useful guide to the formulation of a philosophical argument.

In the second section of Chapter 6 we encountered transcendental analysis, which employs a type of argument frequently used in philosophy and which is closely associated with the work of Immanuel Kant; we worked through exercises constructing transcendental arguments.

The main journey

These detours were needed for us to appreciate the sights of the main journey, which took us through three areas of ontology. In the first of these, reached in Chapter 5, we inquired into the relationship between the reality of physical things and the information provided by our senses. We noted that there were other living creatures which have developed the ability to receive sensory information which our five senses cannot detect. We also noted that there is a difference between the information provided by touch and taste on the one hand, and sight, hearing and smell on the other: the immediacy of touch and taste highlighted the gap, which exists with regard to sight and hearing, between the perceiver on the one hand, and the object perceived on the other.

We found, however, that there is something that all our senses have in common regarding the status of claims that an object exists. Where such a claim is based solely on the information received from the senses, no proof of its existence can be formulated. The strongest form of argument we are able to develop that an object exists can only convince us beyond reasonable doubt. In some theories developed by philosophers, notably George Berkeley, this perennial doubt turned into a denial that anything exists except for our ideas.

Our discussion of Dr Samuel Johnson's famous 'refutation' of Berkeley's theory, by kicking a large stone, led us to consider two further factors which can affect the adequacy of an answer to the question, 'How real are physical things?' Both of the factors are related to our active role in gathering and processing the information from our senses. The first is that we process the information our senses produce; we do not merely absorb it. The second is related to the first: our cognitive experience is directed and purposive; we focus our attention on certain aspects of the content of our minds and process only those aspects. In addition, our senses do not operate at random, being instead purposively directed using 'muscular sense' in order to gather the information that we consider to be appropriate. These two factors provided the central themes for the investigations which we carried out in the final two chapters. In Chapter 7 we investigated the relationship between reality and the ways in which we use our cognitive skills and apparatus in order to interpret information about reality. We provided answers to three questions:

> When are we entitled to call something a 'thing'?

> Can thought generate real 'things'?

> How are knowledge, belief and/or faith related to real 'things'?

In the first section of Chapter 8 we discussed an approach to philosophy which disputes the claim that the phenomena presented to us by our senses provide us with the fundamental building blocks of reality. The discussion focused on the question:

> How real are people?

It started with an examination of the ways in which we can amend our conscious experience. This led on to an investigation into the significance of the purposive aspect of our cognitive experience. In part of the investigation, we asked whether it was possible for an individual to have an experience which she did not direct towards some object. The question led us to discuss the distinction between the experiences of cognitive and non-cognitive beings and, on page 282, we identified one of the central ideas which shapes and directs existentialist philosophy:

> In contrast with a non-cognitive being, the object of experience of a cognitive being is held in consciousness with the possibility that the thought of it might be communicated.

The existentialist believes that the holding of a thought in consciousness is purposive. Our analysis of this purposive aspect of experience introduced us to some of the forces which inspired the phenomenology and existentialism of philosophers such as Franz Brentano, Martin Heidegger and Jean-Paul Sartre. We noted in Discussion Exercise 8.2 that some of the roots of this approach to philosophy are to be found in the work of the scholastic philosopher John Duns Scotus, Doctor Subtilis (the Subtle Doctor).

In the second section of Chapter 8 we discussed the ideas contained in Plato's *Republic*, one of the most renowned texts in European philosophy. Our discussion focused on the question:

> ## How real are ideas?

Plato claimed that the properties of ordinary things were derived from eternal and unchanging ideas, or forms, which have an existence which is separate from the ordinary things. We analysed an outline of his argument. Here, as in the earlier sections of Part II, we were aiming at two targets: the first consisted of an understanding of the philosophical theory we were discussing; the second was the sharpening of our analytical skills. The analysis of the Platonic 'Theory of Forms' was aiming at both targets. As such it was aiming to meet all eight of the aims of philosophical study set out on page 4 above.

Revision Exercises

Revision Exercise 5.1 and 6.1

I smell gas in my garden. The smell is near the place where I remember seeing some workers laying a gas pipe three years ago. I cannot see, taste, touch or hear the gas.

1. Does this mean that, without evidence from my senses of sight, touch, hearing and taste, I can never establish beyond reasonable doubt that there is gas in my garden?

Suppose my neighbour joins me in the garden and he can also smell the gas.

2. Is the corroboration by my neighbour of my claim that there is gas sufficient to establish beyond reasonable doubt that there is gas in the garden?

Suggested answers are on p. 286.

Revision Exercise 5.2 and 6.2

René Descartes was sitting by the fire; he felt the warmth; it made him feel sleepy; he dropped in and out of a light sleep. When half awake, he saw the ashes, the flames and the burning wood; he could hear the crackle and hiss of the burning wood.

1. Is this evidence sufficient to establish beyond reasonable doubt that there was a fire?

2. Is this evidence sufficient to establish beyond reasonable doubt that Descartes existed?

Suggested answers are on p. 287.

Revision Exercise 5.3 and 6.3 (We now return to Discussion Exercise 4.2)

Is the knowledge of the existence of books, which depends on our direct perception, more certain than the knowledge of the existence of electrons, which we cannot perceive directly?

Suggested answers are on p. 288.

Revision Exercise 5.4 and 6.4

The Luddites were a group of people who, during the Industrial Revolution, believed that machines were taking over their work so they set about destroying them. They were known as the machine breakers. Ned Ludd, their leader, was reputed to have his headquarters in Sherwood Forest. There were no verified sightings of him.

. . .

1. Is it logically possible that 'Ned Ludd existed' is true? Does the ponderance of evidence lead us to accept that 'Ned Ludd existed' is true? Is it true beyond reasonable doubt? Or is its truth incontrovertible?

_____

_____

2. Do the same for the statement 'Ned Ludd did not exist'.

_____

_____

Suggested answers are on p. 289.

Revision Exercise 7.1

The sense organs which scientists have today function in the same way as the sense organs of medieval scientists.

What do modern scientists have, in addition to what their medieval predecessors had, which entitles them to claim that things like electrons and DNA molecules exist?

_____

_____

Suggested answers are on p. 290.

Revision Exercise 8.1

Duns Scotus maintained that the mind was a unified entity with a will and an intellect, and that the will was not subject to the laws which govern the production of sense experience. He argued that the thought produced by the arrival of some externally generated stimuli, such as are provided by our senses, would disappear if it were not maintained in consciousness by the will.

. . .

1. Could the imagination function in order to produce new ideas if the will were something which obeyed natural laws?

_____

_____

When an individual's eyes receive an image of a blue sky, the blueness appears to be unchangeable by the individual; it arrives unbidden into the subject of consciousness and cannot be changed.

2. Does the inability to change an impression produced by one of the senses mean that the impression is a more fundamental element of reality than the subject of consciousness?

_____

_____

Suggested answers are on p. 290.

Revision Exercise 8.2

The 'Theory of Forms' is still discussed over two millennia after it was written. Give some reasons why you think it has endured for so long.

_____

_____

Suggested answers are on p. 292.

Further Reading

Berkeley, George: *A New Theory of Vision* (Collins, 1710). The book in which Berkeley sets out his argument about the relationship between experience and the objects experienced.

Plato: *The Republic*. It is essential reading for anyone interested in any area of philosophy. In it Plato sets out his 'Theory of Forms' in a clear and accessible manner. There are various translations, but the one by Francis Cornford is probably the best one to be found in English.

Walsh W. H.: *Kant's Criticism of Metaphysics* (Edinburgh University Press, 1975). One of the clearest expositions of Kant's criticism of speculative metaphysics, it sets out Kant's arguments that any claim that someone has knowledge of objects is limited to judgements about our experiences.

PART III

VALUES and OBLIGATIONS

In the final section of Part II we examined a synopsis of Plato's 'Theory of Forms'. One could question the appropriateness of such an examination in a chapter that deals with reality: a discussion of Plato's theory could easily be situated in a chapter on values, as the theory's main concern is a determination of the nature of the just life. His notion of theory is an integrated one: in it, epistemology and ontology find their unity in the 'form of the good'. In other words, moral values sustain and are sustained by that which we know and think exists. Plato was disparaging about the value of art as a representation of reality, but not about the nature of beauty itself (see the reference to *The Phaedo*, p. 105 above.) The integrated nature of his theory is total: what we now call aesthetic values are inseparable from moral values, and individual moral values are amalgamated with social values.

In our analysis no assumption will be made that any particular theory of value is more acceptable than any other. We acknowledge the possibility that an integrated theory of value may be valid, and that moral and aesthetic values could be different aspects of values in general. We acknowledge the possibility that moral and aesthetic values are independent of each other, and therefore examine them separately. In Chapter 9, in order to discover where the sources of our moral and aesthetic values are found, we do some preliminary work and investigate the rules which govern ordinary behaviour.

In Chapters 10 and 11 we discuss aesthetics and ethics using different approaches. The discussion of aesthetics focuses on the development of the concept of beauty and on answering the question 'What is art?'

[Note: Many general books on philosophy give aesthetics little or no attention. In 790 pages on the history of philosophy, Bertrand Russell mentions aesthetics only three times in passing: on the third occasion it is to inform his readers of John Dewey's influence 'not only among philosophers, but on students of education, aesthetics and political theory' (1946, p. 774). Russell differentiates between students of aesthetics and philosophers. Even Jim Hankinson, in his highly erudite bluffer's guide (1985), does not mention it; perhaps a teacher of aesthetics threatened to sue him.

Despite these and other precedents, aesthetics is included in the topics discussed in this general introduction to philosophy. Two reasons favour its inclusion: firstly, an insight into the theories about aesthetics is needed if we are to have an adequate understanding of the human condition; secondly, the inclusion of aesthetics gives us the opportunity to carry out some fundamental philosophical analysis by asking basic philosophical questions about the nature of a particular human activity. Restrictions of space do not permit us to address the same question in our other discussions. For example, we do not analyse what we mean by epistemology in Chapter 12.]

The discussion of ethics is more extensive, covering five theories. It starts by examining two theories in which moral value and the principles which guide moral action are related to the operations of the faculty of reason. In the first of these we examine Aristotle's ethics, which located moral value in human virtue (human excellence) and moral values in the individual's pursuit of virtue. This is followed by a discussion of Kant's deontology (science of duty) guided by reason, in which the individual is both the moral legislator and the moral agent, and moral value is located in the exercise of freedom as legislator and agent.

These two theories of ethics are then contrasted with those which locate moral value in pleasure: John Stuart Mill's utilitarian ethics, and Henry Sidgwick's ethical egoism. The contrast with the first two theories carries through to the formation and operation of moral rules: in both Mill's and Sidgwick's theories moral rules are seen as similar to the laws of physics as they are determined by the natural desires and impulses of human beings.

In the fifth discussion of theories in ethics we examine a modification of the Kantian notion that moral value and freedom are closely linked. While Kant considered moral value consisted in freely choosing certain maxims of behaviour, the existentialists considered it to consist in a human being's freedom to act. Friedrich Nietzsche's use of this idea as a basis for his reaction against moral rules is contrasted with Kant's and Jean-Paul Sartre's belief that each individual's freedom is achieved through the recognition of the freedom of other individuals.

The discussion of five different theories of ethics creates an opportunity to compare them and thus to develop further some of the analytical skills needed to assess theories. This is done in the final section of Chapter 11.

Value and Values   9

In this brief introductory chapter we do some groundwork in preparation for the main investigations of Part III, which are on the nature of ethics and aesthetics.

On page 42 above we defined 'ethics' (or 'moral philosophy') as 'the branch of philosophy which inquires into the nature of right, wrong, good, evil, duties and responsibilities and into the nature of theories about right, wrong, good, evil, duties and responsibilities'. On page 44, we defined 'aesthetics' as 'the branch of modern philosophy which inquires into the nature of beauty and theories about beauty'. In Chapter 10 we shall understand why the word 'modern' appears in the definition of aesthetics but not in that of ethics. 'Good', 'bad', 'right', 'wrong', 'beauty' and 'ugliness' are all value terms: they each make some reference to a human value, which means that their use can never be neutral. These are, however, not the only value terms, as R. M. Hare (1952, p. 8) pointed out when introducing his discussion into the language of morals:

> for 'bad', is a value-word, and therefore prescriptive. And similarly, teleological theories of ethics which interpret 'right' as 'conducive to Z', where Z is a value word such as 'satisfaction' or 'happiness', only store up for themselves the difficulty of analysing such words.

[Note: 'Teleology' is the study of purposiveness, so a teleological theory of values is one which claims that the value is to be found in the aims of an action, a person or even a biological organism.]

In order to avoid some of these difficulties, we do some preparatory work and inquire into the possible sources of value (worth).

IN THIS CHAPTER

Concepts discussed

- Subjective values
- Rationalist values
- Objective values
- Intrinsic value
- Inter-subjective values
- Extrinsic value

Skills developed

- Analysis of a concept
- Analysis of arguments

Types of argument examined

• Infinite regress

Philosophers whose ideas are discussed

• Aristotle

References made to the following philosophers

• John Locke

Value and the Search for Values

There are two related, yet distinct, notions associated with the words 'value' and 'values'. We need to understand the distinctions if we are to conduct a proper search into the source of value. The use of the term 'value' (worth) which we employ in philosophy is as follows:

> the relative status of a thing, or the estimate in which it is held, according to its real or supposed worth, usefulness, or importance. In Philosophy and Social Sciences, regarded esp. in relation to an individual or group. (*OED*)

The dictionary rightly does not commit itself to whether the worth is real or supposed; producing arguments sustaining a claim that it is either real or supposed is a task for the philosopher. We use the plural term 'values' in a slightly different sense. The dictionary captures this difference by indicating that 'values' refer to: 'the principles or standards of a person or society, the personal or societal judgement of what is valuable and important in life' (*OED*). Values (principles) in this sense are based on a value, and the relationship between the value and the values is independent of experience: once we know what a set of principles is, we do not need experience to determine the human value that sustains them as this is given in the definition of the principles.

Our present concern is to understand the nature of the values or principles which determine what is aesthetically or morally valued. A good place to start is the reasons people give to justify their judgements and actions: a justification of an action only makes sense if it is based on a rule which itself is based on some sort of value. We discussed consequentialist and essentialist reasons for behaving in particular ways in Chapter 2: in Discussion Exercise 2.2 we considered consequentialist and essentialist reasons why a kitchen assistant might have washed some dishes; in Exercise 2.7 we examined the consequentialist and essentialist reasons which inspire people to study chemistry.

The discussions about consequentialism and essentialism restricted our inquiry to two types of reason that we give to justify our actions: those concerning the nature of the action itself and those which focus on the results – the value of the action was found either in the action itself or in something valuable that the action produced. It is possible that these two sources of value are not the only ones which can be used to justify an action. In order to discover whether others exist, let us consider an example to see whether we might find sources of value (worth) in it.

Exercise 9.1

Suppose that a business executive decides to invest a firm's assets in a project that is designed to provide a leisure centre in a deprived city area. The executive claims that the investment she has authorised is justifiable. She could, for example, give a **consequentialist** reason based entirely on her own sentiments in order to justify her claim. She could also give an **essentialist** reason which was independent of her own sentiments.

1. Formulate a **consequentialist** rule of behaviour, which the business executive could have been following, that takes into account only her own sentiments.

2. Formulate a **consequentialist** rule of behaviour, which the business executive could have been following, that is independent of her own sentiments.

3. Formulate an **essentialist** rule of behaviour, which the business executive could have been following, that takes into account only her own sentiments.

· · ·

4. Formulate an **essentialist** rule of behaviour, which the business executive could have been following, that is independent of her own sentiments.

_____

_____

5. In each of the cases 1–4, specify something of value which could be cited to justify the following of the rule.

_____

_____

Suggested answers are on p. 293.

Types of Values (Principles)

Both the questions and the answers for Exercise 9.1 assume that it is possible to have values based on the sentiments of individuals. In the context of values, philosophers use the words 'subjective' and 'objective' in a technical sense with the following meanings:

'Subjective values' are **principles or standards** which are dependent on the cognitive experiences of an individual and which enable her to assess to what extent an action, event or object has worth. For example, the standard of beauty determined by the maxim 'beauty is in the eye of the beholder' is based on subjective values.

'Objective values' are **principles or standards** which are independent of the cognitive experiences of an individual and which enable him to assess to what extent an action, event or object has worth. For example, the principle that what is right is determined by the Ten Commandments is based on objective values.

The following of a rule embodied by either subjective or objective values (principles) is frequently justified by appealing to a source of value (worth) such as a practical sentiment (the pleasure generated), but this is not the only type of justification. Philosophers also cite two other sources of value (worth), both of which are rather abstract. We shall attempt to obtain an understanding of them by considering the answers to two questions based upon the reasons Alice gave for drinking from the bottle with 'a paper label, with the words "DRINK ME" beautifully printed on it in large letters' in Exercise 5.1, Question 3, page 57.

The suggested answer to that question indicated that her reasons for drinking were based upon what all sensible people should do. One should not forget 'the simple rules their friends had taught them: such as, that a red-hot poker will burn you if you hold it too long; and that if you cut your finger *VERY* deeply with a knife, it usually bleeds; and she had never forgotten that, if you drink much from a bottle marked 'poison', it is almost certain to disagree with you, sooner or later'.

Exercise 9.2

Alice was using her faculty of reason in deciding how to act; she was also invoking the rules her friends had taught her. This gives her two possible sources of value which could justify her action.

1. Formulate a rule of behaviour, which Alice could have been following, that is based on the operations of her faculty of reason.

2. Formulate a rule of behaviour, which Alice could have been following, that is based on her reliance on the rules developed by her friends.

Suggested answers are on p. 294.

The two questions and answers indicate that we may have two further types of values in addition to subjective and objective ones: one is the operation of the faculty of 'practical reason' and the other is the mutual agreement of fellow humans. Our analysis of what rules might govern Alice's decision to drink from the bottle has not been rigorously thorough; it was designed to provide an indication of the principles which are used to build rigorously formal value systems. Alice was attempting to be consistent: she wanted to ensure that what she did was in harmony with the rules which determined the proper way to use her reason – a harmony which was valuable to her. Moral value based on this sort of harmony is the type we find in Kant's *Critique of Practical Reason*, which is based on a rationalist value system.

'Rationalist values' are principles or standards, based on the rules which govern a cognitive individual's 'reason', which enable him to assess the extent to which an action, event or object has worth. Kant's 'Categorical Imperative', which we discuss in Chapter 11, provides us with an example.

[Note: We should distinguish between locating 'value' (worth) in the faculty of reason and basing 'values' (principles) on the operations of reason. We shall see in Chapter 11 that Aristotle located value in the faculty of reason while Kant's values – the principles which sustained his system of moral rules – were based on the operations of reason. In *Art and Beauty in the Middle Ages*, Umberto Eco (1986, pp. 85–6) tells us that John Duns Scotus considered beauty to be an aggregate of qualities of size, shape, colour and so on. He states that 'Scotus' theory of the multiplicity of forms, however, meant that his aesthetics had a relational basis. It led him to a more analytical, less unitary conception of beauty.' This moved Scotus away from the Aristotelian concept of value, which we examine in Chapter 11.]

The second question and its answer point us towards the search for values (principles) in the relationships between people. Some Continental philosophers, such as Jürgen Habermas, look for criteria which justify actions in such relationships: they see a source of value as being located in 'intersubjectivity' (see Peter Dews, 1999, p. 124 ff). Due to their complex nature, discussions on intersubjectivity are more appropriate in a post-introductory book on philosophy, but we can keep a definition in mind when discussing the basis of theories of ethics and aesthetics.

'Inter-subjective values' are principles or standards, set by criteria of mutual acceptability, which enable an individual to assess to what extent an action, event or object has worth.

Intrinsic and Extrinsic Value

We started the chapter with an examination of the reasons people give to justify their judgements and actions. By examining possible consequentialist and essentialist justifications we identified four domains where we could find qualities that determined values: objective, subjective, rationalist and inter-subjective. These values (principles governing action) are based on what is valuable, and we have not yet specified what is actually either morally or aesthetically valuable; we do this in the next two chapters. Before doing so, there is one further piece of preparatory work which requires our attention: we need to clarify the distinction between 'intrinsic' and 'extrinsic' value. Indeed, we need to establish whether anything can have intrinsic value.

Exercise 9.3

α (alpha) Every art, every investigation and every practical pursuit or undertaking, seems to aim at some good. Therefore it can properly be said that what everything aims at is the Supreme Good.

· · ·

Aristotle claimed that if there is anything that is valued, then there must be one thing that has intrinsic value (NE 1094a 18–24). Aristotle's argument in support of his claim α (alpha) above consists of the statements α (*alpha*) to ε (*epsilon*), which are paraphrases of the W. D. Ross translation of the original Greek. This means that they might not reflect Aristotle's ideas accurately. He did not use the labels we use here. Study each claim and answer the question which follows it.

α (*alpha*) Every art, every investigation and every practical pursuit or undertaking, seems to aim at some good.

1. This is one of Aristotle's premises. Is it true?

β (*beta*) We find that the arts, practical pursuits and sciences aim at a variety of ends. There are numerous actions, arts and sciences; it follows, therefore, that their ends are correspondingly numerous. For example, the end of the science of medicine is health, that of the art of shipbuilding is a vessel, that of strategy is victory, and that of domestic economy is wealth.

2. Is this statement true? If so, is it true on **rational** or **empirical** grounds?

γ (*gamma*) There are master arts, pursuits and sciences and subordinate arts, pursuits and sciences. For example, bridle making and the other trades concerned with horses' harness are subordinate to horsemanship.

δ (*delta*) The ends of the master arts, pursuits and sciences are things more to be desired than the ends of the subordinate ones. This is because the subordinate ones are only pursued for the sake of the master ones. The aim desired by bridle making is subordinate to the aim desired by horsemanship.

3. Is it possible for someone to practise medicine for reasons other than generating health? If so, does this mean that statement δ could be false?

...

ε (*epsilon*) If every aim were subordinate to some other aim, the process of desiring an end would go on ad infinitum, in which case all desire would be empty and futile. And it makes no difference whether the ends of the pursuits were the activities themselves or some other thing beside these, as in the case of the sciences mentioned.

The process of going on ad infinitum is known in philosophy as an 'infinite regress'. Aristotle is stating that the infinite regress leads to a ridiculous conclusion: when the regress leads to a ridiculous conclusion it is known as a 'vicious regress'; when it leads to a harmless conclusion it is known as a 'benign regress'. To avoid the vicious regress, we must reject the notion that every aim is subordinate to some other aim. By stating that the regress leads to a ridiculous conclusion Aristotle is using a *reductio ad absurdum* argument, but does not explicitly state the conclusion that there must be an end at which all the other ends aim.

4. Is Aristotle describing a 'vicious regress' in Statement ε, or is it possible for people to desire some objects without knowing what good it leads to?

_____

_____

Suggested answers are on p. 295.

ζ (*zeta*) If, therefore, there is some ultimate end of the things we do, which we desire for its own sake (everything else being desired for the sake of this), . . . clearly this must be the good and the Supreme Good.

We postpone the discussion of (ζ), and the claims which follow it in Aristotle's text, to the first section of Chapter 11 where we examine virtue ethics.

Aristotle distinguishes between 'final ends' with intrinsic value, which we will, or desire for their own sake, and 'subordinate ends' with extrinsic value, which we will, or desire for the sake of something else. His argument is designed to support the claim that there must be a single thing which has intrinsic value.

Exercise 9.4

1. Assess Aristotle's argument set out in Exercise 9.3 by giving it a grade A to F, with A being excellent and F being a failure.

2. Give the reasons for your mark.

Suggested answers are on p. 297.

Summary of Chapter

The work carried out in this chapter has been that of an under-labourer. The image of the under-labourer is one which John Locke used when he described a philosopher as someone who clears away the rubble so that the real builders can come along and construct a proper edifice.

> The commonwealth of learning is not at this time without master-builders, whose mighty designs, in advancing the sciences, will leave lasting monuments to the admiration of posterity: but every one must not hope to be a Boyle or a Sydenham; and in an age that produces such masters as the great Huygenius and the incomparable Mr. Newton, with some others of that strain, it is ambition enough to be employed as an under-labourer in clearing the ground a little, and removing some of the rubbish that lies in the way to knowledge. (John Locke 1690: 'Epistle to the Reader')

We have now cleared some of the ground for the master-builders of theories of aesthetics and ethics, who have included the types of human value amongst their construction materials and tools: the notions of good, evil, beauty and ugliness all refer to different types of human value. We have also examined the various ways in which these materials and their components could be used to construct principles which determined how value could be detected. Our brief examination of some aspects of human behaviour has revealed that these principles could be found in: 'subjectivism', 'objectivism', 'inter-subjectivism' and 'rationalism'. We have also noted that the type of component material can vary: a theory can be constructed out of material with 'intrinsic value' and material with 'extrinsic value'.

The under-labouring work will help us to see the work of the master-builders of theories of aesthetics, but space does not permit a detailed examination of their work. Discussions of the theories of Francis Hutcheson, David Hume, Immanuel Kant, Benedetto Croce, Leo Tolstoy, G. E. Moore, R. G. Collingwood and the triumvirate of Fichte, Schelling and Hegel must be left to more specialised studies than our present one. In the next chapter we restrict ourselves to looking at the sort of questions we need to ask if we are either to assess, or construct a theory of aesthetics.

We shall then move on to a discussion of some of the master-builders of theories of moral philosophy (such as Aristotle, Immanuel Kant, John Stuart Mill, and Jean-Paul Sartre) as well as Friedrich Nietzsche's rejection of moral rules.

Theories of Art, Beauty and Taste

10

Our investigation in Chapter 9 into the possible sources of value has prepared us for an examination of some of the ideas which have led philosophers to elaborate their theories of aesthetics. In elaborating their theories, these philosophers are acting in accordance with the second part of our definition of aesthetics set out at the end of Chapter 4.

'Aesthetics' is the branch of modern philosophy which inquires into the nature of beauty and theories about beauty. To the extent that art is concerned with beauty, aesthetics also concerns itself with theories about the nature of art.

In the first section of the chapter we take a brief look back at the significant transformation of academic subjects which took place in European universities in the seventeenth and eighteenth centuries. It was during this period that aesthetics as we know it today was not only born as an academic subject, but also given its name. This section is purely historical and, as such, contains no exercises. It is followed by a section in which we ask ourselves what we mean by 'beauty' and 'art'. In addressing these issues we also discuss the question of what we mean by taste.

IN THIS CHAPTER

Concepts discussed

- Aesthetics
- Beauty
- Art

Skills developed

- Analysis of concepts
- Evaluation of theories

References made to the following philosophers

- Anthony Shaftesbury
- Benedetto Croce
- John Dewey
- Friedrich Nietzsche
- Aristotle
- Karl Marx
- G. E. Moore
- Francis Hutcheson
- Plato
- Plotinius
- Jean-Paul Sartre
- Leo Tolstoy
- Johann Gottlieb Fichte
- Immanuel Kant
- David Hume

The Birth of Aesthetics

The use of the word 'aesthetics' and the academic subject of aesthetics

The subject of aesthetics as an independent subject is relatively new in the history of philosophy. Prior to its use by Alexander Baumgarten in his unfinished treatise *Aesthetica* (1750–8), the word 'aesthetics' had been used exclusively to denote the study of the way our five senses operate. Baumgarten associated the purpose of sensations with beauty, contrasting the aim of logical knowledge with that of sensuous, or aesthetic, knowledge: logical knowledge seeks truth whereas aesthetic knowledge seeks beauty. The word 'aesthetics' comes from the Greek word αισθητικα (*aesthêtica*), which means 'things perceptible by the senses'.

The use of the word 'aesthetics' to denote the study of the relationship between sensations and knowledge of the world was still widespread in the late eighteenth century when, in 1781, Immanuel Kant published his *Kritik der reinen Vernunft* (*Critique of Pure Reason*). In a section entitled 'Die transscendentale Ästhetik' ('the Transcendental Aesthetic'), he analyses the conditions which must prevail if we are to be able to understand the signals which our senses provide for us – here Kant was using the word in its original sense. By 1790, when he published his *Kritik der Urtheilskraft* (*Critique of Judgement*), he was attributing a meaning to the term 'aesthetics' which is closer to our modern one:

> The requisites for fine art are, therefore, *imagination*, *understanding*, *soul* and *taste**. . . . Beauty (whether it be of nature or of art) may be in general termed the *expression* of aesthetic ideas. (*footnote: 'The first three faculties are first brought into union by means of the fourth.') (Kant's emphasis) (C3, p. 320)

In France the 'Philosophes' of the Enlightenment were quick to adopt the word. The new use of the term did not appear in the first edition of the *Encyclopédie* (which was published in eleven volumes between 1751 and 1772) but appeared in the edition published in 1781 – with both editions having been overseen by Denis Diderot.

> Esthétique . . . terme nouveau, inventé pour désigner une science qui n'a été réduite en forme depuis peu d'années. C'est la philosophie des beaux arts. (Aesthetics . . . a new term, developed to designate a science which has only been formalized in the last few years. It is the philosophy of the fine arts.) (Encyclopédie XIII pp. 84–6) (My translation, FCR)

The word took a little more time to cross into the English-speaking world: its use in philosophy throughout Europe and North America started to spread after Hegel's publication of *Aesthetik* in Germany in the 1820s. The date of the first use of the term in English, cited by the *Oxford English Dictionary*, is from 1832: 'Æsthetics (Æsthetik) is the designation given by German writers to a branch of philosophical inquiry, the object of which is a philosophical theory of the beautiful.'

The English-speaking world may have been slow to adopt the word, but it had been in the forefront of the development of the analysis of beauty as a function of the operation of one of our senses. The origins of aesthetics as the subject we know today can be traced back to the writings of Anthony Shaftesbury, one of John Locke's pupils in the late 1690s. However, his main concern was to develop a theory of virtue, rather than one of aesthetics. In doing this he argued, in opposition to Locke, that virtue is based on a 'moral sense' which operates in a similar way to the other senses in that it detects moral qualities. The moral sense recognises benevolence, beauty and justice in a harmonious system. Harmony in the system is recognised by the moral sense in the same way that colour and shape are recognised by the sense of sight. The link between the senses and beauty was established. In 1725 Francis Hutcheson, the Irish philosopher who was one of the leading figures in the Scottish Enlightenment, placed particular emphasis on the link in his theory of beauty (1994, pp. 7–45). He was the first writer to put into systematic form the study of beauty outlined by Kant (see above) although he spoke in terms of a physical sense rather than a human faculty. Hume's analysis of taste, as based on an inner sense (he did not use the term 'aesthetic sense'), was an adaptation of Shaftesbury's and Hutcheson's ideas.

Fine art as an academic subject

The fact that aesthetics was a late developer among subjects in philosophy is related to the late development of fine art as an academic subject. This can be attributed to the endurance of the two aspects of the Greek notion of beauty, which retained a dominant influence in European thought through to the eighteenth century. One of these was concerned with what is beautiful, and the other with the relationships between notions of beauty and morality.

The Greeks viewed the visual arts as being inferior to poetry and music. Their word for the visual arts was τεχνη (*techne*, skill – from which we obtain our words technique, technology etc.). The image is of an artisan's work rather than an artist's. Art was regarded as a skill in which neither the artisan's activity nor the objects he produced were considered to have a meaning which went beyond a reproduction of what the five senses perceived. Virtue and war were both considered to be 'arts': one of living, and the other of victory. Plato does not mention the visual arts when discussing beauty in *The Phaedo*; he sees them instead as a form of imitation (μιμησις (*mimesis*) – from which we derive our word 'mimic') of reality. In his strong attack on art in *The Republic* (Book X), he describes it as being twice removed from reality, since it is only a representation of a copy of a form. The division between poetry and music on the one hand, and the visual arts of painting, sculpture and architecture on the other, was evident in the Middle Ages: poetry and music were studied in academic institutions whereas painting, sculpture and architecture were confined to artisans' guilds.

The move towards the recognition of the visual arts as being more than just a manifestation of a technical skill became evident in sixteenth-century Italy. In Italian universities such as Bologna, which had been established some five hundred years earlier, academics began to debate the relative merits of the different 'liberal arts' (as we understand the term today). A contribution to the debate was provided by Leonardo da Vinci who, in *Il Paragone*, argued for the superiority of painting over poetry. Leonardo was, however, keen to show that painting was a science; the separation between arts and sciences was just beginning, and still had a long way to go. For example, in 1727, the first edition of E. Chambers' *Cyclopaedia* categorised painting, along with optics, architecture and sculpture, under the category of 'mathematical sciences'.

The unification of the liberal arts as we know them today came to fruition in the seventeenth and eighteenth centuries. As we have seen, Anthony Shaftesbury in England, followed in Scotland by Francis Hutcheson and then David Hume, analysed beauty as being based on an inner sense which was applicable to all the liberal arts. In France in 1714, J. P. Crousaz published *La Traite du Beau* in which he analysed the visual arts, poetry and music under a general theory of beauty. This was followed in 1746 by the works of Charles Batteaux in his publication of *Les beaux arts réduits à un même principe* (The fine arts reduced to the same principle).

This last title gives an indication of the changes which were occurring in the seventeenth and eighteenth centuries. Not only were the liberal arts being gathered into a single conceptual framework, but a single principle explaining the nature of beauty in them all was also being sought. This process of unification carried with it a parallel process of separation.

The separation of the academic subject of aesthetics from other theories of value

At the beginning of the eighteenth-century beauty and moral goodness were considered to be different aspects of the same phenomenon, although the signs of a bifurcation were beginning to emerge. The Greek notion that beauty and morality were intertwined in the virtuous life was still firmly entrenched in European consciousness. For example, in 1741 Père André published *L'Essai sur le Beau* in which he discussed the beauty of morality to be found in the works of the spirit, claiming that there were three kinds of beauty: divine, natural and artificial. The link between beauty and morality was maintained by the British philosophers of the time, such as Anthony Shaftesbury, who associated both moral and aesthetic value (worth) with an inner sense – as we noted in the suggested answer to Exercise 7.2 on page 271.

The beginnings of the separation of moral values from aesthetic ones can be seen in Francis Hutcheson's work and later in Kant's. Hutcheson differed from Shaftesbury, suggesting that we had separate inner senses which detected moral goodness and beauty: moral sense generated moral values which were distinct from aesthetic principles generated by the aesthetic sense.

The separation in Kant was not a fundamental separation. It stemmed from his derivation of value from the premises which were needed to be satisfied in order for moral or aesthetic judgements to be possible. Hence the conditions which made moral judgements possible were different from those which make aesthetic judgements possible, but both were based on the operation of the faculty of reason. This led to an apparent separation of moral values and the principles of aesthetics – since both were determined by the operation of a single faculty.

Conclusion

There were three distinct developments which led to the establishment of aesthetics as a separate discipline in eighteenth-century Europe. The first, growing from seeds sown in Renaissance Italy, was the rejection of the view that academic study of beauty should be restricted to poetry and music. The liberal arts were being gathered into a single conceptual framework, and a single unifying principle explaining the nature of beauty was being sought. Secondly, aesthetics was increasingly associated with sensitivity – humans possess an inner sense that detects aesthetic value – hence the use of the word 'aesthetics'. Thirdly, there was a move towards separating moral value from aesthetic value. In all these developments the link between aesthetics and beauty remained constant. What was not constant, however, was the concept of beauty.

What is Beauty?

In our analysis of the sources of value in Chapter 9 we found that value could have its origins either in the person experiencing an object of value, the object itself, or in some interactions between the object and the person. This left us in a certain amount of uncertainty as to what value was. Our brief excursion into history showed us that the definitions of art and beauty tended to change with time, so increasing this uncertainty. The meanings of art and beauty do not appear to be as stable as the meanings of the words related to the natural sciences. The definition of 'solidity' has not generated the sort of discussion that we find in the debates over the meaning of beauty; and while non-philosophers might ask themselves the question 'What is art?' few of them appear to be troubled by the question 'What is physics?'

One way to discover what we mean by solidity is to examine various experiences of things; differentiate between what we call solid and non-solid objects and then specify the criteria for differentiating between solid and non-solid objects. The same can be done with beauty and art. We start with an examination of how we use the word 'beauty', but do so from the particular viewpoint of someone who, like Francis Hutcheson, believes that we have an aesthetic sense which detects beauty in the way the sense of hearing detects sounds. The use of such a method does not, however, commit us to the belief that we have a separate sense of beauty along with the other senses of touch, smell, hearing, taste and sight.

Exercise 10.1

'According to Père André (*Essai sur le Beau*, 1741), there are three kinds of beauty – divine beauty, natural beauty, and artificial beauty.' Tolstoy (1930, p. 95)

The view at sunset of the Painted Desert in Arizona is thought to be beautiful.

1. Describe a natural object, physical feature or event which is thought to be ugly.

_____

_____

2. Describe a human artefact which is thought to be beautiful.

_____

_____

3. Was Père André right to claim that natural and artificial beauty are different?

_____

_____

In the mid-eighteenth century, Francis Hutcheson used an empirical method to analyse beauty by looking at the circumstances in which we, using our 'aesthetic sense', discern alterations in beauty. According to Hutcheson: 'The figures which excite in us the ideas of beauty seem to be those in which there is *uniformity amidst variety*.' (1995, p. 15) He goes on to say that, when we have uniformity, an increase in variety increases the beauty of the object; he gives mathematical examples to illustrate his point. 'The beauty of an equilateral triangle is less than that of a square, which is less than that of a pentagon, and this again is surpassed by the hexagon.'

. . .

4. Was Hutcheson right?

(i) Is uniformity a necessary attribute of beauty? Using Hutcheson's example, is a square always more beautiful than a non-square rectangle?

_____

_____

(ii) Does an increase in variety increase beauty? Using Hutcheson's example, is an octagon always less beautiful than a twenty-sided polygon?

_____

_____

At the turn of the nineteenth century Johann Gottlieb Fichte argued that beauty could be discerned by intuition. Beauty does not exist in the world in the way that yellowness does, ready for our senses to discern it; on the contrary, it exists in the beautiful soul. The soul operates in three realms: the 'sensible' realm of sense experience, the moral realm of spiritual experience and the aesthetic realm, which provides the means for the other two realms to interconnect. Beauty is not just in the eye of the beholder, but also in his soul.

In the story of Snow White and the Seven Dwarves, the wicked queen asks the mirror to tell her who is the most beautiful woman of them all. This question only makes sense if beauty is a universal property which anyone can judge.

5. Is the intelligibility of her question enough for us to justify a claim that beauty is not just in the eye or the soul of the beholder?

_____

_____

Hegel developed Fichte's theory that beauty belonged to the spiritual, rather than the physical realm. According to him only the soul is truly beautiful, which means that nature can only be beautiful if it reflects the natural beauty of the spirit.

· · ·

6. Is the beauty of nature only the reflection of the natural beauty of the spirit?

_____

_____

The two theories considered fall under the general categories encapsulated by the *OED* definition of beauty:

(i) 'That quality or combination of qualities which affords keen pleasure to senses.'

(ii) 'That quality or combination of qualities which charms the intellectual or moral faculties, through inherent grace, or fitness to a desired end.'

Hutcheson's theory falls into the group of theories in which beauty is considered to be a quality which affects the senses, while Fichte's and Hegel's belong to the group which finds beauty in the charmed state of an intellectual or moral faculty.

One 'instrument' we could use to measure one theory against the other is seeing how well it fits in with our own ideas; this would be a subjective instrument.

7. What objective instruments could you employ to help you to decide between these two opposing types of theory?

_____

_____

8. Using the instruments you have set out in Question 7, assess the relative merits of the brief sketches of Hutcheson's and Fichte's theories of aesthetics.

_____

_____

Suggested answers are on p. 298.

What is Art?

Philosophers are generally interested in developing a theory for more reflective reasons than those of scientists: philosophers, like scientists, want to understand the world, but they also want to understand this understanding. Our reasons for inquiring into theories of beauty are not only to understand how to create beautiful things. They go further – as philosophers we wish to deepen our understanding of the human condition. Our last exercise has given us some insight into the ways in which we develop theories about our activities and values. We can now carry out a similar inquiry into the nature of art.

Exercise 10.2

1. Consider art as a pursuit or occupation. Give two characteristics without which an activity could not be considered to be art.

_____

_____

2. Give three possible different aims of art as a pursuit.

_____

_____

3. Which of these views most closely encapsulates what you believe to be the aim of art?

_____

_____

Suggested answers are on p. 302.

The endurance of the use of the word 'art', despite the disagreement over what it is, indicates that art and aesthetics might not be definable in terms of human experience; they are not like physics, where debates on the nature of what physics is, are rare. We now turn to ethics, the second of our two inquiries into theories about human values, and consider whether it has the same intractable quality.

Moral Value, Moral Values and Duty

11

The central aim of this chapter is a dual one: firstly, to gain an understanding of some of the principal theories of moral value; secondly, to become acquainted with particular moral values which have been developed by philosophers since the times of ancient Greece. An awareness of the main characteristics of the theories is needed in order for us to satisfy the subsidiary objective of the chapter, which is to develop critical skills in order to facilitate an assessment or criticism of any of the theories. This is needed because a criticism of a theory of value (worth) or of a system of values (principles) is carried out from the standpoint of a rival theory or system.

In Chapter 4 we defined 'ethics' (or 'moral philosophy') as that branch of philosophy which inquires into the nature of right, wrong, good, evil, duties and responsibilities and into the nature of theories about these concepts. At the beginning of Chapter 9 we noted R.M. Hare's statement that '"bad" is a value-word and is therefore prescriptive'. That is, value-words are not neutral with respect to human behaviour, but put pressure on us to behave in particular ways; simply put, they put us under obligations. Each of the terms 'right', 'wrong', 'good', 'evil', 'duty' and 'responsibility' is also a value-word and is therefore prescriptive'. The moral philosopher studies and tries to explain the nature of the pressure which value-words exert in the same way as the physicist studies and attempts to explain the nature of physical forces, such as the force exerted by gravity. However, just as the physicist is not restricted to the study of gravity, so the moral philosopher is not restricted to the analysis of the role of value-words, although this was the main preoccupation of 'analytic' philosophers such as Hare in the third quarter of the twentieth century.

In this chapter we pose two questions:

> What is the nature of the pressure which a person feels, to act in a moral manner?
>
> How is this pressure related to moral value?

In seeking answers to these questions we consider five theories which offer explanations regarding the nature of the pressure which either a moral value or a system of moral values exerts on humans to behave in particular ways. We examine

Aristotle's virtue ethics, Immanuel Kant's deontology (science of duty), John Stuart Mill's utilitarianism, Henry Sidgwick's ethical egoism and Friedrich Nietzsche's and Jean-Paul Sartre's theories that moral value is found in the individual's exercise of freedom. Of these theories Kant's is the most abstract and may require more time to absorb, since it also incorporates Nietzsche's and Sartre's theories of moral value. It could, however, be tackled after the sections on utilitarianism and ethical egoism.

Although there are five standard theories, there are essentially two categories of explanation in ethics – those centred on the moral agent and those on moral action. Generally speaking, agent-centred explanations find moral value in the person who acts whereas action-centred explanations focus on the action of the person. This division is not, however, clear-cut because agent-centred explanations have to recognise that the moral value of an agent manifests itself through her actions; similarly, action-centred explanations have to recognise that every moral action originates from the behaviour of an agent. One advantage of distinguishing agent-centred from action-centred moral theories is that, by doing so, we can more easily understand Kant's deontology, where moral value is located in the relationship between the agent, as legislator of her own moral laws, and her 'free' actions.

IN THIS CHAPTER

Concepts discussed

- Substance
- *Summum bonum*

Theories discussed

- Virtue ethics
- Freedom as the
  Summum bonum
- Utilitarianism
- Ethical egoism
- Deontology

Skills developed

- Analysis of concepts
- Assessment of theories
- Analysis of text

Types of argument examined

- Infinite regress
- *Ignoratio elenchi*

Philosophers whose ideas are discussed

- Aristotle
- Henry Sidgwick
- Robert Nozick
- Immanuel Kant
- Friedrich Nietzsche
- John Stuart Mill
- Jean-Paul Sartre

Aristotle – A Background

In the opening passages of the *Nicomachean Ethics* Aristotle argued that there exists one thing which has intrinsic value. He formulated his argument in support of statement α (*alpha*) following, in which he located intrinsic value in the aim or purpose at which all activities were eventually directed: 'Every art, every investigation and every practical pursuit or undertaking, seems to aim at some good. Therefore it can properly be said that what everything aims at is the Supreme Good.'

The premise of his argument is contained in the first sentence and the conclusion in the second. Aristotle provided the intermediate steps in the statements we labelled β (*beta*) to ζ (*zeta*) in Exercise 9.3, page 126. We questioned the validity of the premise in Question 1 of the exercise and found that it was not acceptable to us, citing a possible counter-example: the art, activity or practical pursuit of being a thief does not lead to some good. As the suggested answer indicates, it is more than likely that an ancient Greek would have considered that an art, activity or practical pursuit which did not aim at some good was a corruption of a proper pursuit – Aristotle was unlikely to have made the fundamental mistake of considering activities like robbery to be arts which aim at some good.

Aristotle believed that moral value was to be found in the aim or purpose of pursuits or activities. In order to examine the acceptability of this belief, we need to understand it, and in order to do this, we are obliged to digress briefly from moral philosophy to consider how Aristotle linked the aims of an object or activity with its nature and, in particular, how he related our aims as human beings to our nature.

He argued that human beings form part of that group of things which have independent existence; he called such independently existing things 'substances'. For example, a horse was a substance but its whiteness (if it was a white horse) was not, nor was the cart the horse was pulling – the whiteness and the cart did not have independent existence. In order to determine whether something had independent existence, Aristotle invoked his 'Doctrine of the Four "Causes"'. The 'causes' helped to explain both a thing's nature and the mechanisms which induced change in its nature: the first three explained why something was what it was, and the fourth (the final cause) explained why it changed. Aristotle provided examples of each of the four types of cause.

1. A 'material cause' is the material, or stuff, from which something is made. Aristotle cited the bronze of a statue as its material cause. The matter out of which something is made has the potential to take on various forms.
2. A 'formal cause' is the essence or nature of something. Aristotle cited the representation of the Goddess Athena as the formal cause of the statue.
3. An 'efficient cause' is that, by means of which, something comes into existence. Aristotle cited parents as the efficient cause of a child: they were the source of the child's origins.

4. A 'final cause' of a thing or process, its τελος (*telos*), is the purpose for which it exists or is done. Aristotle cited health as the final cause of physical exercise.

He defined a 'substance' as something which contained its own final cause: this meant that the cart being pulled by the horse was not a substance because the purpose for which it was built was in the mind of the artisan who made it. By contrast, the purpose of the horse's existence was to be found only in the horse itself: its final cause was contained in its own essence of 'horseness'. Expressed in the terms a modern scientist would use, Aristotle would say that the horse's final cause is encoded in its genetic structure whereas the genetic or even chemical structure of the cart does not contain its final cause. The driver of the horse and cart is also a substance as his essence contains his own final cause.

Exercise 11.1

What are the material, formal, efficient and final causes of the following objects? Which ones are substances?

1. an automobile   2. a cherry tree   3. a cloud

Suggested answers are on p. 305.

The notion of a human being's final cause, or *telos* (that is, the purpose for which we exist) provided the basis of Aristotle's analysis of moral issues. After a long and detailed analysis in the *Nicomachean Ethics*, he concluded that the purpose for which humans exist is the achievement of ευδαιμονια (*eudaimonia*). The closest translation of *eudaimonia* that we have is 'happiness': in Aristotle's writing, *eudaimonia* was not sensual pleasure, but a happiness which consisted of properly fulfilling one's function as a human being. Along with all other animals, humans had certain faculties whose operations focus on their survival as individuals and as a species – they used their senses to help them feed themselves and reproduce. However, their reason, being a function of the soul, distinguished them from animals. Their purpose as humans, therefore, consisted of nurturing the faculty of reason, and it was in the process of nurturing the faculty of reason that Aristotle looked for, and found, the means to achieve true happiness, or *eudaimonia*.

Aristotle – Virtue and Moral Value

Aristotle's detailed analysis of happiness led him to conclude that 'human good turns out to be the activity of soul in accordance with virtue' (*NE*, Bk I–7). He used the word αρετη (*aretê*), which means excellence of any kind, with two particular forms of virtue in mind. We examine a passage that appears a little later in the *Nicomachean Ethics* to see what these are.

Exercise 11.2

Read the following extract, and then answer the questions.

> Virtue, then, is of two kinds: intellectual and moral. Intellectual virtue in the main owes both its origins and development to teaching; therefore it requires experience and time. Moral virtue, on the other hand, arises as a result of habit, hence its name ηθικη (*êthikê*), which is formed by a minor variation of the word ηθος (*êthos* or habit). From this it is also plain that none of the moral virtues arises in us by nature, for nothing that exists by nature can form a habit contrary to its nature. For instance, the stone which by nature moves downwards cannot be habituated to move upwards, not even if one tries to train it by throwing it up ten thousand times. Similarly, fire cannot be habituated to move downwards, nor can anything else that by nature behaves in one way be trained to behave in another. Neither by nature, then, nor contrary to nature do the virtues arise in us; rather we are adapted by nature to receive them, and are perfected by habit. (Adapted from *NE*, Bk II–1)

1. What reason does Aristotle give for claiming that each moral virtue does not form part of human nature?

_____

_____

2. Is Aristotle right when he says, 'nor can anything else that by nature behaves in one way be trained to behave in another'?

_____

_____

. . .

> 3. According to Aristotle, which part of our moral make-up comes from nature?
>
> _____
>
> _____
>
> **Suggested answers are on p. 305.**

In the passage Aristotle stated that there were two types of virtue, or excellence – intellectual and moral – and intellectual virtue was needed in order for us to know how to obtain moral virtue. He went on to argue that a single type of value was found in these two virtues and it consisted of human happiness (*eudaimonia*). We can see that his theory of value is not restricted to ethical behaviour. Intellectual virtue achieved *eudaimonia* directly, since by developing it humans were attaining their purpose of being human – that is, they were developing their reason. Aristotle believed that the highest form of intellectual virtue was theoretical contemplation and that moral virtue – which is what specifically interests us in this chapter – focused on the behaviour of people and was developed by habit. (It is also interesting to note that the origin of the word 'ethics' is a minor variation of *ethos*, which meant habit.) What, then, did Aristotle mean by moral virtue?

Having told his readers that 'human good turns out to be the activity of soul in accordance with virtue', he told them that moral 'virtue is a state of character concerned with choice' (Bk II–6). The choice was between vice, which was characterised by the extremes of excess and deficiency, and virtue, which was characterised by the avoidance of these extremes. The vices were unrestrained and so were in conflict with the faculty of reason which was governed by rules and, as a result, the vices had to be brought under control. The state of character which was in harmony with reason, thereby generating moral virtue, was a mean, or average, lying between the two unrestrained extremes: the virtue of courage lay between the extremes of cowardice and rashness; proper pride lay between 'the excess of empty vanity', and 'the deficiency of undue humility'.

Just as physical characteristics were particular to an individual, so were the moral means between the unrestrained vices. An individual's *telos* (purpose) was to attain human happiness by the discovery and achievement of her own harmonious moral mean. Let us examine a short passage to see how Aristotle justifies this claim.

Exercise 11.3

Read the following extract from the *Nicomachean Ethics* and answer the questions.

> Now virtue is concerned with passions and actions, in which excess is a form of failure, and so is deficit, while the intermediate is praised and is a form of success; and being praised and being successful are both characteristics of virtue. Therefore virtue is a kind of mean, since, as we have seen, it aims at what is intermediate.
>
> Again, it is possible to fail in many ways,* while to succeed is possible only in one way; for which reason also one is easy and the other difficult – to miss the mark easy, to hit it difficult. For these reasons also, then, excess and deficit are characteristic of vice, and the mean of virtue . . .
>
> Virtue, then, is a state of character concerned with choice, lying in a mean, that is the mean relative to us, this being determined by a rational principle, and by that principle by which the man of practical wisdom would determine it. (*NE*, Bk II–4)
>
> *(for evil belongs to the class of the unlimited . . . and good to that of the limited)

Aristotle gives two different reasons why we should accept that virtue aims at the intermediate. One of these is based on empirical observation of what people do and the other is based on an analysis of the concepts of success, failure, excess, deficit and the intermediate.

1. Do you think the reasons are valid ones? Assess both of them by giving them a grade A to F, with A being excellent and F being a failure.

_____

_____

In the last sentence in the passage, Aristotle states that the state of character concerned with choice is relative; it is not the same for everyone.

2. Does this principle allow me to claim that your virtue generates different moral imperatives from mine? If so, does this make Aristotle's theory of moral virtue unacceptable?

_____

_____

Suggested answers are on p. 307.

We asked ourselves two questions at the beginning of the chapter: 'What is the nature of the pressure which a person feels, to act in a moral manner?' and 'How is this pressure related to moral value?'

Aristotle's explanation of the pressure a person feels to act in a moral manner is based on the harmony of the self and its *telos* (purpose). Our need to feel in harmony with our essential selves as rational beings drives us to nurture two things: intellectual virtue and moral virtue. Moral virtue, or excellence, consists of fostering those characteristics of behaviour which are to be found in the mean between the extremes of unrestrained excess and deficiency. The standard of excellence is not a universal one but is specific to the individual and depends upon his nature or essence (formal cause). The individual's *telos* (final cause) is to harmonise his behaviour with his own standard of excellence. In nurturing this harmonisation he achieves *eudaimonia* – human happiness. We can summarise Aristotle's answers to the two questions with the following two principles:

> As rational beings our aim to achieve 'human happiness' drives us to moral virtue, or excellence.

Aristotle's 'moral value' is found in the natural phenomenon of human happiness; it is agent-centred and objective.

> Moral virtue achieves 'human happiness' by attaining the state of character which is in harmony with the individual's nature.

Aristotle's 'moral values', the principles which guide morally good actions, are therefore also agent-centred and objective.

Kant – Duty and Moral Values

Aristotle's virtue ethics located moral value in the operations of reason: his source of moral value was a rationalist one. The principles which guide action were to be found in the doctrine of the moral mean, which could be discovered and perfected through the development of moral virtue or excellence. Kant went one step further than Aristotle and based both 'moral value' and 'moral values' on rationalist principles. According to Kant, reason provides us with both the foundations and the building materials with which we construct our ethical system. We do, however, find one thing that the Kantian and Aristotelian ethical systems have in common: in both cases the moral worth of actions derives from the extent to which they are in harmony with human rationality.

Duty in Kant's Ethics

In our discussions of Aristotle's moral theory we examined some background material about the Aristotelian 'Four Causes' theory of explanation, before moving on to a discussion of his ethics. In our discussions of Kant we reverse the process and discuss his ethics at the outset, examining the theoretical context in which he places his theory of ethics as we proceed. In doing this we are imitating the Kantian model itself: for example, in the first chapter of Book I of his *Critique of Practical Reason* (C2) he stated one of his central ideas as follows:

> 'Act so that the maxim of your will can always at the same time hold good as a principle of universal legislation.' (C2: Bk I, Chap. I)

This is clearly a command which has to be obeyed – it tells us what our duty is. Because it tells us how to behave, it is an imperative, and has come to be known as the 'Categorical Imperative'. It demands that we accept only those maxims which could become rules for everyone to follow.

It is important to remember that Kant stated that a maxim was a principle and not a command: it was a standard of conduct which was advisable rather than compulsory. When the standard became incorporated into a rule of conduct, the maxim became an imperative.

[Note: The 'Categorical Imperative' underwent a transformation when Kant presented it in the *Fundamental Principles of the Metaphysic of Morals* where he expresses it in the following form:

> 'Act in such a way that you always treat humanity, whether in your own person or in the person of any other, never simply as a means, but always at the same time as an end.' (*FPMM*: Section 2.4)]

Before discussing the significance of either version of the 'Categorical Imperative', we shall examine the relationship between maxims and imperatives.

Exercise 11.4

1. Describe a **maxim** and an **imperative** which regulate how or when you drive a car.

_____

_____

• • •

2. Explain whether it is possible for the **maxim** to become a universal law.

3. Suppose you are an elementary school teacher. Describe a **maxim** and an **imperative** which regulate your behaviour towards a pupil.

4. Explain whether it is possible for the **maxim** to be turned into an **imperative**.

5. Is either the **maxim** or the **imperative** in your answer to Question 3 a moral rule?

Suggested answers are on p. 308.

The suggested answer to the first question shows that not every maxim can be turned into a law: we are prevented by logic from turning some maxims into laws. What Kant does is give us a criterion for deciding whether a rule of behaviour, which we might set ourselves, **could** be a universal moral rule. If a rule failed the test set by the 'Categorical Imperative', then we would know that the rule could not be a moral law.

The suggested answer to the second question indicates that meeting the conditions set by the 'Categorical Imperative' might not be sufficient for a rule of behaviour to become a moral law. On the one hand, we know that keeping hourly records of work (as an elementary school teacher might do) could be made into a law, so the maxim has overcome the first obstacle on its way to becoming a moral law. This is not to say, however, that it has overcome all the obstacles. On the other hand, we know that keeping minute-by-minute records of work could not be made into a universal rule, so insisting on keeping such detailed records fails the test and hence cannot be a moral law.

We can conclude our brief examination of the 'Categorical Imperative' by saying that it gives us a **necessary** condition for a rule to become a moral law, although it does not give a **sufficient** condition. What it does give us, according to Kant, is an imperative to obey, which will guarantee that our behaviour conforms to what we should do. By obeying the 'Categorical Imperative' we know that our behaviour cannot be morally bad, and that it has a **strong chance** of being morally good.

Moral Value in Kant's Ethics

In giving us the 'Categorical Imperative', Kant produced a criterion for determining which of our maxims are worth abiding by. On its own, however, it does not tell us why we should abide by those maxims which conform to it – it does not provide us with an answer to our first question: 'What is the nature of the pressure which a person feels to act in a moral manner?' We must therefore consider **what** makes us obey the instructions given to us by the 'Categorical Imperative'. Kant's basic answer to this question was very similar to Aristotle's. Firstly, we are driven to being moral by our quest to find the *Summum Bonum* (Supreme Good) – that intrinsically good thing which is the ultimate goal of all human action, conduct or behaviour. Secondly, the *Summum Bonum* can be recognised in the harmonious relationship between the self and the operations of the faculty of reason. Kant's analysis differed from Aristotle's, however, in that it equated the *Summum Bonum* with virtue, which he defined as worthiness to be happy, rather than as coinciding exactly with human happiness itself.

> 'Virtue (as worthiness to be happy) is the supreme condition of all
> that can appear to us desirable,
> and consequently of all our pursuit of happiness,
> and is therefore the supreme good.' (C2: Bk II, Chap. II)

Kant had previously indicated that the moral worth of an action was determined by an unconditioned obedience to the moral law.

> 'What is essential in the moral worth of actions is that the moral law
> should directly determine the will.' (C2: Bk I, Chap. III)

The central idea Kant expressed in these two sentences was that no advantage accrued by anyone could be considered when determining the moral worth of an action: morally valuable actions could not be constrained by considerations of the particular circumstances the moral agent was in. In other words, in order for an action to be morally valuable the act had to be one which unconditionally obeyed a rule formulated and accepted by the agent herself. For example, in her normal behaviour the moral agent followed a maxim that she should be honest. She followed her maxim for two reasons: the first was that she knew that the maxim could become a general rule governing all behaviour, thus it could become a categorical imperative; secondly, she behaved honestly and obeyed her maxim because it complied with the 'Categorical Imperative' and not because someone might benefit from her action. There was a direct link between her formulation of a moral rule, her attitude in obeying that moral rule and the moral worth of her action.

Kant argued that this link necessitated that the action should be a free one. The necessity was based on the fact that the moral agent was both the legislator who determined moral rules and the individual who obeyed them. In recognising that moral worth lay in the exercise of his own freedom, the individual's reason also told him that it lay in the recognition of the freedom of others. This would lead him to acknowledge that he could not treat other individuals simply as a means to some end; his behaviour towards them would have to recognise their freedom as moral agents – hence Kant's deduction of the second form of the 'Categorical Imperative' cited above (p. 148):

> 'Act in such a way that you always treat humanity, whether in your own person or in the person of any other, never simply as a means, but always at the same time as an end.'

[Note: We shall discuss the question of moral value and freedom again in the penultimate section of this chapter when we consider Sartre's ideas on morality and Nietzsche's against morality. In the suggested answers to Discussion Exercise 8.2 (p. 283) we alluded to the basis for claims that the individual is free when we referred to John Duns Scotus' theory of a unified mind consisting of a will and an intellect; we did not cite any of Duns Scotus' arguments that the will must be free. His argument and the broader question of whether the individual can be free and the possible nature of that freedom will be discussed briefly in Chapter 16.]

We can summarise Kant's argument on 'moral value' and its relationship with 'moral values' as follows:

1. doing something as a means to an end is not the essence of moral value;
2. the moral world is not a world of means to an end but a world of the ends in themselves – it is a **kingdom of ends;**

3. the moral rules an individual adopts have to aim towards the creation and maintenance of the **kingdom of ends**.

We now ask some questions about the Kantian notion of moral worth and how it is related to the 'Categorical Imperative' and the 'kingdom of ends'.

Exercise 11.5

1. Is duty any the less valuable if it is carried out for selfish motives?

_____

_____

2. Can any cognitive action be carried out with no regard for the consequences?

_____

_____

Kant stated that, in order for an action to have moral worth, 'the moral law should directly determine the will'.

3. Does this mean that he believed that worthy actions are non-reflective?

_____

_____

(**Advanced question**) Suppose I have a maxim of behaviour that I should act in accordance with my duty regardless of any advantages or disadvantages which might result from my actions.

4. (i) Can my maxim 'hold good as a principle of universal legislation' and become a 'Categorical Imperative'?

_____

_____

• • •

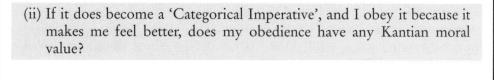

(ii) If it does become a 'Categorical Imperative', and I obey it because it makes me feel better, does my obedience have any Kantian moral value?

_____

_____

Suggested answers are on p. 310.

We can see from the nature of the questions in this exercise that Kant makes life difficult for anyone wishing to criticise his theory. It is possible that the source of our difficulty stems from the fact that Kant places all moral value at a theoretical and abstract level, eliminating the possibility of criticising him on empirical grounds – we cannot turn to particular experiences and say that they are not compatible with his theory of moral value. This contrasts with Aristotle's theory, which can be tested on empirical grounds. Some aspects of experience might not be compatible with Aristotle's notion that the moral mean is peculiar to each individual: we might find by using empirical investigation that all individuals have the same moral mean, which would be an indication that the moral mean was universal. The information gathered from experience could have a bearing on the validity of Aristotle's theory. By contrast, Kant's theory is beyond the reach of the empiricists' tests.

This difference between Aristotle's and Kant's ethics is closely related to another. The teleological nature of Aristotle's theory contrasts with the purely essentialist nature of Kant's. Aristotle's theory is founded on a principle that morally good action is driven by a *'telos'* (purpose), whereas in Kant's theory morally good action is not driven by an aim but accompanies a state of mind. The teleological aspect of Aristotle's ethics is one thing it shares with utilitarian ethics, but, as we shall see, they share very little else.

J. S. Mill – Utilitarianism and Moral Values

Utilitarian ethics are, like Aristotle's, concerned with the achievement of a *telos* which is related to human happiness. There are, however, two fundamental differences between utilitarian and Aristotelian ethics beyond the disagreement about the nature of human happiness. Firstly, the *telos* in Aristotelian ethics is the human happiness of the agent, whilst in utilitarian ethics the *telos* is considered to be **a sum** of all the happiness, or pleasure, of all individuals. Secondly, the means of generating moral value are different. In Aristotle's case the *telos* is achieved by a process of self-discovery and self-development by the individual, using reason to discover the 'mean' for her particular case. In utilitarian ethics, on the other hand, the *telos* is achieved through compliance with a general rule which maximises happiness. In the Aristotelian system of ethics the aim is to **produce** people with moral value, while in utilitarianism the aim is to **induce** behaviour with moral value. This means that the values which guide behaviour in both Aristotelian and utilitarian ethics are objective. They differ in that one system is agent-centred and the other action-centred.

[Note: An adequate understanding of ethical theories requires us to have an appreciation of the distinction between teleological and consequentialist theories. We noted in Chapter 2 that a con-sequentialist explanation considered the outcomes of actions or events while an essentialist one focused on the fundamental properties of things or events. A teleological theory of ethics focuses on the aims of human behaviour: in utilitarianism the aim is to produce events such as experiences of happiness – the theory is therefore consequentialist; in Aristotelian ethics the consequences of actions are not of central importance as the aim is to produce a good human being – the theory is therefore essentialist.]

The action-centred nature of utilitarian ethics is explicitly stated by utilitarian writers. Let us look at the precise wording used by a leading utilitarian, John Stuart Mill, in formulating the action-centred principle which guides action. After some general remarks on the *Summum Bonum* in the first chapter of *Utilitarianism*, he defines the principle which indicates whether an action is right or wrong:

The creed which accepts as the foundations of morals, Utility, or The Greatest Happiness Principle, holds that

> actions are right in proportion as they tend to promote happiness, wrong as they tend to promote unhappiness.

By happiness is intended pleasure, and the absence of pain; by unhappiness, pain and the privation of pleasure. (1962, p. 257) (Formatting added)

In the first sentence Mill identifies the essential characteristics of his moral values: they are the principles which determine the rightness of actions, and are based on promoting the *Summum Bonum* (the Supreme Good). In the second sentence he identifies the *Summum Bonum* as being simply the experience of pleasure and the absence of pain.

In the suggested answer to Exercise 10.1, Question 7 (p. 301) we used two empirical instruments to measure the relative status of rival theories. We shall avail ourselves of these instruments to assess Mill's version of utilitarianism. The first considered which theory corresponded best with what actually happens in the world, while the second was that of explanatory richness, asking which theory gave a richer explanation of all the phenomena we experience. Here we shall use both 'instruments' to measure utilitarianism against the level of acceptability which we expect any adequate theory to attain.

To these two instruments we shall add a third, the thought experiment. The thought experiment is one of the most widely used instruments in the construction of arguments and the testing of theories and hypotheses (within both the sciences and the humanities) and many occur in the discussions of utilitarianism. We can use one of the best known of these, Robert Nozick's 'experience machine', as a powerful addition to our two other instruments to help us to explore Mill's theory of moral value as well as his theory of moral values.

Exercise 11.6

Suppose there were an experience machine that would give you any experience you desired. Superduper neuropsychologists could stimulate your brain so that you would think and feel you were writing a great novel, or making a friend, or reading an interesting book. All the time you would be floating in a tank, with electrodes attached to your brain. Should you plug into this machine for life, preprogramming your life experiences? (Nozick; 1974, p. 42)

Let us assume, for the sake of our argument on utilitarianism, that there are no grounds for disputing the feasibility of Nozick's experience machine.

[Note: Our discussions in Chapter 5 of the significance of the role of muscular sense in the development of a concept of dimensional space could give grounds for questioning the feasibility of the experience machine. The 'superduper' computer simulation would have to be able to anticipate the desires of the individual and have the appropriate response ready for each mental act involving a muscular movement. The possibility of being able to anticipate all the mental acts of a mind involves an assumption that the operations of the brain and the mind are essentially the same, an issue which is still debated by philosophers as well as neuropsychologists.]

1. (i) Nozick's question, 'Should you plug into this machine for life?' tests the validity of utilitarian moral value. In what way does it do this?

_____

_____

. . .

(ii) Formulate a question using Nozick's machine which tests the validity of utilitarian moral values embodied in the Greatest Happiness Principle.

_____

_____

2. (i) Is the duty to build an experience machine contained in utilitarian principles?

_____

_____

(ii) What appears to be the pressure which a person feels to act as a utilitarian?

_____

_____

In an open world where laboratory conditions do not hold, it is not possible to calculate the extent to which actions promote happiness and unhappiness.

3. Does this mean that the Greatest Happiness Principle provides an inadequate basis for moral values?

_____

_____

In the story about Elwood Dowd and Harvey, his six foot three-and-a-half inch (1.94m) white rabbit (p. 94), Elwood is portrayed as an extremely kind person who helps everyone in need and never knowingly harms anyone. The author, Mary Chase, creates great sympathy in her audience for Elwood and invites them to conclude that it would be unjust to commit him to an asylum.

4. Assuming that committing people who have illusions to institutions and obliging them to undergo treatment tends to promote happiness, should Elwood Dowd be committed?

· · ·

5. Does utilitarianism adequately account for people's reactions to the questions about the experience machine and Elwood Dowd?

6. (i) How well does the utilitarian theory of moral value correspond with what people actually value and use in practice to guide their actions? Give it a grade A to F, for empirical content, with A being excellent and F being a failure.

(ii) How well does utilitarianism account for all aspects of the human condition related to moral behaviour? Give it a grade A to F for explanatory richness, with A being excellent and F being a failure.

Suggested answers are on p. 312.

We have found in our brief discussion in this section that the utilitarian notion of human value does not always correspond with what all people hold as morally valuable. Not everyone would plug into an experience machine, and fewer people would be prepared to condemn a kind, harmless person to an asylum even if doing so complied with a rule which tended to promote happiness. The apparent mismatch between the utilitarian concept of value based on pleasure and other possible sources of value was the basis of G. E. Moore's claim that utilitarianism was committing the 'naturalistic fallacy' – by identifying moral value with pleasure, which is a natural phenomenon.

However, as noted in the suggested answer to Exercise 11.6, Question 2 (ii), while Mill associated moral value with pleasure, he shifted away from it and towards a feeling of sympathy as the basis for accepting the Greatest Happiness Principle. A reliance on a feeling of sympathy makes the validity of utilitarianism dependent upon the evidence provided by studies of human motivation. The link is even more evident in the consequentialist branch of ethical egoism – another teleological ethical theory based on the utility of the outcome of actions, which we shall discuss in the next section.

[Note: Mill also moves away from the notion that pleasure forms the sole basis of moral value when he discusses the quality of pleasures – that is, what makes 'one pleasure more valuable than another' (1962, p. 259). This has generated some criticism of his utilitarianism which we shall not discuss here. We shall restrict ourselves to a discussion of the 'naturalistic fallacy' when we assess theories in ethics on p. 165 below.]

Henry Sidgwick – Ethical Egoism

When discussing egoism it must be emphasised at the outset what it is not: it is not egotism, which is 'The vice of thinking too much of oneself; self-conceit, boastfulness; also, selfishness' (*OED*). This is very different from 'ethical egoism' which is the theory which regards self-interest as the foundation of morality.

We need also to distinguish 'ethical egoism' from other types of egoism, such as 'psychological egoism' and 'rational egoism'. Ethical egoism is, as the name suggests, a moral theory which incorporates a theory of moral value and one of moral values, and we shall see that neither of these needs to be egotistical.

There are two forms of ethical egoism: essentialist and consequentialist, and we shall concentrate our attention on the latter. The consequentialist ethical egoist agrees with the utilitarian in ascribing moral value to human happiness, which is also interpreted as pleasure, but disagrees on the nature of moral values. Instead of using the Greatest Happiness Principle, ethical egoism turns it into a principle of the agent's happiness. We can express the basic principle of ethical egoism as the following:

> A moral agent's actions are right in proportion as they tend to promote the happiness of the agent, wrong as they tend to promote his unhappiness.

One of the foremost proponents of ethical egoism, Henry Sidgwick, went so far as to claim that this principle formed the foundation of all ethical systems.

> To sum up: Egoism, if we merely understand by it a method that aims at Self-realisation, seems to be a form into which almost any ethical system may be thrown, without modifying its essential characteristics. (1907, Bk I, Chap. VII, section 2)

The ethical egoist theory of moral value (human pleasure) is identical to the utilitarian one which we discussed in the last section. We shall now examine the ethical egoist theory of moral values.

Exercise 11.7

Consider the suggested answer to Exercise 11.6, Question 1 (ii) (p. 313).

1. Are there any circumstances in which an ethical egoist would plug as many other people as possible into the experience machine?

2. Explain why an ethical egoist is not necessarily an egotist.

3. According to the ethical egoist what is the nature of the pressure which pushes a person to act in a moral manner?

Suggested answers are on p. 316.

The theory of ethical egoism which we have discussed so far aims to promote the happiness of the moral agent – it is a consequentialist theory. Essentialist forms of ethical egoism have also been developed; it is even possible to interpret Aristotelian virtue ethics as being a form of ethical egoism in that the end which it intends to achieve is the happiness of the individual agent. While the moral value of Aristotelian ethics is that of egoism, its moral values are based on the discovery of the 'state of character which makes a man good and which makes him do his own work well' (*NE*, Bk II–3). This is a natural quality which is independent of the experiences of the individual and so is objective, and as such is outside the realm of ethical egoism.

In the next section we persevere with the theme of moral value being agent-dependent, but move from the action-centred characteristics of ethical egoism to the agent-centred theories of ethics which locate moral value in the individual's state of character – a state which is not to be subjugated to moral rules formulated by others. We examine the work of two philosophers, Friedrich Nietzsche and Jean-Paul Sartre, who are both associated with existentialist philosophy.

Nietzsche and Sartre – Moral Value as Freedom

In Friedrich Nietzsche's writings morality itself came under attack. He did not attempt to describe a moral system which would lead his readers to reject other moral theories such as Aristotle's virtue ethics, Kant's deontology or Mill's utilitarianism. Rather than do this, he challenged the very notion that moral principles could be formulated which are consistent with moral value. He considered that moral rules were contrary to nature and prevented individuals from developing their true nature.

> Isn't morality a 'desire for the denial of life', a secret instinct for destruction, a principle of decay, diminution, and slander, a beginning of the end, and thus, the greatest of all dangers? (*TBT*, section 6)

Nietzsche's harsh words against morality are based on his belief that any rules which constrain an individual stand in opposition to the nature of a human being, whose fundamental condition is to act freely. It is only by acting according to one's free will that one can be in harmony with what it is to be truly human. Subjugating oneself to a rule is a sign of weakness, of giving in to a 'herd mentality' – it puts the moral agent beyond good and evil. Nietzsche makes this point equally forcefully in his book *Beyond Good and Evil*.

> The 'non-free will' is mythology; in real life it is only a question of STRONG and WEAK wills – it is almost always a symptom of what is lacking in himself, when a thinker, in every 'causal-connection' and 'psychological necessity,' manifests something of compulsion, indigence, obsequiousness, oppression, and non-freedom; it is suspicious to have such feelings – the person betrays himself. (*BGE*, section 21)

The idea that the ultimate goal of individuals is the expression of a free will is also found in the writing of Jean-Paul Sartre, whose notion of freedom is different from Nietzsche's: Maurice Cranston points out that Sartre's view is 'that freedom is the foundation of all values'. He quotes Sartre as saying:

> that the actions of men of good faith have, as their ultimate significance, the quest for freedom itself as such. . . . We will freedom for freedom's sake, in and

through particular circumstances. And in thus willing freedom, we discover that it depends entirely upon the freedom of others, and that the freedom of others depends upon our freedom. (1962, p. 81)

Here we find that Sartre introduces an element of reciprocity into the notion of freedom – and freedom is the supreme human good. Let us examine the notion that freedom, rather than human happiness, is an individual's supreme good.

Exercise 11.8

1. Is there empirical evidence to support the claim that the ultimate goal of all behaviour is freedom rather than happiness or pleasure?

_____

_____

In Exercise 11.6, Question 4 (p. 156) we asked ourselves whether a utilitarian would have committed the mild-mannered, harmless Elwood Dowd to an asylum.

2. If we accept that freedom is the foundation of value, do we commit Elwood Dowd to the asylum or refrain from doing so?

_____

_____

3. (**Advanced question**) To what extent are moral rules incompatible with the individual's freedom?

_____

_____

Suggested answers are on p. 317.

The suggested answers to Questions 2 and 3 enable us to respond to the question we posed at the beginning of the chapter from the point of view of someone who believes that an individual's ultimate good is to be found in freedom. Sartre's answer to the question 'What is the nature of the pressure which a person feels to act in a moral manner?' is to be found in his declaration that in 'willing freedom, we discover that it depends entirely upon the freedom of others'. The logic involved in acquiring our own freedom necessitates the promotion of the freedom of others.

[Note: Sartre's and Kant's positions on the moral value of an individual's freedom and the moral value of the freedom of others are similar: both philosophers considered that there was a logical connection between 'my' freedom and the freedom of others. The difference between the two is found in the nature of freedom: in the Kantian system it consists of the ability to formulate universal rules and to follow them; whereas in Sartre's system it consists of a recognition that all individuals should not be bound by rules.]

If we take Nietzsche at face value, we should not even consider morality as a guide for action. This would make our question about the nature of the pressure which a person feels to act in a moral manner heavily value-loaded, as it would be assuming the very thing that Nietzsche's theory was denying. In such circumstances our question would be inappropriate, as our critique would be committing the logical fallacy of *ignoratio elenchi*, which involves attributing something to other theories which they do not propound, and then criticising these other theories.

Having briefly analysed five different theories of moral value and moral values, we conclude the chapter with an examination of how we might test the acceptability of a moral theory.

Methods (4) Assessing Theories in Ethics

(Advanced section)

In our earlier discussions of the validity of claims about what really exists, we described four standards of acceptability (Chapter 5, p. 59): the minimum standard to be met was that the claim should be logically possible; the next level of acceptability was that the preponderance of evidence inclined us to accept the claim; next the claim had to convince someone beyond reasonable doubt; and the ultimate level of acceptability was that the claim should be incontrovertible. We shall use the same standards when assessing the theories of ethics which we have discussed in this chapter.

In order to determine how well a theory measures up to each standard, we need to use appropriate instruments. For example, when determining whether the claims made in a theory are logically possible, we must check whether it has used any form of fallacious argument. The most common amongst these are: deductions based on false premises; deductions which lead to unacceptable conclusions; deductions during which there are shifts in the meanings of the terms being used (known as the 'fallacy of equivocation'); and logical fallacies such as the 'affirmation of the consequent'.

When assessing a theory we must be conscious both of the standard against which we are testing the theory and whether the instruments we are using are appropriate. For example, it would be inappropriate to use empirical evidence as an instrument if we wish to discover whether a theory's claims are logically possible. It would be equally inappropriate not to use any empirical evidence if we wish to discover whether the theory is convincing beyond reasonable doubt. Similarly, it would be inappropriate not to use every method available if we wish to show that a theory is incontrovertible.

Testing each of the five theories of ethics against each of the four standards of acceptability would involve us in at least 20 separate processes. In the earlier exercises in the chapter we posed questions about some of the theories in order to test their acceptability. In Questions 2, 3 and 5 of the exercise below we shall re-examine some of the questions with two purposes in mind, first to specify what sort of instrument is being used to test the theory and then to determine which of the four standards the question is aiming at. In Questions 1 and 4 we look at two standard arguments which have been employed by some philosophers to criticise rival theories.

Exercise 11.9 (Advanced exercise)

In a famous passage in his *Treatise of Human Nature*, David Hume criticises moral philosophers for gliding from statements about what **is** and **is not** the case to statements about what **ought** and **ought not** to be the case – this separation of 'is' from 'ought' statements is also referred to as the 'fact-value dichotomy' (see p. 42 above).

> In every system of morality, which I have hitherto met with, I have always remarked, that the author proceeds for some time in the ordinary way of reasoning, and establishes the being of a God, or makes observations concerning human affairs; when of a sudden I am surprized to find, that instead of the usual copulations of propositions, *is*, and *is not*, I meet with no proposition that is not connected with an *ought*, or an *ought not*. This change is imperceptible; but is, however, of the last consequence. For as this *ought*, or *ought not*, expresses some new relation or affirmation, it is necessary that it should be observed and explained; and at the same time that a reason should be given, for what seems altogether inconceivable, how this new relation can be a deduction from others, which are entirely different from it. (1888, p. 469)

Aristotle's *Ethics* starts by claiming that virtue **is** the pursuit of excellence.

• • •

1. (i) What justification is given on p. 147 above that we **ought** to pursue excellence? How can we determine whether the justification is valid?

_____

_____

Hume criticises those theories which glide from statements of fact to statements of value. He uses the 'is/ought' dichotomy as an instrument of analysis to assess whether theories measure up to a standard of acceptability.

(ii) According to which of these standards does the 'is/ought instrument' assess theories: (a) **logical possibility**, (b) the **preponderance of evidence**, (c) **reasonable doubt** or (d) **incontrovertibility**?

_____

_____

The hypothesis of Exercise 11.5, Question 3 (p. 152) questioned Kant's concept of moral worth. It did not cite any empirical evidence.

2. According to which of the four standards was this question measuring Kant's theory?

_____

_____

In Exercise 11.6, Question 3 we discussed the efficacy of the Greatest Happiness Principle by pointing out that, in an open world where laboratory conditions do not hold, it is not possible to calculate the extent to which actions promote happiness.

3. According to which of the four standards was this question assessing utilitarianism?

_____

_____

· · ·

In one of the most influential books on ethics in the twentieth century, G.E. Moore argued that utilitarianism and ethical egoism committed the 'naturalistic fallacy': they both identified goodness with the natural phenomenon of pleasure (1903, pp. 6–17). The fact that the question, 'Is pleasure good?' is not tautological tells us that pleasure is not equivalent to goodness.

> 4. Did the use of the 'naturalistic fallacy' to criticise utilitarianism involve the use of empirical evidence? According to which of the four standards was Moore measuring utilitarianism and ethical egoism?

Existentialist moral value is based on the claim that the ultimate goal of all behaviour is freedom rather than happiness or pleasure. Exercise 11.8, Question 1 asked for empirical evidence to support this claim.

> 5. According to which of the four standards does this request measure existentialist moral value?

Kant's theory of moral philosophy used a single notion (duty) to construct a theory of moral value and moral rules, whereas Mill's utilitarianism used two (pleasure as the *Summum Bonum* and a sentiment of sympathy to sustain the greatest Happiness Principle).

> 6. Does the fact that Kant used fewer concepts to build his theory give us a criterion for preferring it over the rival theory of utilitarianism?

Suggested answers are on p. 319.

In this exercise we have asked questions about how well theories in ethics measure up to certain standards. These are philosophical questions which should help us to gain a better understanding of the nature and status of the theories: they help us to determine whether a theory is merely **logically possible**, whether evidence can be gathered to help us decide if it could be **more acceptable** than rival theories, and whether we can determine if the theory is **incontrovertible**.

We notice from asking these questions that an analysis of the concepts used in a theory can give us some information about its validity. For example, answering Questions 2 and 4 tells us that either Kant's theory of moral value or the utilitarian one might not be logically possible. The answer to Question 5 also indicates that a question could test the practical use of a theory rather than its validity.

The assessment of theories is an important aspect of philosophical activity in general, and the central feature of 'epistemology', which is the branch of philosophy that we tackle next.

Part III: A Summary

In Chapter 9 we familiarised ourselves with the distinction between a value and a set of values. Each theory of aesthetics or ethics is based on an assumption that there is something of value, and by 'value' we mean 'the relative status of a thing, or the estimate in which it is held, according to its real or supposed worth, usefulness, or importance' (*OED*). Whatever is of value then forms the basis of the values, or principles, which determine our judgement in aesthetics and ethics and our ethical behaviour – the term 'values' refers to 'the principles or standards of a person or society', which is different from the plural of 'value'.

The distinction between these two concepts formed the foundation of the analysis of moral theories, which, from the Renaissance onwards, gradually became separate from theories of art and beauty. In Chapter 10 we followed the story of this separation and found that it took place at the same time as two other processes: the demarcations between fields of study and the search for unified principles of explanation for both human behaviour and natural phenomena. The theories of art and beauty which emerged out of their separation from ethics tended to associate them with an aesthetic sense which detected aesthetic qualities – a tendency symbolised by the change of meaning of the word 'aesthetics' in the eighteenth century from a science inquiring into the nature of sensation to one inquiring into the nature of beauty. We noted that the change in meaning of the word 'aesthetics' was triggered by Alexander Baumgarten's use of it to distinguish the study of the intellect from the study of the senses: the former, known as logic, has the knowledge of truth as its object and the latter, known as aesthetics, has the knowledge of beauty as its object.

The historical background provided us with a platform from which to launch investigations into the nature of beauty and of art. In both investigations we found that there was no universal agreement, a consequence of which was that our discussions focused on the nature of the theories rather than on the subject matter. We discussed two broad categories of theory regarding beauty: the first was advocated by the seventeenth and eighteenth-century British empiricists such as Shaftesbury, Hutcheson and Hume, and the second by German idealists such as Fichte and Hegel. The empiricists tended to see beauty as a quality of things which could be detected by a special beauty-detecting sense, analogous to the colour-detecting sense of sight, whereas the idealists tended to see beauty as a quality of the spirit.

In discussing the relative strengths of the opposing theories we rekindled some of the analytical skills developed in Chapter 5 (p. 59) on philosophical methods, where we used four criteria to measure the status of claims about the existence of objects. The criteria for assessing the acceptability of a claim were (1) that it should be **logically possible,** (2) that the **preponderance of evidence** should make it acceptable, (3) that its truth should be **beyond reasonable doubt** and (4) that it should be **incontrovertible.** In Exercise 10.1 we indicated that two empirical instruments could be used to assess how well the theories of beauty measured up to the four criteria: we noted firstly, that we could assess the extent to which each theory's explanation of beauty corresponded to what people actually believe beauty to be; secondly, that we could also assess the extent to which each theory explained the totality of human experience, in other words, the explanatory richness of the theory. In the final section of Chapter 11 we used the same two instruments to assess the ethical theories which we had discussed in the first five sections.

In these five sections we examined five different systems of moral values associated with four theories of moral value. We found that Aristotle's theory of virtue ethics considered moral value to be found in the virtue or excellence of the moral agent, and moral values were located in a mean, or average, lying between the two unrestrained extremes of excesses and deficiencies. Kant's deontology considered moral value to be located in a detached compliance with the moral values embodied in the 'Categorical Imperative'. Mill's utilitarianism and Sidgwick's ethical egoism both considered moral value to consist of pleasure but they diverged on the principles which guide human behaviour: the aim of the utilitarian was to produce the greatest happiness of all individuals while that of the ethical egoist was to produce the greatest happiness of the moral agent. Nietzsche and Sartre (along with Kant) considered moral value to be located in the freedom of the moral agent's actions. This meant that when considering moral values, both of them concluded that the observance of rules of behaviour diminished the moral value of an action – nonetheless Sartre argued that the achievement of one's own freedom necessarily involved the recognition of the freedom of others.

Our aims in the chapter were firstly to achieve an understanding of some of the principal theories of moral value, along with the particular moral values associated with each theory of moral value. We achieved this by seeking the answers to two questions:

> What is the nature of the pressure which a person feels, to act in
> a moral manner?
> How is this pressure related to moral value?

Answering the two questions partly accomplished the second aim of the chapter, which was to develop those critical skills needed to facilitate an assessment or criticism of the theories. In the final section of the chapter we developed these skills further with an assessment of the five different approaches to ethics based on the use of the analytical tools we had described in Exercise 10.1.

Revision Exercises

Revision Exercise 9.1

    1. (i) Make a list of five things, actions or characteristics which are of value to some human beings.

      (ii) Give the reason why each one is valued.

    (iii) Explain how the value of one of them might change (or why it cannot change).

    2. Describe a rule of behaviour which is not linked to something which is of value.

Suggested answers are on p. 324.

Revision Exercise 10.1

Anthony Shaftesbury believed that beauty was a characteristic of things in the world discernible by a human sense in a similar way to the way size, shape or colour are discerned: humans have a beauty-detecting sense similar to the eye which detects colour. He considered the aim of art to be the creation of this natural characteristic and thereby the creation of beautiful things.

Jean-Paul Sartre considered the aim of art to be the liberation of individuals from the constraints of everyday living, and thereby developing their freedom to choose.

1. Describe an empirical method of evaluating the relative merits of these rival claims.

2. Is it reasonable to use an empirical method to compare these claims?

Suggested answers are on p. 325.

Revision Exercise 11.1

The rule 'Do not commit murder' is a law which is found in most ethical systems.

1. Would this be a moral law in the following ethical systems?
   (i)   Aristotle's virtue ethics;
   (ii) Kant's deontological system;
   (iii) Mill's utilitarianism;
   (iv) Sidgwick's ethical egoism;
   (v)   Sartre's theory of freedom as moral value.

. . .

2. In the cases in which it is a moral law explain why it has to be one.

_____

_____

Suggested answers are on p. 326.

Further Reading

Hursthouse, Rosalind: *On Virtue Ethics* (Oxford University Press, 2000). A lucidly written, authoritative and up-to-date examination of all aspects of the subject – a must for anyone who wishes to take this subject further.

Sheppard, Anne: *Aesthetics: an Introduction to the Philosophy of Art* (Oxford University Press, 1987).

Tolstoy, Leo: *What is Art? and Essays on Art,* translated by Aylmer Maude (Oxford University Press, 1930). This little classic is still in print and worth reading, despite being more than a century old.

PART IV

KNOWLEDGE and BELIEF

In Part IV we bring together various themes covered earlier and examine them from a slightly different perspective. In Parts II and III we discussed the type of awareness, understanding and knowledge that we can have of two spheres of human existence, the physical world and the world of values. We switch the focus of attention from the **content** of knowledge and belief to the **nature** of knowledge and belief. This inversion moves us from the philosophical topics of ontology and ethics/aesthetics to epistemology.

There are two fundamental and related challenges which face philosophers concerned with inquiring into the nature of knowledge: the first challenge is to find a way of differentiating knowledge from what is not knowledge, and the second to identify the factors which differentiate knowledge of one type of reality from another – for example, to distinguish between knowledge of nature and knowledge of society.

In Chapter 12 we examine the different sources of knowledge and how these influence, and are influenced by, different categories of knowledge. Traditionally three human faculties have been considered to supply the fundamental sources of knowledge: experience, reason and the imagination. Reason is considered to generate incontrovertible knowledge, experience is considered to generate knowledge which is at best beyond reasonable doubt and there is debate about the nature of knowledge which the imagination might generate. In our analysis we identify four human capacities which can provide us with these sources of knowledge: the physical capacities of the senses; the capacity to interpret information; the capacity to reason about the interpretations and about the conditions which condition the interpretations; and the capacity to conjecture or imagine something which has not been experienced.

In Chapters 12 and 13 we deepen our understanding of the different types of knowledge by examining two different categories: science, which claims to produce knowledge about the physical world we can experience, and the proofs of the existence of God, which claim to produce knowledge about the world which is beyond possible experience. The intention is to develop an understanding which is sufficient to permit a subsequent analysis of any epistemological issue.

Epistemology – The Sources and Status of Knowledge

12

IN THIS CHAPTER

Concepts discussed

- *A priori*
- *A posteriori*
- Analytic judgements
- Synthetic judgements

Philosophers whose ideas are discussed

- Immanuel Kant
- Thomas Reid

References made to the following philosophers

- Aristotle
- Plato
- David Hume

In this chapter we bring together several strands of the investigations which we carried out earlier. In Chapter 4 we briefly discussed 'epistemology', having defined it as the branch of philosophy which inquires into the nature and scope of knowledge and also into the adequacy of claims to knowledge (p. 39). We had our first experience of an exercise in epistemology in Exercise 4.1 when we described some events which could either increase or decrease our confidence that a particular belief we held was true. This exercise paved the way for the discussion of epistemological issues, but it did not address its central question, which is:

> What is knowledge?

This question gives rise to three main topics in epistemology, each of which we have already addressed in previous chapters. Each one of the topics induces philosophers to seek answers to some subordinate questions:

1. **The nature and status of a theory** – which induces questions such as:
   - About what category of subject does the theory make claims?

- What are the sources from which the theory's claims are developed?
- What is the nature of the explanations used by the theory?
- What methods or means are employed in supporting the claims made in the theory?
- How are these methods related to the sources from which the theory is developed?

2. **The scope of a theory** – which induces questions such as:
   - Can the theory's claims justifiably cover the subject areas it professes to cover?
   - What are the limits beyond which the theory's claims cannot legitimately stray?

3. **The adequacy of a theory's claims** – which induces questions such as:
   - What is the level of acceptability of a particular theory's claims?
   - What determines the level of acceptability of a theory's claims?
   - Under which circumstances should a theory be rejected as unacceptable?

In a general introduction to philosophy we cannot expect to find answers to all these questions for all types of theory. We have, however, already sought – and found – answers to some of them. In Chapters 5, 6 and 7 of Part II we examined the basis of claims to knowledge of what reality is. The discussion started with an analysis of Alice's observations about what the world was like on her journey into Wonderland (p. 56), and finished with an evaluation of the argument on the nature of knowledge and reality in Plato's 'Theory of Forms' (p. 107).

Our primary concern then was with how we obtain knowledge of reality; our interest in assessing particular claims about what exists was motivated by a desire to distinguish what is not real from what is real – we wanted to distinguish between appearance and reality. In order to achieve this goal, in the second section of Chapter 5 (p. 59) we discussed the criteria used in assessing claims about what exists. Following on from Exercise 4.1, this was our second experience of epistemology. The third was our recent assessment of theories in ethics in the last section of Chapter 11 (p. 162).

We have also discussed the nature of knowledge, which is another aspect of epistemology. In contrast with the assessments of the adequacy of claims and theories, these discussions have been less frequent. We have, nonetheless, explicitly examined knowledge on two occasions. The first one was in our brief analysis of Plato's 'Theory of Forms' (p. 107), where knowledge was considered to be a state of mind related to the contemplation of abstract 'ideas'. The second discussion of the nature of knowledge occurred when we described Aristotle's 'Doctrine of the Four "Causes"' (p. 142), which is a theory about the nature of explanation. Our motivation for examining Aristotle's theory was primarily to understand the explanation of human behaviour contained in his theory of ethics.

Aristotle's theory of explanation, however, has wider applications: the issue of what an explanation consists of is central to the nature of knowledge and so to epistemology. It is a topic we encounter again in the next chapter on the philosophy of science when we examine the forces which cause scientific explanations to change.

The Sources of Knowledge

An explanation is, however, consequential to the assimilation of the information by means of which the explanation is formulated, and may be conditioned by it; we shall therefore begin our study of epistemology by examining the relationship between knowledge and the ways in which we obtain it.

In Part II we directed our attention towards an examination of the impact which three means of obtaining knowledge could have on a specific type of knowledge – that of our physical environment. They were:

1. An individual's **passive sense experiences** and **active muscular sense**.
2. An individual's **interpretations of sense experience**. For example, in Chapter 5 we discussed how we gather and interpret information from the senses in order to obtain knowledge about the existence of, for example, sheepdogs, roses and bananas.
3. An individual's **use of reason**. For example, in the first section of Chapter 7 we discussed Sir Arthur Eddington's fishy story (p. 85), thus facilitating a discussion of how the operations of our faculty of reason determine the range of issues which we can legitimately examine with sense experience. In doing this we were also investigating the scope of our knowledge.

The discussions in Chapters 5, 6 and 7 contained an implicit assumption that the basic building blocks of our knowledge of reality are provided by sense experience, albeit modified by the use of reason. Two types of theory which have challenged this assumption were discussed in Chapter 8. The first of these, developed by existentialist philosophers, argued that the self (an agent with intentionality) was a fundamental building block which can be used to construct our understanding of reality (p. 99). The second was Plato's challenge, which consisted of the assertion that the use of reason without the polluting influence of the senses was the fundamental and true source of knowledge.

We now build on these not insubstantial beginnings and proceed to an investigation of other possible sources of knowledge, starting with the organisation of experience by reason. In order for reason to organise an individual's experience, certain conditions have to hold; the investigation of these conditions provides us with a possible source of knowledge. Kant is the philosopher who is normally most closely associated with examinations of the conditions which have to apply if certain human activities are to be possible. We shall, however, focus on an argument developed by Thomas Reid, one of Kant's contemporaries. Like Kant, Reid was responding to David Hume's scepticism resulting from his theory that all human knowledge was derived from sense experience.

Exercise 12.1

After retiring from teaching, Thomas Reid published *Essays on the Intellectual Powers of Man* (1785) which contained many of the philosophical ideas he had taught for over 30 years. Alexander Brodie, currently Professor of Logic and Rhetoric at Glasgow University, where Reid was Professor of Moral Philosophy, quotes the following passages from it: 'For, before men can reason together, they must agree in first principles; and it is impossible to reason with a man who has no principles in common with you' (1997, p. 94).
   One of the first principles he goes on to list is that

> qualities must necessarily be in something that is figured, coloured, hard or soft, that moves or resists. It is not to these qualities, but to that which is the subject of them, that we give the name 'body'. If any man should think fit to deny that these things are qualities, or that they require any subject, I leave him to enjoy his opinion as a man who denies first principles, and is not fit to be reasoned with. (ibid., p. 98)

1. According to Reid, how do we know that there are first principles?

_____

_____

2. How do we know that qualities such as colour and motion have to be in a body which is coloured or moving?

_____

_____

Suggested answers are on p. 328.

Reid argued that the processes of reasoning about the way we form concepts and communicate them with others provide us with possible sources of knowledge. This expands our list of possible sources **beyond** the use of physical and cognitive capacities, which were identified by the work we did in Parts II and III above. We can collate these sources of knowledge into the following three categories:

1. Through the use of physical capacities:
   (i)   using our senses to record information;
   (ii) using our muscles to direct the senses.

2. Through the use of cognitive capacities:
   (iii) interpreting sense experience.

3. Through the use of logical capacities:
   (iv) reasoning about the conditions which make sense experience possible;
   (v)   reasoning about the conditions which make thought in general possible;
   (vi) reasoning about the conditions which make discussions with others possible;
   (vii) mathematical and logical reasoning.

This preliminary list is not a comprehensive one of all the sources of knowledge postulated by philosophers, or indeed by non-philosophers. Every element in each category is related to human activities or experiences, each one having some form of empirical content. For example, the association of experience with knowledge in (i) to (iv) resulted from the nature of our discussion in Part II where we were concerned with the nature of reality rather than the nature of knowledge – the focus of such a discussion was bound to be human experience. We shall now expand our inquiry to include the possibility that there is knowledge which claims to have no link with experience.

Exercise 12.2

1. Make a list of other possible sources of knowledge to supplement (i) to (vii) – include any source which may be independent of experience.

2. Specify which of these sources can, and which cannot, lead to incontrovertible knowledge.

Suggested answers are on p. 329.

Our discussion has so far generated ten different possible sources of knowledge: seven on page 179, and three more in the Suggested Answers to Exercise 12.2. We have not, however, analysed the possibility that knowledge might be produced from combinations of these sources – an analysis which would only be appropriate in a text specialising in epistemology. Neither has it produced any arguments which determine the status of the knowledge produced from each of the sources. In addition, it has not addressed the issue of how we distinguish knowledge from belief and we therefore now turn our attention to this question.

Knowledge and Belief

In Chapter 5 we set out four criteria for determining the acceptability of claims about the existence of physical objects, with the most stringent of these criteria being that the claim should be incontrovertible – that 'there should be no available means to show that the claim is false' (p. 59). We are now concerned with determining whether a claim is more than just acceptable – that is, with whether it can be considered to be knowledge. This concern might induce us to stipulate that the claim should be more than incontrovertible, that it should be provable. (The difference between something being incontrovertible and it being provable is small but significant. In mathematics the Riemann hypothesis is at present incontrovertible, but it has neither been proved nor disproved – it has been shown to be true for several thousand million numbers, but so far no-one has demonstrated that it is always true.) In view of this, we now briefly examine what we mean when we say we know something, in order to see whether, in practice, we require that the knowledge should be incontrovertible or even provable.

Exercise 12.3

1. Which of the following claims constitutes knowledge, and which only belief?
   (i)   There are three angles in a triangle.
   (ii)   Michelangelo was the best sculptor of the last millennium.
   (iii) The atom was first split in 1932 by John Cockroft and Ernest Walton.
   (iv)   When I am thinking, I exist.

· · ·

2. For each of the claims give the reasons why it is to be counted as knowledge or as only belief. Indicate whether the reasons are independent of experience.

_____

_____

3. Does a claim have to be incontrovertible for it to count as knowledge?

_____

_____

4. I believe something to be true. Is the fact that I perceive something 'clearly and distinctly' to be true sufficient for me to count it as knowledge?

_____

_____

Suggested answers are on p. 330.

It appears that distinguishing knowledge from belief is not a problem-free activity. Philosophers have used two distinctions to help them decide between knowledge and belief: the **analytic/synthetic** and the _a priori/a posteriori_ distinctions. These form the basis of the discussions in the next two sections.

Analytic and Synthetic Judgements

(Advanced section)
The theorems of mathematics are generally regarded as being incontrovertible and therefore count as knowledge. Similarly, judgements such as 'All Swiss people are European' are incontrovertible because their truth depends solely on the meanings of the terms being used. Judgements of this type were distinguished by Immanuel Kant from those which have a truth value which cannot be determined by an examination of the meanings of the terms being used – such as 'Most Swiss people understand the French language'. He called the former judgements 'analytic' and the latter 'synthetic'.

Analytic judgements (the affirmative) are hence those in which the link of the predicate with the subject is conceived in terms of identity, whereas those in which it is not are called **synthetic judgements**. One could call the former, judgements of clarification and the latter of elaboration; for the former add by their predicate nothing to the concept of the subject. Note: . . . Judgements of experience as such are all synthetic (emphasis added) (*CPR* A7/B10).

This means that, according to the Kantian distinction, being European adds nothing to the concept of being Swiss, while understanding the French language does add something to the concept of being Swiss. In this exercise we examine some judgements in order to determine whether they are 'synthetic' or 'analytic'.

Exercise 12.4

1. These judgements are the ones Kant used when discussing the distinction between analytic and synthetic judgements. Which ones are **analytic** and which **synthetic**?
    (i)   'All bodies are heavy.'
    (ii) 'All bodies are extended (that is, measurable in space).'
    (iii) 'Everything which happens has its cause.'
    (iv) 'The world must have a first beginning.'

    _____

    _____

2. Which of the following judgements are **analytic** and which **synthetic**?
    (i)   The President of the United States is less than 50 years old.
    (ii) God is omniscient (all-knowing).
    (iii) The President of the United States is less than 30 years old.
    (iv) God exists.

    _____

    _____

Suggested answers are on p. 332.

The truth of some of the judgements examined in the last exercise is dependent upon experience: for example, we need to know how old the President of the United States is in order to determine whether Judgement 2(i) is true. The truth of some of the others is unrelated to any form of experience: for example, whether or not God is omniscient is unrelated to any form of experience. Kant claimed that judgements such as 'Everything which happens has its cause' and 'The world must have a first beginning' are independent of experience as well as being synthetic judgements. He argued that the notion that there were no uncaused events was one which could be learnt from experience, yet its truth could not be determined by experience: if scientists had not found a cause, it could be due to the inadequacy of their methods or theory – no test could be devised which determined the absence of a cause.

[Note contributed by Thomas Roberts: This last statement is itself an analytic one because the concept of 'cause and effect' is inherent in the concept of 'test'.]

A *Priori* and A *Posteriori* Knowledge

The independence from experience of some scientific claims was a topic we encountered in the suggested answers to Exercise 7.1 (p. 268), where we discussed two claims made by an ichthyologist who had a net with a two-inch mesh. We regarded his first claim that 'no sea-creature is less than two inches long' as being true *a priori* (independent of any particular experience), and his second that 'all sea-creatures have gills' as being true *a posteriori* (dependent upon experience).

In the next exercise we examine the relationship between the *a priori*/*a posteriori* distinction and Kant's analytic/synthetic distinction.

Exercise 12.5 (Advanced exercise)

Consider the following two *a posteriori* judgements:
(i) The President of the United States is less than 50 years old.
(ii) There are two apples and three pears on the table, so there are five pieces of fruit on the table.

   1.   Under which circumstances would each of them be false?

Consider the following two *a priori* judgements:
(iii) The President of the United States is less than 30 years old.
(iv) 7+5=12 (Kant's example)

   2.   Under what conditions would each of them be false?

...

3. By considering Judgement (iii) and the ichthyologist's claim that 'no sea-creature is less than two inches long', (p. 85) determine under what circumstances, if any, a synthetic judgement can be incontrovertible.

4. What is the difference between the way the ichthyologist attained his knowledge that 'no sea-creature is less than two inches long' and the way he justified it?

Suggested answers are on p. 334.

Two conclusions have emerged from the discussion of the *a priori/a posteriori* distinction. Firstly, two factors can predetermine the truth of a proposition: the first consists of the rules which determine the meanings and correct use of the words we use, and the second consists of the methods we use to gather information about the truth of the proposition. In circumstances where either the rules or the methods can change, as in the examples of the age of the President of the United States and the size of the ichthyologist's net, the truth of a proposition can change – but this truth would nonetheless remain independent of any particular experience. Where either the rules or the methods are immutable, as in the example of the truth of 7+5=12, the truth of the proposition cannot change. Secondly, we do not always use the sources of knowledge in order to validate knowledge: the means we use to gather information (which we then use to formulate true propositions) are not necessarily the same means which we use to determine whether the propositions are true.

[Note: Statement δ (*delta*) of Exercise 8.3 (p. 107) informed us that, in his 'Theory of Forms', Plato distinguished between the sources and the validation of knowledge: inexact and ever-changing experiences provided a source of knowledge, while the knowledge which enabled people to explain them was derived from reason through an understanding of the perfect and unchanging 'forms'.]

We shall return to the distinction between the source of knowledge and the methods of validating knowledge in the next chapter when we discuss the philosophy of science. Before doing so, we shall summarise the points which have emerged from the discussions on epistemology.

Epistemology – A Summary

The central question in epistemology is:

> What is knowledge?

Having knowledge entails making explanatory claims and being able to justify the claims – in other words, asserting and supporting a theory. This means that, in asking themselves what knowledge is, epistemologists investigate the nature of theory construction and validation, processes which involve them in three types of inquiry. These were identified on page 175 as being inquiries into: the nature and status of a theory, the scope of a theory, and the adequacy of a theory's claims.

Before addressing these questions the epistemological analyses we had undertaken when discussing ontology, aesthetics and ethics were brought together. In particular, we had addressed the adequacy of claims in some detail in the Methods (1) section of Chapter 5 on 'Assessing claims about what really exists' (p. 59), and in the Methods (4) section of Chapter 11 on 'Assessing theories in ethics' (p. 162). Further, in discussing Aristotle's 'Doctrine of the Four "Causes"' in Chapter 11 (p. 142) we had examined some aspects of the nature of explanations.

With this previous work as a platform, we proceeded to develop answers to some of the other questions, starting with the possible **sources of knowledge**. Having collated the conclusions reached in earlier sections, and found that we had already discovered seven possible sources, we added three more to the total – producing the following ten possible sources of knowledge:

1. Through the use of physical capacities:
   (i)   using our senses to record information;
   (ii)   using our muscles to direct the senses.

2. Through the use of cognitive capacities:
   (iii) interpreting sense experience.

3. Through the use of logical capacities:
   (iv)   reasoning about the conditions which make sense experience possible;
   (v)   reasoning about the conditions which make thought in general possible;
   (vi)   reasoning about the conditions which make discussions with others possible;
   (vii) mathematical and logical reasoning.

4. Through the exploitation of imaginative capacities:
   (viii) using the imagination (metaphysical speculation and thought experiments);
   (ix) responding to revelation or religious experience (outer or exogenous impulses);
   (x) reacting to an intuition or inspiration (an inner or endogenous impulse).

This list led us to ask whether the use of any of the sources could result in the construction of theories which made incontrovertible claims, and/or an understanding of the distinction between knowledge and belief. The investigations which followed led to the elucidation of the two distinctions which philosophers use to classify knowledge: the **analytic/synthetic** and the *a priori/a posteriori* distinctions.

In this chapter we have examined general questions about the theory of knowledge. In the next two chapters we focus our attention on two specific areas of knowledge: knowledge of nature and knowledge of God.

The Philosophy of Science 13

As with previous topics we shall confine our study of the philosophy of science to a few key areas, giving such sufficient grounding in the subject as to facilitate a follow-up study of greater depth. On page 39 above we defined the 'philosophy of science' as that branch of epistemology which inquires into the nature of our knowledge of the physical world. We noted that it has come to include evaluations and explanations of scientific progress – a subject which more properly belongs to the philosophy of the social sciences. In recognition of this inclusion we examine three main themes in this chapter, each representing an aspect of the three topics in epistemology listed above (p. 175): the nature of science, the nature of scientific explanation and the nature of scientific progress.

IN THIS CHAPTER

Concepts discussed

- Falsifiability
- Scientific revolution
- Paradigm
- Incommensurability
- Normal science

Skills developed

- Assessment of theories

Philosophers whose ideas are discussed

- Carl Hempel
- Karl Popper
- Thomas Kuhn

References made to the following philosophers

- Aristotle
- Plato

In the first two sections we shall examine aspects of the nature, status and scope of scientific theories, asking what distinguishes science from non-science, and also how a scientific explanation differs from other forms of explanation. In the third section we shall discuss some theories which explain how the changes in the acceptability of scientific theories lead to scientific progress. Three questions which are fundamental in the philosophy of science will be asked:

> What differentiates scientific knowledge from other forms of knowledge?

> What is the nature of explanation in science?

and

> What conditions make it possible for a scientific explanation to be considered inadequate?

Science Distinguished from Non-Science

In the discussions in Part I on the nature of philosophy we identified one of the characteristics which distinguished it from, for example, physics and gardening (p. 22). Unlike philosophy, their subject-matter is considered to operate independently of our knowledge of it. This independence, with regard to physics, has an influence on the methods used to study it, with experimental procedures contributing significantly in the production of the physicist's knowledge of how things work.

The non-cognitive nature of the things studied in physics in particular and science in general gives us a criterion for distinguishing physics from other activities. The fact that the things physicists study operate independently of the theories of physics differentiates physics from, say, psychology. The laboratory methods used in science appear to give us another one – as we noted when discussing Thales' Hypothesis 2 (p. 248) and the way J. J. Thompson justified his claim to have discovered the electron (p. 276). The physicist's ability to create special conditions of isolation in a laboratory in order to probe and investigate how things work differentiates physics from sociology, where the interference of the social investigators prevents them from creating the special conditions of isolation.

Modern science is an empirical activity based on the experiences of scientists. These experiences involve scientists in probing for, and gathering, information in special settings and then interpreting that information in order to explain the behaviour of particular things which operate independently of the probing, gathering and interpreting. We now investigate the extent to which science is an empirical activity.

[Note: There are various marginally different meanings of the term science. It can mean a body of knowledge or even a skill. In this chapter it is being used to refer to 'the systematic study of the nature and behaviour of the material and physical universe' (*Collins English Dictionary*). Being a systematic study, science in this context is conceived as an activity.]

Exercise 13.1

1. What sort of event or phenomenon is not investigated by natural science?

2. Which of the following could be the source of an explanation of the way things react to gravity, and which could be a method of validating an explanation?
   (i)   Being hit on the head by an apple.
   (ii) Observing lots of apples hit lots of people on the head.
   (iii) Thinking about lots of apples hitting lots of people on the head.
   (iv) Dropping a bag of feathers and different sized cannonballs from the top of the Leaning Tower of Pisa and observing which reached the ground first.
   (v)   Speculating about the existence of 'bosons' (Higgs particles) which 'give' particles their detectable mass.
   (vi) Consulting the Oracle at Delphi.

[Note: (iv) Galileo's notes state that he conducted experiments like these from several high buildings in Pisa. His results justified his rejection of Aristotle's theory of gravity which stated that heavy things drop more quickly than light things. (vi) The Oracle was a medium through which the gods or goddesses in ancient Greece spoke and made their will known; it was normally represented by a priestess located in a dark mysterious shrine. The Delphi Oracle was the one with the highest reputation in the Greek world.]

3. Modern science uses laboratory methods to validate its claims. Describe a non-scientific method of validating a claim.

Suggested answers are on p. 336.

The responses to the questions in this exercise have given us some clues regarding what differentiates scientific knowledge from other forms of knowledge, but they have not given us a definitive answer. We know that two factors distinguish science from non-scientific activity: the category of object studied in it and the methods used to validate its claims. It is also possible that the sources we can use to produce and develop scientific knowledge provide us with a third factor. The interdependence of these three factors means that none of them on its own is sufficient to produce a criterion to distinguish science from non-science.

The fact that the objects studied operate independently of the type of explanation developed by scientists enables the scientists to use laboratory techniques. These techniques themselves only work if the properties they isolate operate outside the laboratory, in other words, independently of the laboratory. There is a mutual relationship between the technique and that which can be investigated by it: the property being investigated must **invariably** try to operate no matter what context it finds itself in – which is clearly so in the case of an electron which invariably has a negative electric charge.

There is also a symbiotic (mutually interactive) relationship between the type of explanation developed in science and the techniques used to investigate the properties of natural non-cognitive objects. The types of laboratory which scientists can build and the equipment in them determine the range of the types of information which can be gathered. For example, in order to justify claims about the properties of electrons, scientists needed equipment which would alter the paths of electrons as well as equipment which would register their influence on the environment. Without such equipment the electron would have remained, like the boson (Higgs particle) at present, a theoretical entity. The construction and use of the equipment is closely dependent upon the types of explanations offered by scientific activity.

Consequently, the nature of an explanation can limit, if not determine, the nature of the subject being explained. If, on the one hand, an explanation consists of citing events, then the subject being used in the explanation is likely to be limited to events: for example, if a scientist explains the changing tides by citing the pattern of tidal changes over the last thousand years then the subject being used in the explanation is a series of events, that is, tidal patterns; such a scientist will only look for series of events in the search for explanations. If, on the other hand, an explanation consists of describing how things work then the subject being used in the explanation is likely to include things and their operations: the scientist who explains the changing tides by describing the gravitational properties of large masses and the movement of the earth and sun will search for explanations in the properties of objects rather than in series of events. In both cases the method of gathering information and the interpretation of the information reinforce each other and tend to exclude any alternative explanatory system.

We discussed Aristotle's theory of explanation, his 'Doctrine of the Four "Causes"' in the first section of Chapter 11. We now consider some modern theories of explanation which have directed their attention specifically towards scientific explanation.

Explanation in Science

One of the most influential theories of explanation in science has been the deductive model of explanation proposed by Karl Popper (1959) and Carl Hempel (1965). According to the Popper–Hempel theory, when we explain a fact in science we formulate a logical deduction from two types of premise; a universal scientific law and a description of the specific conditions which prevailed prior to the occurrence of the phenomenon. For example, if we wished to explain why a particular loaf of bread rose in the oven while it was being baked we would do the following:

1. invoke a general law that if dough which contained yeast were placed in an environment with a given temperature it would rise;
2. describe the specific conditions that the particular piece of dough was in;
3. use (1) and (2) to **deduce** the result that the dough rose.

The supporters of this theory of explanation claim that it should even apply to non-scientific explanations of ordinary events. For example, an explanation of why a courier delivered a parcel might consist of a statement that an order was placed for a book. There would be an implicit premise left out of this explanation that all orders for books from a certain company were delivered by courier: the explanation would only be giving the specific conditions such as (2), but it would tacitly assume that a general law like (1) was operating.

Scientists, however, often also want to understand **why** laws are adhered to: they require explanations of why dough, which contains yeast and is placed in an environment at a given temperature, rises. They want to have an explanation as to why statement (1) is true.

Exercise 13.2

1. Assess the Popper–Hempel theory of explanation when it is applied to explain a single event by giving it a grade A to F, with A being excellent and F being a failure.

_____

_____

· · ·

2. Assess the Popper–Hempel theory of explanation when it is applied to explain a universal law by giving it a grade A to F, with A being excellent and F being a failure.

_____

_____

[Note: Popper and Hempel claimed that the deductive model only applied to the explanation of facts.]

Suggested answers are on p. 338.

Discussion Exercise 13.3

Is a deductive model appropriate for an explanation of why a general law is valid? Could it be used to explain why free-moving magnets always point towards the north?

_____

_____

Suggested answers are on p. 339.

The question posed in Discussion Exercise 13.3 is an epistemological question because it assesses the adequacy of a model of explanation. Physicists in the nineteenth century began to ask similar epistemological questions about the adequacy of Newtonian mechanics, for so long seen as the definitive description of nature; they began to ask whether the Newtonian model was appropriate for a full explanation of the phenomena they were able to observe.

The questioning resulted in the transformation of physics through the development of quantum mechanics and relativistic physics. This apparent revolution caused many philosophers of science to ask what had caused such a radical change in a subject which had hitherto been regarded as one which made progress through the expansion of existing knowledge. From being considered to be exclusively cumulative and evolutionary, the development of science could also be seen as being discontinuous and revolutionary.

The Development of Science

In the preceding chapter we listed three main topics in epistemology as well as some questions which arise from considering the topics. The very last question was, 'Under which circumstances should a theory be rejected as being unacceptable?' This question lies at the heart of the analyses used to find explanations for scientific change, especially when this is of the revolutionary rather than evolutionary kind. In examining the theories which explain scientific change, we shall modify the question and ask the broader question:

> What conditions make it possible for a scientific
> explanation to be considered inadequate?

One of the leading philosophers of science of the twentieth century, Karl Popper, considered that this type of question stimulated responses which would also answer our previous question about what differentiates science from non-science.

> Popper maintained that for a theory to be considered scientific it
> had to be in principle **falsifiable**: if it was not even theoretically
> possible to show that the theory could be false, then the theory was
> not a scientific one.

For example, 'analytic judgements' (see p. 182) such as 'all bodies are extended' and '7+5=12' are not scientific as they cannot be falsified, whereas 'gravity accelerates a body at a rate of 9.81m/s²' is scientific as it can be falsified.

Popper proceeded to use this criterion to explain how science moves from the acceptance of one theory to the acceptance of another: simply put, he claimed that a theory which was falsifiable, but had not been falsified, remained accepted until evidence was found to falsify it; at this point the theory would be rejected and a new, better, falsifiable theory sought.

Exercise 13.4

1. (i) Give an example of a falsifiable claim which is an **analytic** judgement.

_____

_____

. . .

(ii) Give an example of a non-falsifiable claim which is a **synthetic** judgement.

Popper argued that no matter how many times evidence was shown to be consistent with a theory, the theory could not be proved to be true. By contrast, only one counter-example was needed in order to show that a theory was false. (Verifiability and falsifiability are logically asymmetrical.)

Suppose I drop a cannonball from the Leaning Tower of Pisa, measure its acceleration and find that it is 9.5m/s².

2. (i) Have I falsified the theory that the acceleration due to gravity is 9.81m/s²?

(ii) If this does not falsify the theory, how will I know when it has been falsified?

(**Advanced question**) Scientists are at present attempting to detect 'bosons' (Higgs particles), which explain why elementary particles should have mass. Should there be no known theoretical techniques for detecting 'bosons', scientists would concentrate their efforts on devising such techniques. Until such methods were discovered, the theory postulating its existence would not be falsifiable.

3. Would such a theory be unscientific?

Suggested answers are on p. 340.

The problem of knowing when a theory has been falsified is closely followed by another. How is a new more adequate theory developed? This is a question requiring specialist knowledge in social theory which is beyond our present scope: it requires us to analyse the social forces which lead to innovation in science. Questions about the conditions needed for a social theorist to formulate an answer are, however, legitimate in an introductory text in philosophy; they are questions philosophers tend to ask.

> Given the inadequacy of a particular scientific
> explanation, what conditions make it possible for a
> more adequate one to be developed?

Thomas Kuhn (1970) offered a double-edged notion, consisting of a 'paradigm', to analyse this question. The notion of the 'paradigm' has two cutting edges: the first explains science's evolutionary phases and the second its revolutionary phases. To understand how it performs both functions, we start with a definition of a 'paradigm'.

A 'paradigm' is an achievement – a collection of shared beliefs held by a group of scientists about what the basic problems and methods of scientific inquiry are.

As a scientist I cannot select, evaluate or criticise theories in the absence of a paradigm; and my paradigm has to be shared by other scientists in order for my selection, evaluation and criticism to be accepted. For example, medieval scientists were obliged to set out their theories, conforming to the prevailing orthodoxy of the Church at the time, that the earth was at the centre of the universe and that everything revolved around it. The restriction on science was still in force in 1632 when Galileo was condemned to house arrest and the weekly recitation of Psalms by the Inquisition for stating that the 'sun is the centre of the world and does not move from east to west'.

Assuming that science has to operate within the confines of a paradigm, Kuhn went on to state that there are two possible phases in science: firstly, there is 'normal science', in which the paradigm sets the standards by which scientific activity is carried out and evaluated; secondly, a 'scientific revolution' could occur in which the paradigm itself comes into question. A scientific revolution is a mechanism in an evolutionary process of natural selection in which new paradigms emerge, having originated as proposals from 'young' scientists. The most robust of these theories survive and establish themselves as the new normal science.

In contrast with the radical change inherent in a scientific revolution, Kuhn indicated that the phase of normal science is characterised by a conservatism in science with the accepted paradigm reinforcing the received perception of what a scientific problem is, thus marginalising any proposal to alter the paradigm. It is also characterised by a promise of success in scientific activity. The promise is actualised by:

1. the extension of knowledge in those areas identified as being ripe for development;
2. a reinforcement of the received body of knowledge through confirmation of facts specified within its parameters.

For example, the vision of the world as obeying Newton's laws of motion was one in which force was considered to be proportional to the rate of change of velocity, a view that conditioned physicists not to look for the possibility that the way the rate of change of velocity is measured, could itself alter. This 'paradigm' was overturned by James Clerk Maxwell's equations, which went on to form the basis for Albert Einstein's Theory of Relativity. The overturning of the Newtonian paradigm constituted a 'scientific revolution'. A paradigm is overturned at the point at which there is a crisis of confidence in the prevailing orthodoxy of normal science. Various rival new paradigms are proposed and a process of natural selection ensures that a new prevailing orthodoxy emerges.

[Note: It is not clear what the rival, less robust, theories were which lost out to the 'robust' theories of relativistic physics and quantum mechanics.]

Discussion Exercise 13.5

The common saying 'you cannot teach an old dog new tricks' appears to be stating that, once people have absorbed a way of looking at the world, it is difficult for them to change.

> 1. Was Kuhn just turning common sense into a complicated sounding theory?

_____

_____

Two things are said to be incommensurable if they cannot be measured against each other. Kuhn claimed that successive paradigms were incommensurable, and that one could not say that one was better than the other.

> 2. Is this true? Do we have no way of comparing the medieval theory that the earth is at the centre of the universe with the Copernican theory that the sun is at the centre of a solar system?

_____

_____

Suggested answers are on p. 341.

Attempts to explain the development of science appear to have generated as many problems as the solutions they propose. One area of inquiry which we have not pursued in this chapter is an examination of the relationship between ontology and epistemology. We explored the relationship in Part II when we discussed how Henri Poincaré, a scientist, analysed the relationship between the ways in which we formulate concepts of the world and the ways in which we gather and interpret information. Our interest then was to understand the nature of the reality we can know, whereas here it has been to understand the nature of our knowledge of reality. In both cases, an understanding of the relationship between epistemology and ontology appears to be of central importance. Readers who wish to go further into the subject are likely to find it fruitful to focus on an analysis of this relationship when addressing the issues of the nature of our knowledge of scientific theories and the nature of the criteria we can use for choosing between such theories.

We now move on to an examination of some other theories which claim to produce knowledge of the supernatural rather than the natural world – we discuss the arguments which claim to prove the existence of God.

The Existence of God   14

In this short chapter we discuss four arguments which consider the possibility of establishing the existence of God, a being whose presence cannot be directly perceived with our senses. Arguments which claim to demonstrate that things we cannot perceive exist are not new to us: when discussing the philosophy of science we did not restrict ourselves to an examination of theories about the properties of natural objects which we can perceive. Had we done so, we would have been ignoring the theories physicists use to explain the behaviour of electrons which our senses cannot logically detect (as we noted in Exercise 4.1, p. 39). The theories about the existence of unperceivable particles do, however, claim that there are both perceivable effects of these particles and reliable methods to generate these effects.

The arguments about the existence of God go further than this, claiming that a being exists which is not only not subject to the laws of nature, but also which has power over them. The *OED* defines God as 'a superhuman person who is worshipped as having power over nature and the fortunes of mankind'.

[Note: The power over nature only suggests the possibility that God has the other attributes such as ubiquity (omnipresence), omniscience, and infinite benevolence. By establishing that a being has power over nature, an argument does not necessarily establish that the being also has these other attributes.]

Science investigates the laws of nature: the methods which scientists use to obtain an understanding of nature presuppose that things in nature operate according to fixed rules. The notion that something exists which can change the rules contradicts the basic assumptions of scientific inquiry: arguments based on laboratory activity (involving asking questions of nature by interfering with the pattern of events and then looking for the replies by observing the results) cannot be invoked because God can change the pattern at any point during the experiment. In the laboratory we ask nature questions, and nature replies because it behaves according to unbreakable rules. The infrangibility of the rules of nature is an assumption without which science cannot function; therefore science cannot investigate a being which is not subject to the laws of nature.

This means that arguments supporting claims that God exists have to be different from scientific ones. Different, non-scientific, types of inquiry and argument are needed if we are to establish that a being which has 'power over nature and the fortunes of mankind' exists. A supreme being's power over nature makes its operations as controller of nature undetectable. If we wish to show that God exists, we have two options:

1. to direct the discussion to considering only that which is beyond possible experience;
2. to bridge the gap between experience and what is beyond possible experience.

Religions based on faith opt for (1), while proofs of the existence of God opt for (2). In bridging the gap between the perceivable and unperceivable, the argument goes beyond possible experience; it becomes 'transcendent'.

[Note: Kant used the term 'transcendent' to denote anything that reaches beyond possible experience, and the term 'transcendental' to denote anything that was a condition of possible experience.]

We shall now examine three standard proofs of the existence of God which address option (2). In each case we shall assess the argument by identifying the point at which it bridges the gap between possible experience and what is beyond possible experience.

The Ontological Argument

The ontological argument, dating back to the eleventh century, was first formulated by St Anselm, a Benedictine monk born in Italy who went on to become

Archbishop of Canterbury. It was subsequently revived by Descartes and Leibniz and criticised by Hume and Kant. The argument bridges the gap between what can be perceived and that which is unperceivable by analysing the concepts of existence and perfection. In essence it states that the concept of a non-existent perfect being leads to an incoherent conclusion; this makes it a *reductio ad absurdum* argument. In our first exercise on the arguments for the existence of God, we examine St Anselm's version of the proof.

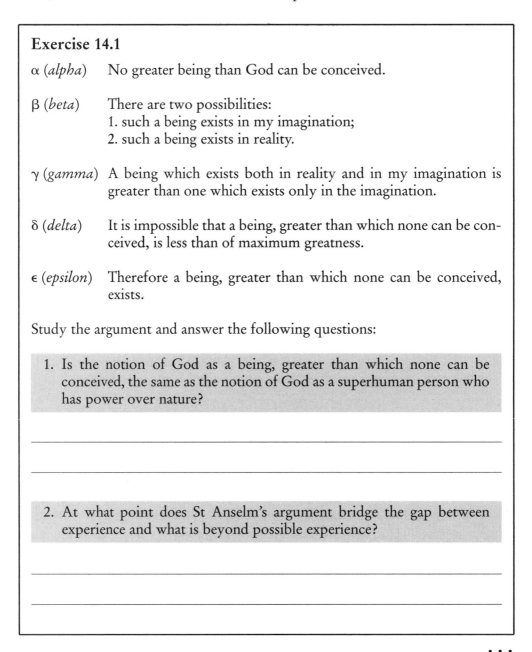

Exercise 14.1

α (*alpha*)   No greater being than God can be conceived.

β (*beta*)   There are two possibilities:
1. such a being exists in my imagination;
2. such a being exists in reality.

γ (*gamma*)   A being which exists both in reality and in my imagination is greater than one which exists only in the imagination.

δ (*delta*)   It is impossible that a being, greater than which none can be conceived, is less than of maximum greatness.

ε (*epsilon*)   Therefore a being, greater than which none can be conceived, exists.

Study the argument and answer the following questions:

1. Is the notion of God as a being, greater than which none can be conceived, the same as the notion of God as a superhuman person who has power over nature?

2. At what point does St Anselm's argument bridge the gap between experience and what is beyond possible experience?

• • •

3. Does an island, greater than which none can be conceived, exist? If it does, can we say that St Anselm's argument fails?

_____

_____

Suggested answers are on p. 343.

The Argument from Design (Teleological Argument)

The argument from design has an even longer history than the ontological argument. The ancient Greeks and Romans produced different versions of it and it was the fifth of Thomas Aquinas' 'five ways' published in 1272 in *Summa Theologica*. One of the most discussed versions was produced by William Paley (1802). Paley started from a simple experience which he described in the opening paragraphs of his book:

> In crossing a heath, suppose I pitched my foot against a *stone*, and were asked how the stone came to be there; I might possibly answer, that, for any thing I knew to the contrary, it had lain there for ever: nor would it perhaps be very easy to show the absurdity of this answer. But suppose I had found a *watch* upon the ground, and it should be inquired how the watch happened to be in that place; I should hardly think of the answer which I had before given, that, for any thing I knew, the watch might have always been there. Yet why should not this answer serve for the watch as well as for the stone? Why is it not as admissible in the second case, as in the first?

Paley used this starting point to construct a simple and, to some, compelling argument. Its main premise was that anything which, like the watch, is well-ordered must have been designed for a purpose. The second premise was that if something has been designed then there must have been a designer, and the third that the universe is well-ordered. From these premises the conclusion he drew was that the universe had a designer, and the designer was God.

[Note: (1) The purposive aspect of design is why the argument from design is also known as the 'teleological argument'. In Aristotle's 'Doctrine of the Four "Causes"' (p. 143), a thing's final cause is its τελος (*telos*) – its purpose. (2) David Hume's *Dialogues on Natural Religion* provides an interesting and well-balanced criticism of the argument from design.]

Exercise 14.2

1. Is Paley's first premise true? Does a well-ordered mechanism have to have been designed for a purpose?

_____

_____

2. Is Paley's third premise true? Is the universe well-ordered?

_____

_____

Paley's conclusion bridged the gap between experience and what is beyond possible experience by stating that the universe's designer was God.

3. Does the designer of the universe have to have power over nature and the fortunes of mankind?

_____

_____

Suggested answers are on p. 345.

The Cosmological Argument

(Advanced section)

Like the argument from design, the Cosmological Argument has its roots in ancient Greece: Plato in the _Laws_ (section 10) and Aristotle in _Metaphysics_ (section 12) developed versions of it. In the Middle Ages St Aquinas, the scholar who revived Aristotelian philosophy, also revived Aristotle's cosmological proof, as did Duns Scotus a few years after him. Leibniz, basing his argument on the notion of pre-established harmony, also reproduced a version of it. Kant (_CPR_, Chap. 3, section 5) provides us with powerful criticisms of the proof.

All versions of the proof start with premises describing something **which exists** and move to a deduction of what **must have caused it to exist** – this gives them the form of a 'transcendental argument' which looks for the conditions which must hold if a given occurrence is to be possible. In our final exercise on the proofs of the existence of God we examine an adaptation of Duns Scotus' version of the proof – the subtle nature of the argument tells us why medieval scholars knew him as Doctor Subtilis.

Exercise 14.3 (Advanced exercise)

Study the following six propositions paraphrasing Duns Scotus' proof. (Explanatory comments in brackets have been added.)

α (*alpha*)   Changes which are effects occur in the world – this is a given occurrence.
(This is the X **which exists**)

β (*beta*)   Each effected change must be caused by something other than itself because:
1. no effect can be produced by itself;
2. a loop of causes bringing about an effect is impossible.
(This is something, call it Y, that **must have caused X to exist.**)

γ (*gamma*)   Therefore each effect forms part of a series of caused effects.
(This series, call it S, **must exist** if X exists.)
(and S is either a randomly occurring or an ordered series.)

δ (*delta*)   If S is a series of randomly occurring causes then there is an ordered, non-random, series of causes OS. We accept this statement because:
1. a caused event in series S occurs because of the operation of a certain procedure P.
2. procedures do not operate randomly.
From 1 and 2 we can conclude that:
3. the procedure P must be part of an ordered series of causes, call it OS, which is different from the random series S.
(This ordered series OS **must exist** if S exists.)
(Therefore an ordered series, either S or OS, **must exist** if X exists.)

ϵ (*epsilon*)   An infinite series of ordered, non-random, causes is impossible because:
1. it is logically possible for causal agent Y to possess its own causal power in a perfect way;
2. an agent possessing its causal power because it has received it from another causal agent further back in the chain is dependent upon this other agent;

• • •

3. dependence is an imperfection;

4. if it is not possible for any causal agent such as Y to possess the transmittable causal power without dependence then every Y possesses its causal power in an imperfect way;

(Statements ϵ (1) and ϵ (4) contradict each other.)

(Statement ϵ (4) is false because statement ϵ (1) is necessarily true.)

(The finite ordered series OS **must exist** if X exists.)

ζ *(zeta)*   Therefore a prime mover (an initial causal agent), which possesses its causal power with no imperfections, exists. In other words God exists.

1. Are propositions β (1) and (2) **analytic** or **synthetic**?

_____

_____

2. Why does Duns Scotus need to go through step δ and show that random sequences can only exist if there are non-random ones backing them up?

_____

_____

Duns Scotus bridges the gap between what can be perceived and what is beyond perception at stage ϵ claiming that statement ϵ (1) must be true and ϵ (4) false.

3. Assess the value of the deduction by giving it a grade A to F, with A being excellent and F being a failure.

_____

_____

Suggested answers are on p. 346.

[Note: The subtlety of Duns Scotus' argument is not the only thing worth noting. He considered causal power to be transferable to the next agent in the causal series; he also considered the agent who received the causal power to be a dependent (and thus imperfect) causal agent. In analysing causation in terms of a transferable causal power he drew a distinction between the **causal agent** who exercised causal powers and the **series of caused events**: it was not the previous event which brought about the current one, but the exercise of a causal power by the preceding causal agent.

This analysis also enabled him to distinguish between a random series and an ordered series of events – a distinction which lies at the heart of modern laboratory practice which is designed to detect this very distinction.]

Transcendent and Transcendental Arguments

We noted above that the arguments which address the question of the existence of God face the problem of bridging the gap between experience and that which lies beyond possible experience – their purpose is to extend knowledge beyond the bounds of sense experience. Each of the arguments starts with the content of human consciousness: the ontological argument starts from an understanding of concepts of existence and perfection; the teleological (design) argument's starting point is conscious experience, together with an understanding of the concepts of design and purpose; and the cosmological proof's starting point is conscious experience together with an understanding of the concept of causation.

The cosmological argument uses its starting point as a premise to deduce what lies beyond experience: the concept of perfection allows us to formulate the concept of a perfect being. In doing this it attempts to transcend the bounds of experience; in Kantian terms it is 'transcendent'. By contrast, the teleological and ontological arguments use their starting points to infer the existence of the conditions which make a process either intelligible or possible. The teleological argument infers the existence of God as the only thing that makes the order of the universe intelligible to us, while the cosmological argument infers the existence of God as the only thing that makes a causal chain possible; in Kantian terms they are 'transcendental arguments'.

There is a fourth type of argument, not discussed in this chapter, which attempts to prove the existence of God – the moral proof. It is a subjective rather than universally applicable argument which also takes the form of a transcendental argument: it is based on the claim that God is the necessary condition for an individual to be able to justify being a moral agent or having moral experience. Having criticised the other three objective arguments, Kant formulated a subjective moral proof of his own (*CPR* A809/B837 ff).

Part IV: A Summary

At the beginning of Part IV we set out to deepen our understanding of the nature of knowledge, affirming that this could be achieved by discovering the different possible categories or types of knowledge, and our understanding of how to differentiate knowledge from what is not knowledge. After some preliminary discussions (pp. 187–80) we developed a working hypothesis that knowledge entails making explanatory claims and being able to justify the claims. We used this to investigate the notion in more depth in Chapter 12 (see the summary of the chapter on p. 185). We drew on the results of our previous discussions in Part II on *a priori* and *a posteriori* knowledge of reality, expanding them through an analysis of the Kantian notions of 'analytic' and 'synthetic judgements'.

Armed with an understanding of these Kantian notions, we went on to examine the nature of a scientific explanation and also the development of science. We identified some of the limitations of the deductive model of explanation of a scientific fact proposed by Karl Popper and Carl Hempel, noting that the model applied only to individual facts describable in the special circumstances of a laboratory and not to universal theories. We then discussed the notion of what constituted a scientific fact, and in particular Popper's use of the criterion of falsifiability which he used to identify a scientific theory. We found that, while this notion was useful in distinguishing a scientific from a non-scientific theory, we ran into difficulties when attempting to use it to explain the nature of scientific progress.

The analysis of the Popperian explanation of scientific progress and change led to an examination of Thomas Kuhn's notion of a 'paradigm' shift from one episode of 'normal science' to another via the mechanism of a 'scientific revolution'. We found that, while Kuhn's explanation had the advantage of explaining some of the upheavals in science in the last two centuries, it had two major weaknesses: firstly, it omitted to consider the effect the Kuhnian theory might have on the social forces which it was explaining – the knowledge that normal science was by nature conservative would itself change the nature of normal science; secondly, Kuhn's notion of 'incommensurability', whereby theories in different types of normal science could not be measured against each other. In particular, this meant that scientific change could not be explained in terms of the rationality of the scientist who chooses quantum mechanics rather than Newtonian mechanics and yet understands both these allegedly incommensurable paradigms.

The discussion about our knowledge of nature was followed by an examination of the arguments which claim to establish knowledge of transcendent entities, that is, of entities which lie beyond possible experience. We analysed three standard arguments which claim to prove the existence of God. We ascertained that the teleological (argument from design) and cosmological proofs were forms of 'transcendental argument', while the ontological proof was a *reductio ad absurdum*. In all three cases the arguments did not provide an incontrovertible bridge between experience and what lies beyond possible experience.

The absence of certainty was an unstated recurrent theme of the discussions in all three chapters; we noted in the suggested answers to Exercise 12.3 that even René Descartes had doubts about the application of his criterion of certainty in knowledge when he observed, 'however, that there is some difficulty in rightly determining the objects which we distinctly conceive' (p. 332).

We dealt with the absence of certainty by invoking the four criteria for assessing claims and theories which we outlined in the second section of Chapter 5 (p. 59), and by assuming that these were not controversial. Only one of these criteria, that a claim or theory should be incontrovertible measured up to the Cartesian standards of certainty; the other three all left us with differing degrees of doubt concerning the acceptability of a claim or theory. All of these less strict criteria invoked the concept of a normal person for their application, which means that the concept of a person is a pivotal concept even in epistemology. It is to a discussion of a person that we now direct our attention.

Revision Exercises

Revision Exercise 12.1

In James Barrie's story of Peter Pan, a little girl Wendy is questioned by her mother about the state of the nursery floor.

> Some leaves of a tree had been found on the nursery floor, which certainly were not there when the children went to bed, and Mrs. Darling was puzzling over them when Wendy said with a tolerant smile:
> 'I do believe it is that Peter again!'
> 'Whatever do you mean, Wendy?'
> 'It is so naughty of him not to wipe his feet,' Wendy said, sighing. She was a tidy child.
> She explained in quite a matter-of-fact way that she thought Peter sometimes came to the nursery in the night and sat on the foot of her bed and played on his pipes to her. Unfortunately she never woke, so she didn't know how she knew, she just knew.

· · ·

Barrie tells us that Wendy knew that the tree's leaves had been left by Peter Pan.

1. (i) What was the basis of Wendy's knowledge?

_____

_____

(ii) What was the source of Wendy's knowledge?

_____

_____

(iii) Was Wendy justified in her claim to know that Peter Pan visited the nursery?

_____

_____

2. (i) Does the fact that Wendy did not know how she knew that Peter came into the nursery in the night affect the status of her claim that she knew?

_____

_____

(ii) In what way, if any, was Wendy's knowledge different from Descartes', which was based on his 'clear and distinct ideas'?

_____

_____

Suggested answers are on p. 349.

Revision Exercise 12.2 and 13.2

Consider Sir Arthur Eddington's fishy story of the ichthyologist whom we first met on p. 85.

In the suggested answer to Exercise 7.1, Question 1 (p. 268) it was stated that the ichthyologist's second generalisation was *a posteriori* knowledge (as a result of experience), while the first was *a priori* (independent of experience) because it depended upon the nature of his net.

1. How do **we** know that the nature of the ichyologist's net affects the truth of the statements?

2. Assuming the ichthyologist is not aware of our alternative methods of examining sea creatures, should it be important to him to know that the nature of his catch is determined by the type of equipment he uses?

Suggested answers are on p. 350.

Revision Exercise 13.1

Consider Thomas Kuhn's claim:

Theories formulated in different scientific 'paradigms' are 'incommensurable'. (Claim TK)

1. (i) Is Claim TK an **analytic** or a **synthetic** proposition?

. . .

(ii) According to Karl Popper's criterion of falsifiability, is Claim TK a scientific claim?

_____

_____

In answering this question, assume that Kuhn's theory of scientific change from one form of 'normal science' to another via a 'scientific revolution' is true.

2. Is the knowledge that, in the nineteenth century, science moved from one 'paradigm' to another *a priori* or *a posteriori* knowledge?

_____

_____

Suggested answers are on p. 351.

Revision Exercise 14.1

Consider the following paraphrase of René Descartes' proof of the existence of God:

α (*alpha*)   I know I am an imperfect being because I am able to doubt.
β (*beta*)   I have a concept of perfection and of a perfect being.
γ (*gamma*) Since I am imperfect I cannot have generated this concept of perfection.
δ (*delta*)   The concept of perfection must have been generated by a perfect being.
ε (*epsilon*) Therefore, a perfect being exists.

1. Is Descartes' proof an **ontological, teleological** or a **cosmological** proof?

_____

_____

2. Identify the premises in the argument and state whether they are necessarily true.

_____

_____

3. At what point does Descartes bridge the gap between experience and what is beyond possible experience?

_____

_____

Suggested answers are on p. 352.

Revision Exercise 14.2

We now return to the question asked in Discussion Exercise 3.2.

1. What is the relationship between **wisdom** and **knowledge?**

_____

_____

and

2. Does having infinite **wisdom** necessarily involve having infinite **knowledge?**

_____

_____

Suggested answers are on p. 353.

Further Reading

Descartes, René: *Discourse on Method*, and *Meditations on First Philosophy* (Wordsworth Classics, 1997). These are classics and necessary reading for any serious student of philosophy.

Hume, David: *Dialogues on Natural Religion* (Baron David Hume, Hume's nephew, posthumously, 1777). This is a classic text on the argument from design, with Hume at his subtle best.

Kuhn, Thomas: *The Structure of Scientific Revolutions* (University of Chicago Press, 1970). A highly influential book which is rewarding to read.

Popper, Karl: *The Logic of Scientific Discovery* (Hutchinson, London, 1959). Another highly influential and rewarding book.

Radcliffe-Richards, Janet: *Human Nature after Darwin* (Routledge, London, 2000). This is a comprehensive and illuminating discussion of criticisms of Darwin's theory.

Walsh, W. H.: *Kant's Criticism of Metaphysics* (Edinburgh University Press, 1975). Provides an excellent commentary on the central argument of the 'Critique of Pure Reason', as well as giving a newcomer access to Kant's thought which the existing translations sometimes obscure.

PART V

PEOPLE and FREEDOM

In the final part of this introduction to philosophy we discuss the concept of a person – a subject which, as we shall see, has underpinned various strands of our earlier discussions. Philosophers throughout the ages have analysed the concept of a person precisely because it lies beneath the surface of virtually every philosophical problem. The principal aim of our discussion here is to identify the different approaches to the question of personal identity and to understand the different theories resulting from them. The evaluation of the theories is a secondary aim, and these are, like all the evaluations in the previous sections, open to criticism.

In Chapter 15 we answer two different but related questions concerning personal identity. The first asks what we mean by a 'person' and the second what is involved in remaining the same person during periods when physical and mental attributes change. The answers to these questions form the basis of the discussions in Chapter 16 when we examine the related topics of a person's capacity to act freely and a person's responsibility for her own actions.

Personal Identity

15

The following interdependent questions form the basis of the discussions in this chapter:

> What is a person?

and

> How do we identify a person
> as the same one on different
> occasions?

IN THIS CHAPTER

Concepts discussed

- Personal Identity

Theories discussed

- Dualism
- Physicalism/materialism

Skills developed

- Assessment of arguments
- Analysis of concepts
- Analysis of arguments

Types of arguments examined

- Those based on Thought experiments

Philosophers whose ideas are discussed

- René Descartes
- Derek Parfit
- John Locke
- David Armstrong

References made to the following philosophers

- Aristotle
- Thomas Reid
- Jean-Paul Sartre
- John Duns Scotus
- David Hume
- Thomas Kuhn
- Immanuel Kant
- John Stuart Mill

What is a Person?

At the end of Part IV we noted that the processes by which we assess claims and theories require us to have a notion of what it is to be an ordinary person – even Descartes' criterion to determine whether he knows something (that he should perceive clearly and distinctly that it is true) requires that there be someone who is able to perceive clearly and distinctly. Philosophical analysis would be impossible without the ability to assess and evaluate theories, and we are as such obliged to reject any concept of a person which defined a person in a way that made it impossible for the person to assess a theory – such a definition of a person would exclude philosophers from being persons! Some of our other philosophical analyses also place conditions upon a workable concept of a person.

In studying epistemology we discerned various requirements regarding the nature of a person:

1. Hume's empiricism required that a person should be a subject who could be perceived (p. 98);
2. our own assessment of the degree of acceptability of a theory required a subject who could classify it as being incontrovertible, beyond reasonable doubt or merely logically possible (p. 59);
3. Descartes' rationalism required that there be a subject who perceived clear and distinct ideas (p. 333);
4. Reid's analysis of the 'Intellectual Powers of Man' (p. 178) required a subject who accepted first principles so that he would be 'fit to be reasoned with';
5. Kuhn's analysis of 'normal science' or a 'scientific revolution' (p. 195) required a scientist who selected, evaluated and criticised theories in existing scientific paradigms or changed them for new ones during a scientific revolution.

In studying ontology we discerned more requirements regarding the nature of a person:

6. the existence of the social structures which we use required persons who communicated with each other in order to sustain those structures (p. 267);

7. existentialist philosophy required a subject with an intellect and a free will who would act as one of the fundamental building blocks of reality (p. 283).

In studying ethics we discerned further requirements:

8. Aristotle's virtue ethics required a person to be a 'substance' (p. 142);
9. Kant's deontology required a person to choose freely to obey those of her maxims of behaviour which could be made into universal laws (p. 148);
10. Mill's utilitarianism (p. 153) and ethical egoism (p. 158) required a person to be someone who valued and calculated the units of his pleasure;
11. Sartre's and Nietzsche's ethics required a person to be a subject whose free actions constituted moral value (p. 160).

These eleven requirements of what a person should be have arisen from our various philosophical inquiries (though it is also possible that different philosophical inquiries from the ones carried out above would have produced other requirements). The result is that some of the requirements can contradict each other: for example, a Cartesian perceiver of incontrovertible clear and distinct ideas of Requirement (3) might not be consistent with a Kuhnian scientist of Requirement (5), who participates in a scientific revolution.

Should a concept of a person conflict with any of the above requirements we would have to either reject that concept or alternatively question the principle which generated the requirement. For example, if a concept of a person permitted the splitting of a person into two people, we might find that the existentialist notion of a subject whose free actions constitute moral value would become untenable. We would be faced with a choice between the theory that persons can split into two people and the notion that moral value is found in the free actions of an individual.

When faced with a discussion containing the variety of possibilities such as those included in the above list, a good strategy is to look for an analytical tool which permits the problem to be broken down into manageable components. The Aristotelian notion of a 'substance' (a separately existing thing) provides us with such a tool. It also has the advantage of providing an analysis of personal identity similar to the more modern question which asks whether the concept of a person is an 'intrinsic' or an 'extrinsic' one. Aristotle defined a substance as something which contained its own final cause – a cart was not a substance but the driver of the cart was. This was because the purpose for which the cart existed (its final cause) was in the mind of the artisan who built it and so not part of the cart, whereas the purpose for which the driver existed was essentially part of him. The essential parts of the definitions were 'extrinsic' in the case of the cart and 'intrinsic' in the case of the driver.

An 'intrinsic' property belongs to a thing independently of its relations with other things whereas 'extrinsic' properties depend upon the existence of other things.

An extrinsic concept would be one in which all the properties of the thing defined depended upon its relations with other things. Some philosophers argue that the concept of a person is an extrinsic one – for example, Brian Garret in his entry in the *Routledge Encyclopaedia of Philosophy*. In the following exercise we inquire into the extent to which the distinction between intrinsic and extrinsic properties forms part of the use of commonplace descriptions of people.

Exercise 15.1

Being taller than someone else and being a good conversationalist are **extrinsic** qualities of a person, both being relations which are dependent upon other people.

1. List four other properties of persons which are **extrinsic**.

David Armstrong (1968) argued that **all** properties of persons are extrinsic whereas Descartes argued (*Meditations*) that some properties are intrinsic.

2. List four properties of persons which could be said to be **intrinsic**.

3. Are there any characteristics which differentiate the possible **intrinsic** properties from the **extrinsic** ones?

Suggested answers are on p. 355.

The claim by philosophers such as Armstrong, that all mental properties of people can be reduced to physical ones, is an example of 'reductionism': his materialist theory of the mind, which explains mental properties of people in terms of properties of physical entities, is said to have 'reduced' psychology to a physical science.

Aristotle's notion of a substance is a non-reductionist one since the substance's final purpose could not be found in anything but itself: one could not find the explanation for the horse's purpose in anything but the horse, whereas the explanation for the final purpose of the cart was to be found in the mind of the artisan who made it.

In the next sections we examine two non-reductionist and one reductionist theory of personal identity. All three take human experience and reason as their starting point: in Cartesian dualism they lead to the concept of an immaterial self; in Locke's theory they lead to the concept of a self as a unitary continuous conscious being; and in materialist theories of the mind they lead to a concept of the person as a physical object. We have already discussed some aspects of the theories which include human freedom along with reason and experience as their starting point (p. 99). We return to them briefly again in the next chapter.

Dualism – Mind and Body

The idea that a person has a body and a soul is deeply ingrained in many cultural systems, the soul being a simple (indivisible) spiritual 'substance'. According to Aristotle the soul was the formal cause (essence) of a person, which was inseparable from the person. Plato argued that essences in general, and the soul of the person in particular, had an existence separate from physical things. We shall focus our attention on the Cartesian theory which, like Plato's, claimed that a person's simple spiritual essence was distinct and separable from his body. Descartes examined the relationship between mind and body in the *Meditations*, concluding that the two were separate and separable entities. This separability is known as 'Cartesian dualism'.

Exercise 15.2

Examine the following argument from *Meditation VI* (section 9) and answer the questions.

α (*alpha*) 'I have a clear and distinct idea of myself, in as far as I am only a thinking and unextended thing'
(By 'unextended' he means 'cannot be measured in space')

β (*beta*) 'and as, on the other hand, I possess a distinct idea of body, in as far as it is only an extended and unthinking thing'

γ (*gamma*) 'it is certain that I, that is, my mind, by which I am what I am, is entirely and truly distinct from my body, and may exist without it.'

. . .

1. Does the fact that Descartes had a clear and distinct idea of himself as a thinking and 'unextended' (with no length, area or volume) thing mean that we all must have similar clear and distinct ideas of ourselves? If not, is Descartes' argument only valid for people who have such clear and distinct ideas of themselves?

_____

_____

2. Does the fact that a mind might be analysed separately from the body with which it interacts mean that the body and the mind can exist separately?

_____

_____

3. In Statement γ Descartes suggests that his mind is that by which he is what he is. Does this claim assume the conclusion that his body may exist without his mind?

_____

_____

Suggested answers are on p. 356.

Descartes' argument in *Meditation VI* has been hotly debated over the centuries – it was famously parodied by Gilbert Ryle (1949, p. 17 ff.) as 'the ghost in the machine'. More recent criticisms have centred on the use of 'thought experiments' in which the splitting of a person into two continuing, but separate, persons is postulated. Various versions of the person-splitting thought experiment have been postulated; we shall focus on Derek Parfit's rendering of it, involving a set of triplets (1984, p. 253).

My Division. My body is fatally injured, as are the brains of my two brothers. My brain is divided, and each half successfully transplanted into the body of one of my brothers. Each of the resulting people believes that he is me, seems to remember leading my life, has my character, and is in every other way psychologically continuous with me. And he has a body that is very like mine.

Parfit went on to ask what would happen to him in these circumstances, deducing that both surviving people would be him. The reason he gives is that if either twin had been the only to survive, that person would have been the surviving Derek Parfit. The argument has implications which affect the question of how we identify a person as the same one on different occasions, which we discuss below. For the present we focus on the implications it might have on Cartesian dualism.

Exercise 15.3 (Advanced exercise)

In Questions 1 and 2 assume that Parfit's thought experiment is valid. It is logically possible for two distinct Cartesian thinking and 'unextended' subjects to be given access to two different half brains.

1. Is it logically possible for a single Cartesian thinking and 'unextended' subject to split into two versions of itself?

At some point between conception and birth a Cartesian thinking subject is said to enter into the body of a person.

2. Is it logically possible for my 'unextended' Cartesian subject to be transferred into one of my brothers' bodies and for another different 'unextended' subject to enter the body of my other brother when the brain transplants are being carried out?

3. Do the arguments based on the person-splitting thought experiment repudiate the validity of Cartesian dualism?

. . .

4. If Cartesian dualism were true, what would the outcome of Parfit's experiment be? Would such an outcome be logically impossible?

_____

_____

Suggested answers are on p. 357.

CARTESIAN DUALISM?

The criticism of Cartesian dualism was only one of three uses to which Parfit put his thought experiment – the other two were the construction of Parfit's own theory of personal identity and a criticism of John Locke's theory.

Continuity – Body and Consciousness

Locke agreed with Descartes that a person was a subject of consciousness, but did not accept that the essence of this subject, which endured as the same subject during the passage of time, consisted of a 'thinking and unextended thing'. Unlike Descartes, Locke distinguished between what it was to be a person and the criteria which were needed to identify a person; he addressed the two questions we asked at the beginning of the chapter. The first was:

> What is a person?

In *An Essay Concerning Human Understanding* Locke wrote:

> we must consider what a person stands for – which, I think, is a thinking intelligent being, that has reason and reflection, and can consider itself as itself, the same thinking thing, in different times and places (1690, II, Chap. 27, section 9)

In the first clause Locke refers to an ability to consider 'itself as itself': this is an **intrinsic** property of the person. The last clause shows that Locke was also concerned with the second question, which was posed earlier:

> How do we identify a person
> as the same one on different
> occasions?

Locke addressed this question in the next section of the *Essay*: 'For, it being the same consciousness that makes a man be himself to himself, personal identity depends on that only, . . . ' which indicates that he believed that the continuity of consciousness determined the continuing identity of a person. He concluded the sentence by stating: '. . . whether it be annexed solely to one individual substance, or can be continued in a succession of several substances' (1690, Chap. 27, section 10). This indicates that he believed, like Parfit, that consciousness could reside in different bodies – a factor significant for anyone who believed in the resurrection of a body which had decomposed.

In this exercise we examine the differences between Parfit and Locke and ask whether a thought experiment is a valid instrument for analysing the nature of a person.

Exercise 15.4

In Questions 1 and 2 assume that Parfit's thought experiment is valid.

1. Does the division of Parfit's consciousness mean that Locke's definition of a person as 'a thinking intelligent being, that has reason and reflection, and can consider itself as itself, the same thinking thing, in different times and places' was mistaken?

_____

_____

2. Does the division of Parfit's consciousness mean that we cannot use the continuity of consciousness to identify him as the same person on different occasions?

_____

_____

3. (Advanced question) Consider the following thought experiment:
   A hydrogen atom divides to form two new atoms which are identical in every way to the previous single atom. There is no nuclear explosion and no energy is given off or absorbed by the atoms during the metamorphosis. The two new atoms are continuous in every way to the original single atom; scientists observing the change name the original atom 'Atom-One', the atom which moved off to the left 'Atom-Lefty' and the one which moved off to the right 'Atom-Righty'. Both Atom-Lefty and Atom-Righty have histories which are continuous with that of Atom-One.

   This atom-splitting thought experiment violates the principle of the conservation of mass and energy.

   (i) Is it legitimate to conclude from it that we cannot use the continuity of an atom's history to identify it as the same atom on different occasions?

_____

_____

. . .

> (ii) Does Parfit's person-splitting thought experiment violate any principles?
>
> _____
>
> _____
>
> **Suggested answers are on p. 359.**

The discussion of the person-splitting thought experiment might not be conclusive in terms of telling us what a person is or even how to identify someone as being the same person on different occasions. Nevertheless, it has given us an opportunity to sharpen some analytical skills in assessing arguments. When presented with an argument involving the speculative use of the imagination as a source of knowledge, we should examine all of the assumptions implicit in it.

The next theory of personal identity we examine states its assumptions explicitly; indeed, it only makes one assumption, which is, that all mental phenomena can be explained in terms of physical ones.

Materialism – Mind as Body

'Materialism' is a term which has more than one meaning. In common usage it refers to a philosophy in which value is ascribed to physical objects rather than to moral or aesthetic qualities. With regard to philosophy it is used in at least two areas: in the philosophy of mind and in Marxist philosophy. In the former it refers to the theory that matter alone exists and that minds and spirits can be explained in terms of changes in matter. In Marxist philosophy, where it is qualified as being either dialectical or historical, it refers to the mechanisms which generate social change.

Here we are concerned with its meaning in the context of theories of persons in general, and those dealing with the mind in particular. In outline, materialist theories of the mind consist of the six steps set out in the following exercise.

[Note: The wording used to represent an argument in summary form can predetermine the results of any criticism. It is possible to rewrite the argument in such a manner as to make it less amenable to either anti-materialist or pro-materialist criticism.]

Exercise 15.5

Examine the following argument and answer the questions.

α (*alpha*)   The body is made of matter and the brain is part of the body.

···

β (*beta*)   The behaviour of matter complies with the laws of nature therefore the behaviour of the brain complies with the laws of nature.

γ (*gamma*) The mind functions through the operations of the brain.

From these premises we draw the following conclusions:

δ (*delta*) The mind's functions have to comply with the laws of nature.

ε (*epsilon*) The mind's functions can be explained by explaining the brain's functions.

ζ (*zeta*)   A person is nothing but a physical object.

A driver has to comply with the laws governing motoring.

1. Does this mean that the driver's behaviour can be explained by using the laws governing motoring?

2. Does the brain's compliance with the laws of nature mean that the behaviour of the mind can be explained by using the laws of nature?

(Advanced questions)

3. The argument α to ζ may have been formulated in a manner prejudicial to the materialist case. How might a materialist amend it?

4. Questions 1 and 2 may have been formulated in a manner prejudicial to the materialist case. How might a materialist amend them?

Suggested answers are on p. 361.

The suggested answers to Questions 1 and 2 show that compliance with a law does not give sufficient grounds for supporting a claim that something is determined by the law. They also suggest that rigorous philosophical support for the materialist case requires us to demonstrate that the mind is regulated **completely** by the physical functions of the brain. It is at this point that philosophers tend to go their separate ways.

One group is formed by materialists (such as David Armstrong) who claim that the confirmation that the mind is regulated completely by the physical functions of the brain will eventually come from neuroscience; in other words, they claim that all the human sciences can be 'reduced' to physics. The success of modern computer technology in imitating analytic behaviour of intelligent people is seen as providing support for the hypothesis that a physical mechanism such as the human brain can reproduce all the mental phenomena we associate with the human mind.

The second group of philosophers consists of those who have followed in the footsteps of Franz Brentano (and his 'Intentionality Thesis') claiming that there is a difference between two types of function of the mind: one involves the processing of information and is subject to the laws of nature, while the other involves intentionality and is free from some of the restrictions imposed by physical laws. During our examination of Brentano's nineteenth-century notion of intentionality (p. 283), we also discussed its medieval predecessor, the 'unconditioned' will which accompanied a 'conditioned' intellect in Duns Scotus' analysis of a unified mind (p. 283).

The theories of one member of this second group, Simone de Beauvoir, will be discussed in the next chapter, but first we shall summarise this chapter's discussion on the theories about identity which take the combination of reason and human experience as their starting point.

Summary

Starting with his reason and the evidence from his conscious experience, Descartes concluded that he was an immaterial substance that was separable from his material body. As a thinking thing, he noticed that he was 'unextended' but that his body was 'extended' and therefore separable. In Exercises 15.2 and 15.3 we questioned the logic of using the distinction between that which is 'unextended' and that which is 'extended' as a basis for deducing their separability.

Locke accepted Descartes' notion of a person as 'a thinking thing' that found itself in a body. He assumed that a person was 'a thinking, reasoning and reflective being' whose self-awareness permitted him to consider himself to be the same thing, in different times and places. Locke did not deduce from this that the mind and body were separable. His main concern was to establish the criteria for determining the continued identity of a person over time. His analysis led him to conclude that this was to be found in the continuity of a unitary consciousness, a conclusion challenged by Derek Parfit. We examined Parfit's use of a thought experiment involving the division of a person and found that it made some assumptions that prevented it from providing incontrovertible refutations of either Locke's or Descartes' theories.

In Exercise 15.5 we examined an argument designed to establish a materialist (physicalist) theory of a person. We analysed the formulation of the argument and of the questions designed to evaluate it, finding that both of these could prejudice the evaluation. A full evaluation of materialist theories would need to be carried out in the same way as that for any theory in the natural sciences, using the evaluative techniques appropriate to science. In our present state of knowledge, however, the practical laboratory appraisals of the physicalist theory of a person cannot be carried out. Some of the theoretical appraisals of the theory can be attempted, however, and we finished by indicating that the rival philosophical position articulated by existentialist philosophers claimed that the physicalist theory would not be able to explain the intentionality of conscious experience. We shall touch on this theme in the final chapter.

Freedom and Responsibility 16

For in every action what is primarily intended by the doer whether he acts as a result of natural necessity or out of free will, is the disclosure of his own image. Hence it comes about that every doer, in so far as he does, takes delight in doing; since everything that is desires its own being, and since in action the being of the doer is somehow intensified, delight necessarily follows . . . Thus nothing acts unless by acting it makes patent its latent self.

(Dante, from *de Monarchia*, as quoted and translated from the original Latin by Hannah Arendt (1958, p. 175) in a section on the agent as disclosed in action)

Hannah Arendt used the quotation from Dante to introduce a discussion of the agent as disclosed in action, arguing that action was not just a response to external stimuli but was itself a creative stimulus through which an individual defined herself and was defined by others. The notion of an individual disclosing herself through action forms the central idea which is examined in our final chapter.

We start with a reminder of the previous discussions which were connected with the notion of freedom. These occurred in Chapters 8 and 11 where the autonomy of the individual was assumed as a given fact and the implications of that assumption were analysed; in this chapter we challenge that assumption and examine some responses to the challenge. A review of these discussions will help to pinpoint the questions which have led existentialist philosophers to place freedom at the core of the concept of a person.

In Chapter 8 we discussed two theories which challenged the empiricist notion that the fundamental building blocks from which reality is built are solely the phenomena of cognitive experience. In the first we observed that the existentialist challenge to this empiricist position claimed that the individual with a unified mind consisting of an intellect and a will constituted such a fundamental building block. We also observed that the notion of a will which directs the analyses carried out by the intellect did not originate with Brentano's intentionality thesis but had its roots in the writings of the medieval scholar Duns Scotus (p. 283).

Modern existentialist philosophers have looked into the basis for making the claim that the mind consists of a will and intellect; they consider that a unified mind consisting of a will and an intellect provides the answer to the Kantian (transcendental) question:

> What are the conditions which make it possible for
> us to ascribe meaning to the signals we perceive
> through the senses? [Q1]

In the examinations of moral theories in Chapter 11 we also discussed the theory that moral value was to be found in the free actions of individuals, focusing on the ideas of Jean-Paul Sartre and Friedrich Nietzsche. In all the discussions of moral theories the main aim was to understand the principles on which they were built and the standard criticisms of each theory; we did not consider the conditions which made the ascription of value possible. These considerations would have produced a second Kantian question which is also asked by modern existentialist philosophers:

> What are the conditions which make it possible for
> us to ascribe value? [Q2]

[Note: (i) Neither of these two questions has been formulated with these words by existentialist philosophers. (ii) The sort of question which inquires into the basis of a philosophical activity is sometimes given the prefix 'meta'; so this is a question posed in 'meta-ethics' because it asks a question about the nature of ethics. These further subdivisions of the subjects in philosophy into meta-philosophical subjects often do little more than create barriers for a novice to overcome; they tend to hide the meaning of a philosophical claim in a mesh of abstruse sub-categories.]

Various different answers have been given to the two questions. Here we shall focus on Simone de Beauvoir's answers which are in harmony with the principle underlying Hannah Arendt's use of the quotation from Dante cited above; her answers are more optimistic than the ones produced by her contemporary and life-long companion, Jean-Paul Sartre, although we shall not be examining this aspect of the difference between them. The optimism contained in consenting to Dante's notion that 'every doer, in so far as he does, takes delight in doing' has at least two merits: firstly, it avoids the pessimist's internal conflict of willing an action and knowing that the action must fail to achieve its aim; secondly, and perhaps more significantly, the optimism allows one to make sense of attempts to emancipate socially oppressed human beings – in the absence of optimism all attempts at social reform would be worse than futile, they would be nonsensical.

Freedom of Thought and Action

De Beauvoir regarded Q1 and Q2 as being inexorably interlinked. In the section on 'Ambiguity and Freedom' from her book *The Ethics of Ambiguity* she recognised that:

> existentialism merely carries on the tradition of Kant, Fichte and Hegel, who, in the words of Hegel himself *'have taken for their point of departure the principle according to which the essence of right and duty and the essence of thinking and willing are absolutely identical.'* The idea that defines all humans is that the world is not a given world foreign to man, one to which he has to force himself to yield from without. It is the world willed by man, insofar as his will expresses his genuine reality. (MacDonald, 2000, p. 282)

[Note: The translator has chosen to translate *homme* as 'man' rather than 'person'. However, gender is not as specifically related to males and females in French as it is in English. For example, in French one does not say 'his' or 'her' when referring to a person's presidency, one says *sa* ('her') *présidence* for both males and females because *présidence* is a feminine word.]

In accepting Hegel's claim that the point of departure for moral values and cognitive processes were absolutely identical, de Beauvoir was merging the answers to Q1 and Q2. She did not, however, merely state that there was a single point of departure, she produced arguments to support her statement. We now examine some of these arguments.

Exercise 16.1

The extracts for Questions 1–3 are from *The Ethics of Ambiguity*.

Freedom is the source from which all significations [The designation of meaning, focusing on the qualities or properties of a concept as it is perceived in consciousness, rather than meaning seen in terms of the things which fall under the concept.] and all values spring. It is the original condition of all justification of existence. The person who seeks to justify his life must want freedom itself absolutely and above everything else. (p. 283)

When we learn to speak as children we are told what the meanings of words are: we are told, for example, that the word 'bread' refers to something we eat and that 'hard' refers to something which resists attempts to change its shape.

1. (i) In allocating meaning could I be merely processing data in the same way as a computer does?

_____

_____

(ii) Do I have to be free to allocate meaning?

_____

_____

Man cannot decide between the negation and assumption of his freedom, for as soon as he decides, he assumes it. He cannot positively will not to be free for such a willing would be self destructive. (p. 283)

2. Does the fact that I cannot will my freedom away mean that I must be free?

_____

_____

However, man does not create the world. He succeeds in disclosing it only through the resistance which the world opposes to him. The will

· · ·

is defined only by raising obstacles, and because the facts in the world are open to different outcomes certain obstacles let themselves be conquered, and others not. (adapted) (p. 285)

[Note: In order to make the last sentence accessible to readers who are unfamiliar with philosophical jargon, I have substituted 'by the contingency of facticity' with 'because facts in the world are open to different outcomes'. (FCR)]

3. (i) Does the world have to resist me in order for me to obtain knowledge of it (disclose it)?

_____

_____

(ii) If so, does this mean that I must exercise some freedom when I act?

_____

_____

In the last quotation de Beauvoir argues that freedom is situated in a world in which other things behave independently of it – freedom always functions in a particular context and it is said to be 'situated'. This means that an individual's freedom is dependent upon her ability to interact not only with a resistant world but also with other individuals who, like her, are free. De Beauvoir argues that in order to realise our own freedom we **must** recognise the freedom of others.

4. If in order to be free I do not have to recognise that the world which resists me is free, am I obliged to recognise that other cognitive individuals are free?

_____

_____

Suggested answers are on p. 363.

The suggested answer to 4 indicates that de Beauvoir considered the relationship between a free individual and the world of objects to be different from the relationship between the individual and other free individuals. This difference implies that she believed that there were **two types of freedom**: a freedom to interact with a physical world which either resisted or acceded to the individual's will, and a freedom to give meaning to existence.

De Beauvoir considered the freedom of the individual to interact with the physical world to be independent of the laws of nature, although constrained by them; perhaps this was similar to the freedom of the driver we discussed in Exercise 15.5 (p. 226), whose behaviour had to comply with the laws of motoring but was not determined by them. We can contrast this sort of freedom with the freedom which is 'the source from which all significations and all values spring' – that is, the basis from which we give meaning to all we do.

It was this latter type of freedom which de Beauvoir considered to be dependent upon the freedom of other individuals, and which through being the source of all 'significations' and values was inherently linked to the existence of other beings. This is pointed out by Linda Bell in her examination of de Beauvoir's and Sartre's analysis of willing one's own freedom and that of others. Bell quotes de Beauvoir as saying: 'To will that there be being is also to will that there be people for whom the world is endowed with human significance' (1999, p. 164). De Beauvoir argued that an individual, in willing her own ends and recognising her own freedom, had also to will the active support of others. Since the freedom of others was a precondition of obtaining this support, willing one's own freedom necessitated willing the freedom of others. Thus, in order to give meaning to the world, an individual would be obliged to promote the freedom of others; de Beauvoir provided a single answer to Q1 and Q2 (p. 230).

Exercise 16.2

Is it logically possible for God to be the source from which all 'significations' and all values spring?

_____

_____

Suggested answers are on p. 366.

The arguments on freedom developed by existentialist thinkers such as de Beauvoir were 'transcendental arguments' – they looked for the conditions which make something possible. In their case the something was the designations of meanings to concepts ('significations'). These arguments contrast with the deductive ones supporting the theories of personal identity which we discussed in Chapter 15. An existentialist philosopher would challenge the very possibility of finding definitive criteria for personal identity as these would be based on a concept of the self as defined extrinsically; an extrinsic definition of the self would be inconsistent with the conditions which made the designations of meanings to concepts possible – in other words, extrinsic definitions of the self would render the conceptualisation of the world in human terms impossible. The consequence of this would be that the actions of a person (defined in completely extrinsic terms) could not achieve what was 'intended by the doer whether he acts as a result of natural necessity or out of free will', namely 'the disclosure of his own image' (Dante, from p. 229).

Responsibility

We saw earlier that Kant developed a transcendental argument which stipulated that freedom was the precondition of a human activity (p. 151). Kant's argument was more specifically focused on moral values and moral rules, citing freedom as a condition for the possibility of actions having moral value. We shall pursue this Kantian theme in the final discussion on freedom by asking whether freedom is a precondition of moral responsibility for actions.

Exercise 16.3

Various legal jurisdictions allow people accused of committing criminal acts to plead that they were not guilty on the grounds that they were unable to choose to act otherwise.

1. Is the claim that people are responsible for their actions only if they are able to act otherwise an analytic or synthetic claim?

_____

_____

2. Are people responsible for their actions when they break the law only if they are able to act otherwise?

_____

_____

3. Describe an activity which you cannot do without assuming the responsibility for your actions.

_____

_____

Suggested answers are on p. 366.

The suggested answer to 3 indicates that learning and teaching are symbiotic interactive activities rather than activities involving a distinct cause and a distinct effect. The approach to learning philosophy in this introduction to the subject has been an interactive one and, notwithstanding the limitations imposed by the written word, has attempted to show that learning philosophy is part of the subject itself. Socrates put this process at the heart of his philosophy, and the Socratic method has guided the production of this book.

Part V: A Summary

In Part V we have explored personal identity and freedom. Although these themes were central to many of the arguments discussed in the previous chapters, they remained below the surface, concealed by the immediacy of the discussions of the topic in hand. Indeed, at the beginning of Chapter 15 we noted eleven different conditions that the concept of a person had to meet in order to comply with the requirements of various different approaches to philosophical analysis. Among these conditions we found that Aristotle's analysis of knowledge required a person to be a 'substance'; Kant's ethical system required a person who could choose freely to obey those of her maxims of behaviour which could be made into universal laws; Descartes' theory of knowledge required the individual to be capable of having incontrovertible 'clear and distinct ideas'; and Mill's utilitarianism required a person to be someone who valued and calculated the units of his pleasure.

The varying requirements of the properties which a person should have led to the formation of two questions which subsequently directed the discussions on personal identity:

> ## What is a person?

and

> ## How do we identify a person
> ## as the same one on different
> ## occasions?

We examined two categories of answer to the first question: the first considered people to be subjects of experience and the second considered them to be physical or material things. We examined Descartes' claim that the subject of experience is an immaterial 'thing' which was both 'unextended' and separable from the body. This was followed by an examination of the materialist claim that the person is a material object like all other material objects. Both these opposing claims were subjected to scrutiny by using a thought experiment in which it was assumed that a person could bifurcate, or split into two replicas of itself.

The person-splitting experiment was also used to scrutinise answers to the second question, in particular Locke's answer that a person's identity over time was constituted by a continuity of consciousness. The limitations of using such thought experiments were also discussed.

In the final chapter we returned to the theme of the person as a subject of experience and discussed the existentialist claim that subjects of experience are necessarily agents who disclose both themselves and the environment which they experience through their free actions. This led naturally to a discussion, albeit very brief, of the relationship between freedom and responsibility.

This final discussion had a dual purpose: the first was informative and the second formative. The informative purpose was the introduction of the reader to a philosophical issue which lies at the heart of both ethics and epistemology. Kant, for example, considered that freedom, and the responsibility that is an indispensable part of freedom, underpinned knowledge as well as moral value. The formative purpose was to endorse the notion that learning is a process in which the learner is an active participant. This endorsement returns the reader to the vision of philosophy set out in the first chapter as an activity in which the participants take a active part, one in which the present practitioners invite newcomers to join them, rather than just listen to them. This does not mean that readers have to accept Simone de Beauvoir's claim that the individual is free, but that, if they reject the claim, it is because they have worked through the arguments themselves.

Revision Exercises

Revision Exercise 15.1 and 16.1

When an animal is cloned, the clone is genetically indistinguishable from the original.

> 1. Does this mean that a cloned human being would be the same person as the one from whom he was cloned?

Descartes claimed that he had 'a clear and distinct idea of myself, in as far as I am only a thinking and unextended thing'.

· · ·

2. Can a 'thing' be unextended (non-measurable in space)?

Kant's deontology required a person to choose freely to obey any of the person's own maxims of behaviour which could be made into universal laws. David Armstrong claimed that a person is fully definable as a material object.

3. (i) Can a material object freely choose to obey universal laws?

(ii) Given the answer to (i), do we reject Kant's theory, Armstrong's or neither?

Suggested answers are on p. 368.

Revision Discussion Exercise 16.2

When we see the symbols 10 and 100 we normally interpret them as the numbers 'ten' and 'one hundred'. However, if we were mathematicians working in a different number base, for example with binary numbers, we would interpret them as the numbers 'two and four'.

The symbols written as 10+10=100 would form the same image on the eye but would be interpreted with one meaning in one set of circumstances and a different meaning in another – the different meanings would make the symbols represent falsehood in one case and truth in the other.

Working in the standard number base non-mathematicians use, the set of symbols would catch the eye as being out of place; we would focus on them and look for an explanation as to why a false statement were there. Working in binary numbers we might not even notice them.

Cognitive beings have the ability to interpret the images they gather from their environment in different ways. They also have the ability to focus the mind on the different interpretations and meanings of these images.

1. Does the fact that cognitive beings have these abilities mean that they have a free will which is able to alter the content of consciousness?

_____

_____

2. Does an individual's ability to give different meanings to the same images she gathers from her environment depend upon the existence of other individuals who have the same ability?

_____

_____

Suggested answers are on p. 370.

Further Reading

Descartes, René: *Discourse on Method*, and *Meditations on First Philosophy* (Wordsworth Classics, 1997). These are classics and necessary reading for any serious student of philosophy.

Parfit, Derek: *Reasons and Persons* (Clarendon Press, 1974). A highly provocative and stimulating book which also analyses the leading theories of Personal Identity in depth.

Bell, Linda: 'Existential Ethics', in *The Edinburgh Encyclopedia of Continental Philosophy*, Simon Glendenning (ed.) (Edinburgh University Press, 1999, pp. 163–73). A lucid examination of existential ethics which explains its central role in existentialism.

Burwood, S., Gilbert, P. and Lennon, K.: *Philosophy of Mind* (UCL Press, 1999). A comprehensive analysis of the subject ideal for the interested student who wishes to study the subject in detail.

Suggested Answers – Part I

Exercise 2.1 (p. 12)

1. Describe two human activities which can be understood well by doing them and without thinking about how the activity works.

    (i) Hitting a forehand topspin when playing tennis requires practice. A player can come to understand that hitting the ball in a particular way makes it spin, which in turn makes its trajectory a dipping one. No understanding of the physics involved in the flight of a spinning ball is needed to understand what is involved in playing a topspin shot.

    (ii) Grapes have been successfully fermented to make wine for thousands of years without the majority of wine-makers being able to understand the chemical processes of fermentation. The winemakers nonetheless have a deep understanding of what activities and conditions are likely to produce good wine.

Comment

_____

_____

2. Describe a human activity which can be understood well even without ever having done the activity.

    Many physicists who have never been in space understand the principles of space travel.

Comment

_____

_____

3. Assess Claim 1 and amend it if necessary.

The answers to Question 1 support the acceptability of Claim 1, but they are not sufficient to validate it properly. It is still possible that there may be an activity which can be completely understood by some method which does not involve doing it. The example of the physicists who have never been in a spacecraft, and yet who understand space travel, will suffice. This single example is enough for us to reject Claim 1, as there is an activity which is not best understood by doing it. On this basis a grade C or D seems to be appropriate.

This single counter-example may lead us to amend Claim 1 and produce a counterclaim.

Claim 2: Taking part in a human activity is a good way to understand what it is. An alternative way to understand a human activity is to use a model to simulate the activity.

Comment

_____

_____

Exercise 2.3 (p. 16)

1. Give three **consequentialist** and three **essentialist** reasons for studying history.

Firstly, the study of history leads to a deeper understanding of our present culture than we would have had without studying history. Secondly, the study of history enables us to avoid some of the mistakes our predecessors have made. Thirdly, the study of history leads to a better understanding of human nature than the one we would have had without studying history.

The following are three essentialist reasons for studying history: we study history because it is interesting; we study history because it is a compulsory part of the curriculum; we study history because the history teacher is good-looking.

Comment

_____

_____

2. Give one **consequentialist** and one **essentialist** reason why a car driver might stop at a red traffic light.

Consequentialist reasons might be that the driver wanted to avoid an accident, or that she wanted to avoid getting a fine. An essentialist reason might be that her sense of duty prevents her from breaking the law.

Comment

_____

_____

3. Formulate a question which can have only an **essentialist** answer.

Why is the number 4 a factor of the number 12?

Comment

_____

_____

4. Are there any human activities which have no **consequentialist** aspects? Give reasons for your answer.

No. Every human activity will have some consequentialist aspect, and all activities change the world in some way. This necessarily means that there will be consequences associated with the changes. Naturally, the consequences of some actions will be longer lasting and/or more significant than others. Dropping a brick on a glass roof will have more long-lasting and significant effects where the roof breaks than where it remains intact.

It may also be important for us to know whether the consequences were intended or unintended. In the case where I meant to break the roof, the moral and legal implications for me would generally be more serious than they would be if I dropped the brick unintentionally.

Comment

_____

_____

Exercise 2.5 (p. 17)

1. What are the consequences, for the person involved, of learning about gardening?

People who learn about gardening increase their understanding of how plants grow in particular seasons, weather conditions, different soils, conditions of light and proximity to other plants. They may also learn about the aesthetic aspects of plant arrangements in gardens of different sizes and in different locations. They will be able to use this knowledge in order to decide when and how to plant seeds, when and how to transfer seedlings from pots to a prepared flowerbed, when and how to prune or cut back a plant, when and how to feed the plants and when to remove plants from different parts of the garden and which to remove.

Comment

_____

_____

2. What exactly is gardening?

Gardening is the activity in which one plants out and cultivates fruit, vegetables and/or flowers in a defined plot of land. The activity is governed by certain principles: those which establish criteria by which to judge how well the plot has been laid out, and those which establish the conditions which need to be met if the cultivation is to produce the desired effects.

Comment

_____

_____

Exercise 2.7 (p. 19)

1. According to the text (line 1), what processes are studied in chemistry? And why do chemists seek to understand these processes (lines 4–7)?

Processes which involve transformation of matter are studied in chemistry. There are two reasons why chemists seek to understand these processes.

The first, and main one, is so that they may **control** the course and outcome of the processes. The second reason is that chemists may wish to understand other sciences. Chemistry is essential to understanding many other sciences: the transformation processes occur everywhere, in the earth and living systems and in the stars, so understanding them is essential for anyone who may wish to understand other sciences.

Comment

2. According to the text, what are the **consequentialist** reasons which should encourage someone to study chemistry?

The first consequentialist reason cited in the text which should encourage someone to study chemistry is given in the answer to Question 1. In lines 4–7 of the Weinberg College text, we are told that the study of chemistry leads to the ability to control the course and outcome of transformations of matter.

The second consequentialist reason cited in the text is also given in the answer to (1). Also in lines 4–7, we are told that the study of chemistry leads to a better understanding of other sciences. The same idea is repeated in lines 13–15: 'Some study chemistry because it provides the language and the conceptual framework for a deeper understanding of other subject areas – geology, biology, physiology, astronomy, environmental science, and energy studies.'

A third consequentialist reason given (lines 16–17) is that it is an essential part of the preparation for their professions, as chemists, engineers, physicians, dentists, consultants, etc. The study of chemistry opens up possible careers for the student. All three of these reasons cite the **results** of studying chemistry as the reasons why someone should study it. This makes them consequentialist reasons.

Comment

3. According to the text, what are the **essentialist** reasons which lead some people to study chemistry?

The only essentialist reason cited in the text (lines 11–12), which leads some people to study chemistry is that 'they find the subject interesting and challenging. There is great appeal in both the scientific rigor and the usefulness of chemistry.'

Comment

_____

_____

4. Give some reasons why someone might **not** want to study chemistry. Contrast these negative reasons with the positive reasons given in the text. Can each negative reason be paired with a positive one?

It is possible to give a great number of different answers to this question. Only a few are given here. Among the most obvious reasons are the ones which are the direct negatives of those given in the text.

A prospective student might not wish to have a better understanding of other sciences, or to control the course and outcome of transformations of matter, or to prepare for a profession as a chemist, engineer, physician, dentist, etc. or might not find the subject interesting and challenging.

But each of these is not a **sufficient reason** on its own not to study chemistry. Someone who does not 'find the subject interesting and challenging' might still study it because she wishes to follow one of the professions which requires chemistry. This is possible, but unlikely.

It is also possible that someone may decide not to study chemistry because he does not wish to do what his father or mother did.

Comment

_____

_____

Exercise 2.9 (p. 23)

(i) What are the consequences, for the person involved, of studying philosophy?

In answering Question (i) we might say that the students of philosophy, like those of physics, increase their understanding of the world. But they increase their understanding of different aspects of the world. Instead of focusing on the world itself, they focus on the relationships between the world and the way we humans perceive the world.

In particular, they will increase their understanding of how we humans come to value things and actions – how we come to ascribe beauty to art and how we come to decide that certain actions are right or wrong. They will also increase their understanding of how we humans come to accept particular claims to knowledge, whether scientific or not, as being valid.

Students of philosophy will improve their ability to analyse the relationships between ideas and the relationships between ideas and the objects the ideas refer to. In other words, they improve their ability to reason. In particular, they will increase their understanding of both formal abstract reasoning, logic, and the less abstract reasoning used in formulating sound arguments.

Comment

_____

_____

Exercise 3.1 (p. 27)

1. Describe a situation in which someone has **wisdom** without **knowledge**. Readers should attempt to describe other situations.

A senior politician, who advises new party members to delay making pronouncements for a day until they have had time to sleep on them, has wisdom. She is aware that what people say without fully considering their words often has a different effect from the one that is intended by the speaker. It is possible, however, that she does not understand either the psychological or physiological impact on a person of waiting for a day – she lacks knowledge.

Comment

_____

_____

2. Describe a situation in which someone has **knowledge** without **wisdom**.

A scientist who understands all the theories of elementary particle physics sufficiently well to build his own portable atomic bomb has knowledge. If he does not appreciate that the possessor of this knowledge cannot indiscriminately allow access to this knowledge, then he does not also possess wisdom.

Comment

_____

_____

Exercise 3.3 (p. 29)

Thales' Hypothesis 2: The one fundamental, or primary, substance is water. Everything we see, touch, smell, taste or hear is a mutation of water.

1. Assess Thales' Hypothesis 2 by giving it a grade A to F, with A being excellent and F being a failure.

The personal answer of the author of this text is to award a B.

If Thales had been living in the twenty-first century, then the mark would have been nearer to an F. The reason is that accepting Hypothesis 2 would make nonsense of modern science. Accepting the notion that the one fundamental substance is water would mean that we would have to reject modern scientific methods and practices, and science would be nonsensical. The teaching of laboratory techniques, the interpretation of the results of laboratory experiments and the application of the knowledge we gain in laboratories would no longer have meaning. Accepting Thales' Hypothesis 2 would entail our sacrificing the intelligibility of modern science and would lead us into absurdity. This sacrifice is too great, so we reject Thales' hypothesis – and we would expect Thales himself to reject it if he were alive today.

[Note: The type of argument set out in these two paragraphs is a 'reductio ad absurdum argument'. The intelligibility of laboratory activity has been invoked by Roy Bhaskar (1978) as a principle from which we can conclude that science investigates a world which is necessarily independent of our conceptualisations.]

Comment

_____

_____

2. Give the reasons for your mark.

The justification for grade B comes from the fact that Thales was operating at a significant disadvantage. He did not have the experience of modern science which would enable him to assess his own theory as effectively as we can. He could observe the cycle of water evaporating into the air and then returning to the ground in the form of rain much of which would immediately re-evaporate. He may also have seen ice and known that it melted to form water. This would have given him the knowledge that the same substance changes from gas to liquid and to solid. He would not have known how this change took place.

This lack of knowledge obliged him to guess, and in guessing he was forming an hypothesis. He had no way of testing the hypothesis, so all his other 'knowledge' also had to remain as a series of hypotheses, or guesses. His Hypothesis 2 brings together all of these guesses into a single hypothesis and makes his acceptance of Hypothesis 1 rational. The reason for being impressed by this hypothesis is that it accepts that Hypothesis 1 is valid.

Comment

_____

_____

_____

Exercise 3.4 (p. 30)

Thales' Hypothesis 1: Everything is made of one fundamental, or primary, substance. Each thing we see is a mutation of the fundamental substance.

The personal answer of the author of this text is to award an A.

1. Assess Thales' Hypothesis 1 (p. 28) by giving it a grade A to F, with A being excellent, and F being a failure.

Comment

_____

_____

2. Give the reasons for your mark.

The justification for the A grade is based on the difficulty, if not impossibility, of explaining any change without assuming that there is something stable against which the change can be measured – and Thales' Hypothesis 1 stated that water was that stable substance. Without an assumption of a stable setting against which we can detect changes, we cannot assess whether a change has taken place: we have no way of experimenting to evaluate how good our description is; the only explanation we are left with is a dogmatic assertion based on something like religious faith. Thales' Hypothesis 1 makes scientific investigation possible.

Comment

_____

_____

Exercise 3.5 (p. 32)

α Suppose that one of the known elements, such as earth, fire, air or water, is the **primary substance**.

β The elements are in opposition to each other: air is cold, water is moist, and fire is hot.

γ If one element were the **primary substance**, it would conquer the others. The **primary substance** would become infinite; the rest would have ceased to exist by now.

δ Elements which are in opposition to each other have not ceased to exist.

ε We can conclude that α is false. The **primary substance** is neutral and cannot be one of the elements which is in opposition to the others.

1. Is Anaximander's argument a **valid** one? Justify your answer.

[Note: Anaximander's argument is a 'proof by contradiction', using a *reductio ad absurdum*. The statement α is the 'contrapositive' of what Anaximander wishes to prove.]

The stated premises of this argument are the first four statements: α, β, γ and δ. The first of these, (α), is a supposition which Thales wishes to show is false. He intends to do this by showing that it leads to an unacceptable conclusion. Statement β is an **observation** about the properties of things in the world. Statement γ is a **reasoned claim** about how the world is ordered – in particular about how the properties of the substances mentioned in β – that the primary substance would conquer all the other substances. Statement δ is an **observation** about what we actually find in the world, which contradicts the claim γ.

Since we accept this observation (δ) as true, we can conclude that one or more of the four premises is false. We have to choose between accepting the supposition α and the observations, β and δ, about what happens in the world. This means that the argument is logically valid, but not that its conclusion is necessarily true.

The acceptability of an argument depends upon the truth of the conclusions, which in turn depends upon the truth of the premises. If we were prepared to accept all of Anaximander's premises, the argument would be **acceptable**. This takes us on to assessing the acceptability of the argument.

Comment

---

2. Determine whether Anaximander's argument is an **acceptable** one.

The second premise (β) is necessarily true. We can ask why elements have to be in opposition. Could they not just co-exist peacefully? There seems to be no contradiction in the suggestion that air could be hot or moist, although moist fire does seem to be a contradiction. The acceptability of the argument will depend upon whether we can determine if the elements can, in practice, co-exist peacefully. Evidence produced from modern laboratory techniques indicates that the elements can co-exist. This indicates, therefore, that the premise is not acceptable to someone who accepts modern scientific practice as providing methods to determine how elements behave.

The acceptability of the argument is also weakened by the third premise, statement (γ). This statement cannot be accepted without reservation. If two things are in opposition, it does not follow that one would conquer the other. If the forces are evenly balanced, it is possible that neither will prevail – draws between sporting opponents are not unusual.

On balance, we can say that the argument is not an acceptable one. Too many factors need to be ascertained as being true in order for the premises to hold.

Comment

Exercise 3.6 (p. 34)

1. Assess Anaximander's first principle by giving it a grade A to F, with A being excellent, and F being a failure.

The personal answer of the author of this text is to award an A.

The reason for giving a higher mark than was awarded to Thales is that Anaximander avoids Thales' problem: he makes it possible to understand how substances might change their form to produce what we see as water, rocks, wood, air, grain, heat etc. Anaximander lays the foundations for science. He makes it possible for people to investigate how the world works: after him, science could start to look for underlying causes of the phenomena we experience.

Comment

_____

_____

2. Assess Anaximander's second principle by giving it a grade A to F, with A being excellent, and F being a failure.

The assessment of the claim was carried out in the previous exercise when assessing Anaximander's argument that no single element could be the 'primary substance'.

Comment

_____

_____

3. Describe something which can be seen yet is usually accepted as being **unreal.**

A mirage in the desert looks like a lake. This 'lake' can be seen, but it is not real.

Comment

_____

_____

4. Describe something which cannot be seen yet is normally thought to be **real**.

A 'black hole' cannot be seen as no light can emerge from it. Scientists infer that one exists from the fact that light from distant stars bends round something on its way to us. They calculate the mass of this 'thing' by the extent to which the light bends. They then calculate the gravitational pull of the 'thing' and find that this is consistent with it pulling all light back into itself. No light can emerge from the 'thing'. This means that it cannot be seen yet it is thought to exist.

Comment

Revision Exercises
Revision Exercise 2.1 (p. 47)

1. Specify which of the events (i) to (v) are accidental consequences of the bird's successful foraging expedition and which are not accidental.
   (i)   A small hole is found in the earth at the point where the bird caught the worm.
   (ii)   The bird flies back to its nest carrying the worm.
   (iii) The bird feeds the worm to its chicks.
   (iv)   The bird's chicks are no longer making as much noise as they were before being fed.

All four of these events are not accidental: (i) the bird's aim was to pull the worm out of the ground, thus leaving a hole where the worm was; (ii) any definition of a bird foraging will include a description of the return trip; (iii) an integral part of a foraging expedition is the feeding of the bird's chicks; (iv) chicks make more noise when they are hungry so a consequence of a successful foraging expedition necessarily involves a diminution of their hunger and so of the noise they will make.

Comment

_____

_____

(v) Having fed its chicks, the bird is standing on the edge of its nest. It is casting a shadow on a squirrel which is at the foot of the tree.

This is an accidental consequence: no definition of foraging, as understood by humans, will include a requirement that shadows should be cast at any point during the expedition.

Comment

_____

_____

2. Are the accidental consequences of foraging related to the essential features of foraging?

The relationship between the essential and accidental features turns on the definition of foraging. This is true of any object or event. Our understanding of what something is will determine the parameters that delineate the thing's essential characteristics. Anything that is not an essential characteristic will be an accidental one.

Comment

_____

_____

Revision Exercise 2.2 (p. 48)

The following two dictionary definitions of philosophy were given:

(i) 'the study of the general principles of some particular branch of knowledge, experience or activity'
(ii) 'that department of knowledge or study which deals with ultimate reality, or with the most general causes and principles of things'

Decide whether each of the following claims is a philosophical claim and justify your decision.

2. The existence of God can be neither proved nor disproved.

This is a philosophical claim which comes under definition (ii) as it says something about a particular aspect of our knowledge of reality.

Comment

_____

_____

3. Modern physicists are near to finding the fundamental building blocks of matter.

This is a philosophical claim which comes under definition (ii) as it also says something about a particular aspect of our knowledge of reality.

Comment

_____

_____

4. 'Do not commit murder' is a fundamental law which applies to all human beings.

This is a philosophical claim and it comes under definition (i) as it claims to be a general principle of ethics, which is a particular branch of knowledge.

Comment

_____

_____

Revision Exercise 2.3 (p. 49)

Are Claims 1 and 2 in Revision Exercise 2.2 **valid** claims?

Claim 1 is valid. Ornithologists' activities only make sense if the behaviour of the birds they are observing follows certain patterns, implying that the birds' environment has an effect on that behaviour. The presence of the ornithologists alters that environment so it is reasonable to assume that their presence may affect the behaviour of the birds they are observing and so affect the data they are gathering.

Comment

_____

_____

Claim 2 is also valid as it makes a well-founded claim about the status of another claim: stating that the 'existence of God' was blue would not have been a well-founded claim and so would not be philosophically valid.

Comment

_____

_____

Revision Exercise 2.4 (p. 50)

1. Is Kant giving an **essentialist** or a **consequentialist** reason for writing the *Critique of Pure Reason*?

   Kant's reasons are consequentialist as the result of writing the *Critique of Pure Reason* was that he did not do something else.

Comment

_____

_____

2. Give an example of a negative reason for doing something which is **essentialist**.

   The government passed a law protecting children from economic exploitation because not doing so would have contravened the principles of natural justice.

Comment

_____

_____

Revision Exercise 3.1 (p. 50)

> 1. Is it possible for something to change completely on its own without out-side influences? In other words, does Anaximander's claim hold true for all the changes of things?

Yes, it is logically possible. There are philosophers who argue that the human will operates in such a way that it can change without external causes obliging it to do so, although there are philosophers who disagree (see Chapters 15 and 16).

Comment

_____

_____

> 2. When you change your mind, is it always because of an outside influence?

As the answer to Question 1 indicates, this is a disputed issue. Duns Scotus' answer would have been 'No' (see Chapter 8) and David Armstrong's would be 'Yes' (see Chapter 15).

Comment

_____

_____

Revision Exercise 3.2 (p. 51)

> 1. Is a partial absence of order in the world possible? In other words, could the world still function with just a little bit of disorder?

Yes. It is possible for laws to apply universally and yet for there to be disorder: in a controlled laboratory environment there is order, but if the universe is open and infinitely vast it becomes logically impossible to control all environments, so the operations of laws will not necessarily lead to a laboratory type of order.

Comment

_____

_____

2. Can a bit of disorder be thought of as a good thing? In other words, does **justice** always have to involve total order?

No. It is logically possible for justice to operate in some disorder; indeed, the very reasons why civil and religious laws exist is because there is an absence of total order.

William Paley argued that, not only was a little disorder a good thing, it was also a necessary condition for us to be able to appreciate God's infinite justice.

Comment

_____

_____

[Note: This question is directly related to arguments about the existence of God, in particular to the 'teleological argument' (argument from design), which we discuss in Chapter 14.]

3. Let us suppose that nature operates according to a principle of **justice**. Does this mean that there must be something, or some being, beyond nature which generates or maintains the justice?

Not necessarily.

Comment

_____

_____

_____

Revision Exercise 3.3 (p. 52)

Are ideas just as real, more real, or less real than mountains, trees and houses?

The answer to this question depends, in part, on what is meant by an idea. We shall restrict ourselves to the two meanings that are part of everyday usage: a mental image and an archetype or pattern.

The reality of mental images seems to be more certain than the reality of mountains, trees and houses because we have less work to do to establish their existence. The mental image is inside our consciousness while the mountains, trees and houses are outside it. However, this subjective idea needs a subject who holds it in consciousness; it has a dependent sort of existence which mountains, trees and houses do not have.

The reality of an idea as an archetype or pattern, as something a designer has, is more difficult to determine. This sort of idea is not dependent on an individual subject in the same way as the mental image; but it does not seem to have the same sort of independent permanence as mountains, trees and houses. We examine Plato's claim that ideas do have independent existence in the second section of Chapter 8.

Comment

Suggested Answers – Part II

Exercise 5.1 (p. 56)

1. (i) Identify the statement in the first paragraph which connects some of Alice's specific experiences to the general properties of her environment:

   'So many out-of-the-way things had happened lately, that Alice had begun to think that very few things indeed were really impossible.'

   Comment

   _____

   _____

   (ii) State why she believes the claim to be true.

   Alice's belief, in this case, is based on her own experience. Out-of-the-way things had happened, so she was prepared to believe that other out-of-the-way things could also happen.

   Comment

   _____

   _____

2. (i) Identify the statement in the last paragraph which makes a claim about the appearance of a specific object.

   'This bottle was *NOT* marked "poison".'

   Comment

   _____

   _____

(ii) State why Alice believes the claim to be true.

Alice believes this claim to be true because she had decided to 'look first, and see whether it's marked "poison" or not'. She had seen that the bottle was not marked 'poison', so she based her belief, in part, on her faith in the proper functioning of her sense of sight.

Comment

_____

_____

3. (i) Identify three claims Alice makes in the third paragraph about the general properties of some types of object or occurrence.

'A red-hot poker will burn you if you hold it too long.'
'If you cut your finger VERY deeply with a knife, it usually bleeds.'
'If you drink much from a bottle marked "poison", it is almost certain to disagree with you, sooner or later.'

Comment

_____

_____

(ii) State why she believes the claims to be true.

Alice believes these to be true because they were 'the simple rules their (that is, her) friends had taught them (that is, her)'. She was relying on other people's experience and accepting the rule that this experience had produced.

Comment

_____

_____

_____

4. Assess the validity and/or acceptability of each of Alice's five claims, by giving it a grade A to F.

The three claims in Question 3(i): Believing something to be true because your friends had taught you is valid as long as your friends are trustworthy. The assessment of the validity shifts to the trustworthiness of the friends. The claims are reasonable, but Alice could have made them more acceptable by adding evidence from her own experience. They each deserve about a grade C.

The claim in Question 2(i): Believing something to be true because you have checked it yourself is normally more reliable than trusting your friends, as you do not need to check anyone else's trustworthiness. Alice looked at the bottle; in order to make sense of the world, she has to have basic faith in the reliability of her sense experience. This claim is more acceptable than the last ones; it deserves a grade B.

The claim in Question 1(i): Alice's belief that this claim is valid was based on her own recent direct experiences **and on an interpretation of those experiences**. This extra requirement enables her to make her experiences more intelligible to her, but it also increases the risk of error – she could have interpreted what happened to her incorrectly. This claim is better than the claims in Question 3(i), but is not as risk-free as the one in Question 2(i); it deserves a grade B.

Comment

_____

_____

Exercise 5.2 (p. 60)

Information acquired by seeing and hearing real things

1. Does **seeing** or **hearing** a sheepdog provide us with:
   (i) **logically possible** reasons that the sheepdog exists?

The absence of logical contradictions is all that is needed for something to be logically possible. There is no logical contradiction involved in suggesting that I can see or hear something which I believe is a sheepdog. There is also no logical contradiction involved in using this suggestion to back up a claim that a sheepdog exists.

Comment

_____

_____

(ii) reasons that put the sheepdog's existence **beyond reasonable doubt?**

The evidence from hearing on its own does not normally provide us with reasons that put the sheepdog's existence beyond reasonable doubt.

In normal circumstances, the use of sight can provide us with reasons that put the sheepdog's existence beyond reasonable doubt. We would expect sight to count as sufficient evidence of its existence, and we would only reject it if there were reasons to believe that the visual senses have malfunctioned or that something has interfered with the signals the eye is receiving.

By contrast, in normal circumstances, hearing may not be sufficient – hearing is not normally as well developed and as reliable a source of information as sight. For example, if I should hear a dog but not be able to see one, a significant doubt remains that the sound that I hear is not a sheepdog but some other dog, or even a recording. However, if the person hearing the sound has an acute sense of hearing, and has maybe studied dogs and recordings of dogs, then the evidence might be sufficient to put the sheepdog's existence beyond reasonable doubt.

Comment

_____

_____

(iii) reasons that **prove** that the sheepdog exists?

In normal circumstances, either sight or hearing can be challenged as providing proof. The evidence they give is not incontrovertible since the organs could have malfunctioned, and the malfunction could be correctable. It can be argued that, in the abnormal circumstances of the controlled environment of a laboratory, the evidence from one of these senses may be incontrovertible, but this puts the burden of proof partly on the nature and use of the controlled environment. The significance of a controlled laboratory environment is discussed at various points throughout the book, for example, in the discussion on the proofs of the existence of God on p. 199.

Comment

_____

_____

Exercise 5.4 (p. 63)

Information acquired by touching real things

1. Can **touching**, or **kicking**, a rock provide us with reasons that put the rock's existence **beyond reasonable doubt?**

The sense of touch seems to be more reliable than the other senses in telling us that something exists; this could be because it is more immediate than the other senses. There is no intermediate medium between the thing sensed and the sense organ, that is no air through which light or sound travels, so, at impact, there is no opportunity for interference with the signal before it reaches the sense organ. The question of possible illusion applies equally to all the senses, so the sense of touch is more likely than the senses of sight and hearing to provide a correct impression that a real rock exists.

Comment

_____

_____

2. Did Dr Johnson succeed in refuting Berkeley's theory that physical things exist only as ideas in people's and God's minds?

By refuting a theory we mean that we have provided incontrovertible reasons demonstrating it to be untenable. It is logically possible that both Boswell and Johnson were simultaneously struck by a hallucination, harmonised either by chance or by God; indeed, the harmonisation by God of our experiences is the nub of Berkeley's idealist theory. The confirmation or refutation of the theory depends upon whether or not we can prove the existence of God.

Comment

_____

_____

Exercise 6.2 (p. 79)

1. (i) What physical or other characteristics must money have to have in order for it to be **practically possible** for it to be used as a means of exchange?

In order for it to be practically possible for money to be used as a means of exchange, it must be:

(a) **durable**: If we could not rely on money still being there at a future time we would not accept it as a means of payment because it could not act as a store of value.

(b) **easily transportable**: If money were not easily transportable a trader would find it difficult to buy and sell.

(c) **divisible into basic units** with (d) **each basic unit having the same value as every other basic unit**: If there were no basic units of money, then no-one would know the price of the thing which was being traded; buying and selling would therefore be impossible.

Comment

_____

_____

(ii) Which of these characteristics, if any, are needed in order for it to be **logically possible** for money to be used as a means of exchange?

The only characteristic which is clearly not essential is that it should be (b) easily transportable. It is logically possible for people to use two ton pieces of concrete as money; the problem involved in handing over money in any transaction would be practical rather than logical.

It is arguable whether money has to be durable. In his satirical novel, _The Hitchhiker's Guide to the Galaxy_, Douglas Adams (1993), describes a community which had made the leaf legal tender. There were resulting problems of inflation, as anyone who needed money simply had to pluck a leaf from the nearest tree!

Comment

_____

_____

2. (i) What physical or other characteristics does money have to have in order for it to be **practically possible** for it to be used as a store of value?

In order for it to function at a practical level as a store of value, money must be (a) durable, (b) transportable and (c) divisible into basic units with (d) each basic unit having the same value as every other basic unit. The arguments are the same as the ones set out in Question 1(i).

Comment

_____

_____

(ii) Which of these characteristics, if any, are needed in order for it to be **logically possible** for money to be used as a store of value?

A store of value must be something which maintains a characteristic over time. This means that the thing has to be durable. Quality (a) is essential for money to be a store of value.

The arguments here with regard to (c) and (d) are the same as in Question 1(i). If there were no basic units of money then no-one would know the value of a certain quantity of money; without knowledge of its value, money could not function as a store of value.

Comment

_____

_____

_____

Discussion Exercise 6.3 (Advanced exercise) (p. 81)

> 1. A physical object is bought. What relationship must the object have with the seller before the sale?

The object must be owned by the seller or the person whom the seller represents. If the object is not owned, then the transaction is fraudulent; the object has not been bought.

Comment

_____

_____

[Note contributed by Thomas Roberts: According to the provisions of German law, an object can be bought even in cases where the seller does not own the physical object. Should the seller not be entitled to sell the object, the true owner could only reclaim the value of the sold object from the seller. Buyers are entitled to ownership of the purchased object as long as they were in good faith at the time of the sale.]

> 2. Describe a society in which trading is **logically impossible**.

Since trading involves the transfer of ownership of property, in any society in which such transfers cannot occur trading would be logically impossible. Naturally, in a society where there is no ownership of property, trading would be logically impossible.

Comment

_____

_____

(A more general advanced question)

> 3. What characteristics or processes does a society have to have in order for it to be able to function as a society?

One process, without which a society could not function, is 'concept communication' between individuals, a condition that is unlikely to be disputed by many philosophers.

[Note: There is, however, some disagreement about the nature of the relationship between concept communication and the existence of society: Continental philosophers would argue that this dependence is two-way, that is, that concept communication could not function outwith the context of a society; philosophers in the analytic tradition would argue that society is a product of the interactions between people, rather than a condition which makes the interactions possible.]

This is not a comprehensive answer to the question. It may be that other relationships such as economic interdependence may have to exist in order for there to be a society. Considerations like these will, however, go beyond the scope of an introductory book in philosophy.

Comment

_____

_____

Exercise 7.1 (p. 85)

1. No sea-creature is less than two inches long.
2. All sea-creatures have gills.

1. Are both, either or neither Statements 1 and 2 true? Give reasons for your answer.

Neither statement is true.

It is possible to find sea-creatures which are less than two inches long. To do this we need to use some other method to gather evidence about sea-creatures. Perhaps if the ichthyologist were to dive down into the sea with some form of illumination, he might see some sea-creatures which were less than two inches long.

If the ichthyologist has **only** his net and no other means of obtaining information about sea-creatures, then Statement 1 is true and can never be false. No experiences can ever contradict it: this means that it is true *a priori*, or independently of all experience.

We know that whales and dolphins do not have gills, and they could have been caught in his net. The ichthyologist is only entitled to claim that the sea-creatures he has so far seen do not have gills. This claim is true of his experience so far: it is true *a posteriori*, or on the basis of experience.

Comment

_____

_____

Eddington tells us that the ichthyologist has a net with a two-inch mesh, and it cannot catch sea-creatures which are less than two inches long.

2. Does the nature of the net affect what type of creatures there are in the sea?

It is difficult to envisage a situation in which a fishing net might determine the nature of creatures which live in the sea. Further, if the ichthyologist is to make claims about sea-creatures that exist independently of his research methods, then his net ought not to affect what type of creatures there are in the sea.

[Note contributed by Thomas Roberts: It is, however, possible that even if all fish were originally more than two inches long, the presence of the fishing net might cause fish to evolve which were less than two inches long in order to evade capture! The nature of the net would then affect the type of creatures there are in the sea.]

Comment

_____

_____

3. How, if at all, does the nature of the net affect what type of creatures the ichthyologist can determine there are in the sea?

If using the net with the two-inch mesh is the **only** method of gathering information about sea-creatures, then this limits the ichthyologist's knowledge of sea-creatures. It would restrict the nature of the catch, and so of any conclusions drawn from the evidence produced by the catch.

Comment

_____

_____

4. How, if at all, does the nature of the net affect the truth of the statements?

If there were no other means of gathering information about sea-creatures at our disposal, then the nature of the net would affect the truth of Statement 1: there would be no means available to contradict Statement 1;

it would be **incontrovertible**. **Incontrovertibility** was cited above (p. 59) as the criterion which determines whether a claim has been proved. Statement 1 would have been proved as being true. Note: This type of proof is known as a transcendental proof.

Comment

_____

_____

Exercise 7.2 (p. 87)

Let us coin an Eddingtonian phrase: 'What my five sense organs can't detect isn't real'.

1. Describe something **physical** that my sense organs can't detect.

Radio waves are disturbances in the atmosphere which seem to affect certain pieces of equipment but have no detectable effect on my sense organs.

Comment

_____

_____

2. Describe an **emotion** that my five sense organs can't detect.

Other people's happiness is not directly detectable by the sense organs, which can only pick up signs of happiness, although eighteenth-century philosophers, led by Anthony Shaftesbury, claimed that there is a special moral sense which detects moral and aesthetic value in the same way as the eye detects light. However, they did not find a specific organ which detected the feeling of happiness.

Comment

_____

_____

3. Describe a social entity that my five sense organs can't detect.

We cannot see a government or a university, but only government buildings and officials, university buildings, laboratories, students and university staff.

Comment

_____

_____

4. Describe something whose existence is independent of what my five sense organs can detect.

All the types of thing cited in the answers to Questions 1–3 are assumed to be present because of some sort of effect which can be detected by our sense organs. We see happy expressions denoting the presence of happiness; we can see, hear and touch government buildings and officials, university buildings, laboratories, students and university staff.

It is possible to argue that the existence of God is not dependent upon what my five sense organs can detect. It may be that the very concept of God precludes the possibility that the senses can detect God. (The proofs of the existence of God are examined in Chapter 14.)

Comment

_____

_____

5. Is the statement 'What my five sense organs can't detect isn't real' true or false?

The statement is false.

There is more than one possible way of showing that the statement is false. We can, for example, base our argument on how science is practised. We do this by using a _reductio ad absurdum_ argument to show that the statement is false: we assume that it is true and proceed to show that this assumption leads us to an absurd conclusion.

Let us assume that the statement is true. Since we cannot detect radio waves directly with our senses, we would have to believe that they do not exist. Such an assumption would therefore oblige us to believe that science does not describe what is real. This belief would mean that tuning a radio would not make sense; that is to say, I would be trying to match my hand movements to something which did not exist. My behaviour in tuning my radio would therefore be absurd. It would, in fact, make as much sense as lining up a golf shot while believing that the golf ball did not exist. We can conclude, therefore, that radio waves are as real as golf balls.

Comment

_____

_____

Exercise 7.3 (Advanced exercise) (p. 91)

1. Describe how a police force might change without any of the force's equipment or buildings changing.

There are several possible answers to this question. The make up of the personnel of the force might change, for example, because there are more female officers among the new recruits. The shift pattern of the force might change, for example, through the reduction of the rest periods after a night shift, thereby putting greater strain on the officers. Both of these changes result in a change in the behaviour of the force and, consequently, in a change in the effect of the force's behaviour.

Comment

_____

_____

2. Describe an effect of the change identified in Question 1.

An increase in the proportion of female officers may lead to a greater willingness of female victims of crime to report the crimes.

Comment

_____

_____

Discussion Exercise 7.4 (Advanced exercise) (p. 92)

> Is there such a thing as society?

This suggested answer is likely to be controversial.

Margaret Thatcher was right, there is no such thing as society.

The suggested answer to Exercise 7.3, Question 3 shows why society ought not to be called a 'thing'. It does not interact with people, other social entities or with physical things. Rather than interacting with people, other social entities and physical things, it provides the context in which people and other social entities interact with each other and with physical things. Banks, governments, schools and police forces are 'things' but society is not. Thatcher was saying 'You are a metaphysician. Bah!' to the people who believe that society is a 'thing'. She was right.

It is also possible to formulate a proof demonstrating that society is not a 'thing'. We can show that society needs to be viewed in the same way as the universe is viewed in physics. The universe is the context in which physical things exist and interact; it is not a 'thing'. Similarly, society is the context, or social universe, in which social objects exist and interact. The argument which demonstrates that society **needs** to be viewed in this way is a 'transcendental proof' and formed part of the author's doctoral thesis. Roughly speaking, the argument in the thesis points out that learning processes would be impossible in the absence of such a social 'universe'. Some of the implications of this argument were developed in a later publication (Roberts, 1993).

Comment

Exercise 7.5 (Advanced exercise) (p. 94)

Elwood Dowd lived in a small town in the Mid-West of the USA in the 1940s. He had a constant companion, Harvey, a six foot three and a half inch (1.94m) white rabbit.

> 1. Does the fact that Elwood could interact with Harvey provide us with sufficient grounds for saying that Harvey really existed?

The answer is simply 'No'. The arguments presented in Chapter 5 indicated that more than one person was needed in order to establish the existence of animals in general and rabbits, in particular, beyond reasonable doubt.

Comment

_____

_____

Both Harvey and Elwood were created by Mary Chase for her theatre play *Harvey*. No one else apart from Elwood could see Harvey. A film of the play was made by Universal in 1950; the part of Elwood was played by James Stewart and Josephine Hull played the part of his sister Veta, who wanted to have him committed to an asylum. Eventually Veta admits to having seen Harvey, so she is committed instead of Elwood.

2. If Elwood and Veta had been real people, rather than characters in a play and a film, would we be justified in saying that Harvey was also real?

In this case, we would have more than one person. However, there would be many others who could give evidence that they were unable to detect Harvey's presence. As in the cases argued in Chapter 5, the contradictory evidence means that we would not be able to establish Harvey's existence beyond reasonable doubt.

Comment

_____

_____

Suppose a group of James Stewart fans were to form a Harvey Society. Suppose they were to hold annual dinners at which Harvey was the guest of honour with a special reserved seat at the top table.

3. Would we now be justified in saying that Harvey existed?

The fact that more people than just Elwood and Veta behave as though Harvey exists still does not establish his existence beyond reasonable doubt. There would be others who would provide opposing testimony stating that they could not detect Harvey's presence.

Comment

_____

_____

Mickey Mouse was the product of Walt Disney's imagination. He seems to meet many of the conditions needed to be real: real things are imitated and so is 'he', 'he' gives children's parties and 'he' is registered as a trademark.

4. Is it possible to create a real thing just by using the imagination?

Mickey Mouse would be what sociologists call a 'social construct'. He was, and still is, constructed by mental effort and through social mechanisms. Whether this social construct is able to interact with people and other 'things', is less certain. It may be that the best we can do is say that we cannot ascribe thinghood to Mickey Mouse **beyond reasonable doubt**, but that the **preponderance of evidence** indicates that we should.

Comment

_____

_____

_____

Exercise 7.6 (Advanced exercise) (p. 96)

1. Make a list of five things which some people believe are real, or have been real, yet which their senses have never directly detected.

Some people believe that the following entities exist (or have existed):
(a) dinosaurs
(b) the soul
(c) electrons
(d) Yale University
(e) thought waves
None of these has been detected by our senses, although dinosaur fossils have been.

Comment

_____

_____

_____

2. Consider two of the things you have described in Question 1. Describe a theory, belief or form of behaviour which implicitly commits people to accepting that these things exist.

(a) Studying palaeontology and searching for fossils commits one to accepting the existence of prehistoric animals in general and of dinosaurs in particular.

Comment

_____

_____

(b) Many different religions conduct funeral ceremonies which commit the departed person's soul to a future existence. Taking part in such a ceremony commits the participants to a belief in the existence of the soul.

Comment

_____

_____

(c) J. J. Thomson, who was awarded the Nobel Prize for physics in 1906 for his discovery of the electron, justified his belief in its existence by referring to a set of laboratory experiments – experiments which classified him as a scientist rather than, say, an illusionist. Modern scientists who conduct experiments using electron microscopes are also committed to the belief that electrons exist, and the same is true for all of us who switch a television set on and expect to see something which is being broadcast: taking part in these activities commits the participants to the belief in the existence of those things without which the activities would not make sense.

Comment

_____

_____

(d) Making a donation to Yale University to fund a scholarship commits the donor to the belief in the existence of the university. Despite being able to see things owned by Yale, such as its fine library, we cannot see Yale University itself.

Comment

_____

_____

(e) An identical twin who is suddenly convinced that her twin is calling for help and tries to find her, is committed to a belief in the transfer of thought.

Comment

_____

_____

Exercise 8.1 (Advanced exercise) (p. 100)

Suppose you have experienced something for the first time. The experience is either positive or negative or neutral. A second or subsequent experience will also be either positive or negative or neutral.

1. Indicate whether this subsequent experience would be more or less positive than the first, more or less negative, or of equal value to the first experience.

First experience	Subsequently more/less positive/negative
(i) Eating an ice cream	usually this is less positive
(ii) Hearing a particular joke	it loses nearly all its appeal
(iii) Re-reading a particular thriller	usually this is less positive
(iv) Seeing a multi-coloured sunset	this might be more positive the second time
(v) Proving Pythagoras' Theorem	this is distinctly less positive
(vi) Responding to questioning after being arrested	usually this is less negative
(vii) Riding a bicycle in a straight line	this is less positive
(viii) Acting a particular part in a play	this could be either, but it is unlikely to be the same.

Comment

_____

_____

2. Specify which of the above repeated experiences can become more positive or less negative through your own mental effort? Describe how one of these experiences can be made more positive.

Every one of the experiences can be affected positively by controlling the reaction to it: we can savour a positive experience or resist the effects of a negative one, and the fact that this might be difficult in particular circumstances does not mean that it cannot be achieved. For example, the mundane experience of riding a bicycle in a straight line for someone who learnt to do so as a child can be enhanced simply by recalling the pleasure of having achieved the feat for the first time. This ability to associate pleasurable experiences with any current experience gives individuals the ability to enhance an experience.

Comment

_____

_____

3. If you claim that one experience cannot be enhanced, explain why it is impossible in that particular instance.

The answer to Question 2 eliminates the need for an answer.

Comment

_____

_____

4. Does the fact that we can modify an experience mean that we are more fundamental entities than the experience?

This certainly provides us with a prima facie case for suggesting that our existence as conscious individuals is at least as fundamental as the phenomena of our internal experience. If we can modify something, then that something's existence cannot be more fundamental than ours is. Since the content of consciousness modifies an individual's future experiences, this argument works in two directions: the phenomena of our internal experience cannot consist of a less fundamental entity than the subject of the experiences.

Comment

Discussion Exercise 8.2 (Advanced exercise) (p. 103)

1. Is it possible for an individual to have an experience which he does not direct towards some object?

This question asks us to examine Franz Brentano's 'Intentionality Thesis' that every mental event is directed towards some object.

We shall use the schema for answering a question outlined on p. 67.

Specify the framework which guides the analysis of the question.
Firstly, we assume that it is possible for an individual to direct his experience towards some object. This assumption is implicitly accepted by anyone who answers Question 1. In philosophy we examine even our implicit assumptions, and perhaps dispute their validity. In this particular case we do not need to examine the assumption in great depth since contesting its validity would be self-negating. Contesting something involves directing one's attention to it; therefore we cannot contest the assumption that it is possible to direct one's attention to an experience. Such a contestation would be self-negating.

The answer to Exercise 8.1 enables us to extend the scope of this assumption. We noted that an individual is able to enhance or mitigate the effect of an experience, which means that he can do more than just direct his attention to some object of experience, that is, he can focus on the memory of the first time he rode a bicycle in order to enhance the pleasure of the present bicycle ride. Secondly, we specify the meanings of any terms we are going to use. In order to answer Question 2, we need to specify what we mean by the term 'fundamental entity'. In the introduction to Part II, on p. 53 above, the term 'fundamental entity' was defined as something which has separate existence or whose existence cannot be determined by referring to other entities.

Comment

_____

_____

Decompose (or 'deconstruct') the question into sub-questions.
It is possible to analyse the question differently from the way it is done in this suggested answer. In whichever way it is done, the deconstruction of a question is, however, the essence of the analysis which permits one subsequently to construct an answer.

The specification of the parameters which guide the analysis of the questions allows us to break the first part of our problem up into component parts.

We can reduce these to five preliminary questions:

(i)   Are there any examples of everyday behaviour which show that we normally assume that individuals are able to contribute to their own experiences?
(ii)   What can count as an object of experience?
(iii)   In what way, if at all, is the object of experience of a cognitive being different from that of a non-cognitive being?
(iv)   Does an experience have to be directed towards an object?
(v)   Is the individual's will an indispensable component of experience?

and, with the answer to Question 2 in mind:

(vi)   Do the answers to (i) to (v) help us to establish whether or not the individual's existence can be completely determined by referring to other entities?

Comment

_____

_____

Form the answers to the sub-questions and ensure the sub-answers conform to the parameters which guide the analysis of the question.

(i)   We saw in Exercise 8.1 that individuals can enhance or diminish the impact of an experience. This means that an experience can feed back onto itself and modify the experience.

We can go further. Some of our everyday behaviour assumes that we can deliberately affect our own experiences; most forms of social education assume that we are able to affect them. Parents teach their children to be aware of the effect of their actions both on other people and, significantly, on themselves. If we do not accept that individuals contribute to their own experience we have to deny that the ordinary behaviour of a parent teaching a child makes sense.

Comment

This ordinary behaviour makes the same assumption of the individual's ability to affect her own experiences as is made in clinical practices in psychoanalysis. These practices take things a stage further: they assume that individuals are able to contribute to their own experience without being aware of doing so; experience without such awareness is known as 'unconscious experience'.

The existence of 'unconscious experience' now forms part of standard theory and practice in psychoanalysis. Sigmund Freud (1949, p. 20) described mental unconscious processes by saying: 'What is unconscious can, as a result of our efforts, be made conscious, though in the process we may have an impression that we are overcoming what are often very strong resistances.' In attempting to teach patients to come to terms with their unconscious experiences, psychoanalytical practice makes an assumption that these unconscious experiences can be brought into consciousness so that the patient can reduce their negative effects. What the clinical psychoanalyst is doing is very similar to the parent who is trying to make his children aware of the effect that their own behaviour has on themselves. The intelligibility of practices in psychoanalysis depend upon the same assumption as the one which makes parental teaching intelligible: that individuals have the ability to affect their own experiences.

[Note: This last sentence provides an example of a 'transcendental argument'.]

Comment

(ii) There are at least five possible types of 'object' of experience.

Firstly, physical things in material form could be the objects of experience, although philosophers such as George Berkeley argued that physical objects were merely assemblages of 'ideas', or images, found in consciousness.

Secondly, whatever comes from our senses could be an object of experience. As we noted in the example of sharks which sense electromagnetic fields (p. 58), our sense organs are not necessarily restricted to the five senses. Further, philosophers such as Francis Hutcheson and David Hume argue that humans have a moral and an aesthetic sense which detect moral and aesthetic qualities; these qualities could equally be the objects of experience.

Thirdly, an emotion could also be the object of experience.

Fourthly, it is possible that the individual subject of the experience could be the object of his own experience.

Fifthly, abstract ideas such as mathematical concepts and general ideas such as circularity and goodness (also known as 'universals' because they can be applied throughout the universe and sometimes known as forms, because of Plato's 'Theory of Forms') could be objects of experience.

Finally, the object of experience could be a combination of these five objects. For example, the contemplation of a work of art is likely to involve more than one of these 'objects'.

Comment

_____

_____

(iii) In contrast with a non-cognitive being, the object of experience of a cognitive being is held in consciousness with the possibility that the thought of it might be communicated.

This sentence encapsulates one of the central ideas which shapes and directs existentialist philosophy.

Comment

_____

_____

_____

(iv) and (v) The fourth and fifth questions overlap; it is possible to answer them jointly. In doing so we ask ourselves a subordinate question: 'Can the content of experience arrive unbidden into consciousness?' The possibility that it might arrive unbidden suggests that experience could be directed towards an object by something other than the subject of the experience.

The issue is one which Alexander Brodie (2000, Chap. 3) discusses when he considers John Duns Scotus' influence on the development of Scottish philosophy. It leads us to a discussion of the role the human will plays in experience. The subject of the operation of the will in human experience has engaged the attention of philosophers of all periods, from medieval scholastic philosophers, such as Scotus, to philosophers of the last two centuries who were interested in phenomenology and existentialism, such as Franz Brentano and Martin Heidegger.

[Note: Paul MacDonald (2000, p. 229) traces the link between these two distant strands of European philosophical thought when he states that, in Duns Scotus, both Brentano and Heidegger had 'discovered a medieval precursor to the phenomenological concept of intentionality'.]

Brodie summarises Scotus' argument about the role of the will in experience in very clear and accessible language. Scotus accepted that experiences arrive unbidden into consciousness; our senses are receivers of information and some of it arrives whether we like it or not. Scotus points out that what happens after the arrival is dependent upon the operation of the will: the thought produced by the arrival of some externally generated stimulus would disappear if it were not maintained in consciousness by the will. Scotus makes a second, and related point: the intellect could not start to do its work on these thoughts unless something told it to and unless something kept them in consciousness. This something is the will. Brodie tells us that Scotus compares the function of the will in controlling the direction of our thoughts with the control of our physical bodies.

If there were not physical movements that take place unbidden, that take place entirely by nature or by instinct, there would not be the possibility of our willing to perform acts in the physical world. Likewise though some thoughts that come into our minds come unbidden, nevertheless almost all of our mental life is willed, for we have control over the direction that our thought takes at any instant. (Brodie, 2000, p. 23).

[Note: Scotus uses a transcendental argument: if we are to be able to make sense of the difference between unbidden and bidden experience, the operation of human will is a condition which must be fulfilled. Without the operation of the will, the words 'voluntary' and 'involuntary' would have no meaning.]

(vi)   Scotus' two arguments enable us to conclude that the human will is a faculty which operates in every mental act. The will is needed in order for thought to be sustained in consciousness and it is needed for reason to be given the impetus to do its work on one set of ideas rather than another. In other words, every experience must be directed by the will.

(e)   Form the answer to the question. The original question asked whether it is possible for an individual to have an experience which she does not direct towards some object. In the light of Scotus' arguments, the direct answer we give is 'No'; but we add the proviso that the directed experience can be triggered by something other than the individual's will.

Comment

_____

_____

2. What impact does the answer to Question 1 have on the question of whether the individual is a fundamental entity?

The criteria for the individual to be a fundamental entity seem to have been fulfilled. We cannot determine the existence of human experience completely without reference to the faculties of the will and the intellect. We have identified the source of the problem which Hume faced in finding a sense impression which corresponded to the subject of experience. The images provided by the senses may well be fundamental entities, but they are inadequate to the task of accounting for the subject of experience. Indeed, in order for them to form part of an experience there must be a subject with both a will and an intellect. The individual is a fundamental entity.

Comment

_____

_____

_____

Exercise 8.3 (Advanced exercise) (p. 108)

The following are suggested answers which have been formulated with a twenty-first century perspective and come from an interpretation of Plato's work gained by reading it in translation. Full text on pp. 106–7.

1. Indicate whether each statement makes a claim about our experiences, the nature of reality and/or our knowledge of reality. Where possible, indicate also whether you believe the statement to be true or false.

Statement	Experience	Reality	Knowledge	True or false
α	✓			T
β	✓	✓	✓	
γ		✓		T
δ	✓	✓	✓	
ε			✓	T
ζ	✓	✓		F
η		✓		F
θ			✓	T
ι		✓	✓	

[Note: A full discussion of Plato's theory is needed before we can determine whether β, δ and ι are true or false.]

Comment

The suggested answers to Question 1 indicate that Plato wanted to understand the human condition and to discover the principles which lead us to a better life. The way humans experience the world was an integral part of

Plato's philosophy. His theory claims that a more fundamental reality beyond experience helps us achieve both goals, but it does not say that the world we experience is not real.

2. Basing your answer on what you have learnt so far of Plato's 'Theory of Forms', how do you think Plato himself would have answered the question in the cartoon? Do you think he would have accepted that the book is real?

Like all physical things, the book is real. Plato's theory states that its properties are derived from more fundamental entities which exist independently of the book; for example, its rectangularity is derived from the 'form' of rectangularity.

Comment

_____

_____

Revision Exercises

Revision Exercise 5.1 and 6.1 (p. 114)

I smell gas in my garden. The smell is near the place where I remember seeing some workers laying a gas pipe three years ago. I cannot see, taste, touch or hear the gas.

1. Does this mean that, without evidence from my senses of sight, touch, hearing and taste, I can never establish beyond reasonable doubt that there is gas in my garden?

No. In normal circumstances the evidence from one of the senses is insufficient to establish beyond reasonable doubt that something exists. However, if I happen to be an expert chemist or gas technician the evidence from one sense alone might be sufficient because it is supported by reasoning which is based on expert experience. The expert can interpret information in a manner which is beyond the capabilities of non experts; this interpretation adds reliability to the information supplied by a single sense.

Comment

_____

_____

[Note: This example is derived from a real experience in an episode during which several people confirmed the smell of gas in a garden. Subsequent tests could not detect a gas leakage. (FCR)]

2. Is the corroboration by my neighbour of my claim that there is gas sufficient to establish beyond reasonable doubt that there is gas in the garden?

The answer is 'perhaps' as it depends upon my expertise as well as that of the neighbour: if neither of us has the expertise referred to in Question 1, then the corroboration strengthens the claim but still might not be sufficient to establish it beyond reasonable doubt.

Comment

_____

_____

Revision Exercise 5.2 and 6.2 (p. 115)

René Descartes was sitting by the fire; he felt the warmth; it made him feel sleepy; he dropped in and out of a light sleep. When half awake, he saw the ashes, the flames and the burning wood; he could hear the crackle and hiss of the burning wood.

1. Is this evidence sufficient to establish beyond reasonable doubt that there was a fire.

Yes, as there is corroborative evidence from more than one of the senses, together with sound reasoning which interprets the information the senses provide. Descartes, however, wanted there not to be any doubt at all: in *Meditation 1* (section 2) he stated that he would reject any proposition if even a part of it gave him 'some ground for doubt'. This constitutes his famous 'method of doubt'.

Comment

_____

_____

2. Is this evidence sufficient to establish beyond reasonable doubt that Descartes existed?

Yes. Even Descartes would have agreed, but he would not have used the evidence of his feeling heat or seeing the fire; he would have relied on the fact that he was thinking in order to establish that he existed. In *Meditation 1* (section 5) he expressed doubt about the existence of his body:

> I extend this hand consciously and with express purpose, and I perceive it; the occurrences in sleep are not so distinct as all this. But I cannot forget that, at other times I have been deceived in sleep by similar illusions; and, attentively considering those cases, I perceive so clearly that there exist no certain marks by which the state of waking can ever be distinguished from sleep, that I feel greatly astonished; and in amazement I almost persuade myself that I am now dreaming.

Descartes' argument here establishes that there is insufficient evidence to establish incontrovertibly that he existed.

Comment

_____

_____

Revision Exercise 5.3 and 6.3 (p. 115)

Is the knowledge of the existence of books, which depends on our direct perception, more certain than the knowledge of the existence of electrons, which we cannot perceive directly?

Yes. The knowledge of the existence of electrons, and that of books is supported in each case by observation, but the claim that an electron exists requires corroboration. This is provided by reasoning based on a theory with which we use to interpret the information gathered in experiments.

As was pointed out by Thomas Kuhn, the interpretation of scientific information depends upon the 'paradigm' scientists accept as the one which determines the meaning of the information gathered in experiments, and a modification of the paradigm can lead to a modification of the interpretations – see Chapter 13 (p. 195). The fact that the theory can be modified reduces the reliability of the interpretations based on the theory.

Comment

Revision Exercise 5.4 and 6.4 (p. 116)

The Luddites were a group of people who, during the Industrial Revolution, believed that machines were taking over their work so they set about destroying them. They were known as the machine breakers. Ned Ludd, their leader, was reputed to have his headquarters in Sherwood Forest. There were no verified sightings of him.

1. Is it logically possible that 'Ned Ludd existed' is true? Does the preponderance of evidence lead us to accept that 'Ned Ludd existed' is true? Is it true beyond reasonable doubt? Or is its truth incontrovertible?

2. Do the same for the statement 'Ned Ludd did not exist'.

Let us label 'Ned Ludd existed' as NLT and 'Ned Ludd did not exist ' as NLF. There is no logical inconsistency in claiming that Ned Ludd existed, so it is logically possible that statement NLT is true. Similarly, it is logically possible that NLF is true.

The preponderance of evidence suggests that Ned Ludd did not exist (NLF is true). This is because there is likely to have been an historian somewhere who, by now, would have found and published a document indicating Ned Ludd's birthplace or even a record of where he had worked. Records of this nature did exist in early nineteenth-century England.

Since the preponderance of evidence indicates that Ned Ludd did not exist (NLF is true), it is impossible for NLT to be accepted as true beyond reasonable doubt. The only issue which remains is whether NLF would be accepted by a jury as being established beyond reasonable doubt. This question should be answered by an expert historian.

Neither of the two claims is incontrovertible since it is possible that evidence could be found that indicates that he actually existed, or that there was a conspiracy to create the myth that he existed.

Comment

_____

_____

Revision Exercise 7.1 (p. 116)

What do modern scientists have, in addition to what their medieval predecessors had, which entitles them to claim that things like electrons and DNA molecules exist?

Our discussions in Chapters 5, 6 and 7 have led us to conclude that the basis of any claim that something exists rests on two things: the information obtained through using our sense organs and the interpretation of that information. There is a significant difference between modern and medieval scientists in both these areas.

The information provided by the sense organs does not arrive by chance; we gather it in accordance with what we assume will be useful. Modern scientists have a distinct advantage over their medieval predecessors. Firstly, the information which modern scientists obtain is richer in meaning than that obtained by medieval scientists; modern scientists have more extensive explanations of the information provided by their sense organs at their disposal. Secondly, these more extensive explanations enable them to develop more extensive techniques for searching for information, which can be interpreted using the more extensive explanations.

Comment

_____

_____

Revision Exercise 8.1 (p. 117)

1. Could the imagination function in order to produce new ideas if the will were something which obeyed natural laws?

Yes. The notion that physical entities obeying immutable laws could combine to produce situations which had never been formed before is not contradictory: novelty and the adherence to unchangeable laws are not mutually exclusive.

[Note: This tells us that the physicalist thesis that the operations of the will can be fully explained is logically possible; it does not, however, tell us whether the physicalist thesis is true.]

Comment

_____

_____

2. Does the inability to change an impression produced by one of the senses mean that the impression is a more fundamental element of reality than the subject of consciousness?

No. The impression would only be more fundamental if the reception of information from the senses were to describe fully all aspects of conscious experience. Duns Scotus pointed out that this is not the case: in order to reason about any experience, the subject of experience has to have the capability of retaining a thought even when there is no external stimulus to generate it. In the introduction to Part II (p. 53) the term 'fundamental entity' was defined as something which has separate existence or whose existence cannot be determined by referring to other entities. This indicates that the subject of experience is a fundamental entity which cannot form the content of a sense impression.

[Note: We cannot deduce from this answer that the empiricist analysis of the origins of all knowledge is false. What can be deduced is that there must be a subject of experience which cannot be experienced as a sense impression. This accounts for Hume's failure to find a subject of experience, as was noted in the answers to Exercise 8.2, Question 2 (p. 284). It remains possible, however, that the subject of these experiences has no source of knowledge except the experiences generated by the senses, so Hume's failure does not compromise his claim that all knowledge is derived from sense experience.]

Comment

_____

_____

_____

Revision Exercise 8.2 (p. 117)

> The 'Theory of Forms' is still discussed over two millennia after it was written. Give some reasons why you think it has endured for so long.

Plato's 'Theory of Forms' addresses most of the fundamental issues which still concern anyone who wants to understand the human condition. It offers a basis for explaining the physical world at the same time as offering one for explaining the foundations of our systems of moral values. These explanations can be challenged, but what is significant about them is that they pinpoint the central role reason plays in the development of any form of explanation.

Naturally this is only the beginning of an answer. To answer it fully we should need to discuss the part reason and experience play in the production of knowledge, the relationship between reason and moral value, and the nature of reality – in other words, all the main areas of philosophy. It is in the sheer breadth of the 'Theory of Forms' that we perhaps find one of the reasons for its enduring nature.

Comment

Suggested Answers – Part III

Exercise 9.1 (p. 123)

Suppose that a business executive decides to invest a firm's assets in a project that is designed to provide a leisure centre in a deprived city area. The executive claims that the investment she has authorised is justifiable. She could, for example, give a **consequentialist** reason based entirely on her own sentiments in order to justify her claim. She could also give an **essentialist** reason which was independent of her own sentiments.

1. Formulate a **consequentialist** rule of behaviour which the business executive could have been following, that takes into account only her own sentiments.

   I should act in such a way as to ensure that I will feel better afterwards.

Comment

_____

_____

2. Formulate a **consequentialist** rule of behaviour, which the business executive could have been following, that is independent of her sentiments.

   I should act in such a way as to increase the earnings of as many people as possible.

Comment

_____

_____

_____

3. Formulate an **essentialist** rule of behaviour, which the business executive could have been following, that is independent of her sentiments..

   I should act in such a way as to be true to my inner self, to my concept of what I am as a person.

Comment

_____

_____

4. Formulate an **essentialist** rule of behaviour, which the business executive could have been following, that is independent of her sentiments.

   I should act in such a way as to be true to my role as a business executive.

Comment

_____

_____

5. In each of the cases 1–4, specify something of value which could be cited to justify the following of the rule.

   (i)   My own feelings provide a source of values to which I, as an individual, can refer.
   (ii)   The happiness of all individuals provides us with a source of values.
   (iii) Fulfilling the function of one's true being is valuable.
   (iv)   The proper performance of one's social role is valuable.

Comment

_____

_____

Exercise 9.2 (p. 125)

Alice was using her faculty of reason in deciding how to act; she was also invoking the rules her friends had taught her. This gives her two possible sources of value which could justify her action.

1. Formulate a rule of behaviour, which Alice could have been following, that is based on the operations of her faculty of reason.

Always behave in such a way as to be consistent with the aims and analysis of your faculty of **practical reason**. (It is not clear whether Alice knew what her practical reason was.)

Comment

_____

_____

2. Formulate a rule of behaviour, which Alice could have been following, that is based on her reliance on the rules developed by her friends.

Always behave in such a way as to be consistent with the principles which your friends have agreed are the best guides for action.

Comment

_____

_____

Exercise 9.3 (p. 126)

α (alpha) Every art, every investigation and every practical pursuit or undertaking, seems to aim at some good. Therefore it can properly be said that what everything aims at is the Supreme Good.

1. This is one of Aristotle's premises. Is it true?

This seems to be patently false, as there are occupations such as that of robbery which do not aim at some good. It seems likely that the concept of an art, or a science or a practical pursuit had an element of propriety included in the ancient Greek meaning; Aristotle is unlikely to have made such a basic error as to consider all occupations as aiming towards some good.

Comment

_____

_____

β (*beta*) We find that the arts, practical pursuits and sciences aim at a variety of ends. There are numerous actions, arts and sciences; it follows, therefore, that their ends are correspondingly numerous. For example, the end of the science of medicine is health, that of the art of shipbuilding is a vessel, that of strategy is victory, and that of domestic economy is wealth.

2. Is Statement β true? If so, is it true on **rational** or **empirical** grounds?

Yes, it is true, and Aristotle gives three examples to illustrate its truth: medical science, shipbuilding and domestic economy. The fact that it is an empirical truth means that his argument is valid only as long as the empirical truth holds.

Comment

γ (*gamma*) There are master arts, pursuits and sciences and subordinate arts, pursuits and sciences. For example, bridle making and the other trades concerned with horses' harness are subordinate to horsemanship.

δ (*delta*) The ends of the master arts, pursuits and sciences are things more to be desired than the ends of the subordinate ones. This is because the subordinate ones are only pursued for the sake of the master ones. The aim desired by bridle making is subordinate to the aim desired by horsemanship.

3. Is it possible for someone to practise medicine for reasons other than generating health? If so, does this mean that Statement δ could be false?

An individual could practise medicine for personal reasons which are unrelated to the promotion of health. For example, someone might do so in order to obtain social status. This does not mean that Statement δ is false since Aristotle was referring to the aim of medical science and not to the aims of a medical scientist.

Comment

ε (*epsilon*) If every aim were subordinate to some other aim, the process of desiring an end would go on ad infinitum, in which case all desire would be empty and futile. And it makes no difference whether the ends of the pursuits were the activities themselves or some other thing beside these, as in the case of the sciences mentioned.

4. Is Aristotle describing a vicious regress in Statement ε, or is it possible for people to desire some objects without knowing what good it leads to?

This question also fails to distinguish between the aims of the individual and those of an art, occupation or a science. In order for something to be an occupation it must have a defined aim.

Comment

_____

_____

[Note: (i) The distinction between an individual's aims and those of his occupation lie at the heart of the Marxist concept of alienation: when the two aims do not coincide, the individual is said to be alienated – a garbage collector's reasons for collecting garbage are rarely the same as the reasons garbage is collected! (ii) If we were to criticise Aristotle's argument on the grounds that the aims of the people who practise an art or occupation do not coincide with the aims of the art or occupation, we would be committing the logical fallacy of *ignoratio elenchi*: in other words, we would be attributing another argument to our adversary and showing that this other argument is invalid.]

Exercise 9.4 (p. 129)

1. Assess Aristotle's argument set out in Exercise 9.3 by giving it a grade A to F, with A being excellent and F being a failure.

A personal answer of the author of this text is to award a B.

Comment

_____

_____

_____

2. Give the reasons for your mark.

The reason for not giving a higher grade is that the move from Statements ε to ζ is not as sound as the argument up to Statement ε. Aristotle has established that there must be at least one thing which is valued for its own sake, but he has not established that there is only one thing. The fact that values conflict with each other indicates that it is not self-evident that they are all based on one absolute value.

Comment

_____

_____

Exercise 10.1 (p. 136)

'According to Père André (*Essai sur le Beau*, 1741), there are three kinds of beauty – divine beauty, natural beauty, and artificial beauty.' Tolstoy (1930, p. 95)

1. Describe a natural object, physical feature or event which is thought to be ugly.

A slug is thought to be ugly.

Comment

_____

_____

2. Describe a human artefact which is thought to be beautiful.

The Taj Mahal, the mausoleum of the Mughal Empress Mumtaz Mahal on the banks on the River Yamuna in Agra, India, is universally thought to be beautiful.

Comment

_____

_____

3. Was Père André right to claim that natural and artificial beauty are different?

On the one hand, the fact that it makes sense to use two different adjectives to qualify the single word 'beauty' indicates that it is possible for there to be two types of beauty; it may be that André was focusing on this difference. On the other hand, the fact that we use the single word 'beauty' indicates that the two types of beauty share some common characteristics.

Comment

In the mid-eighteenth century, Francis Hutcheson used an empirical method to analyse beauty by looking at the circumstances in which we, using our 'aesthetic sense', discern alterations in beauty. According to Hutcheson: 'The figures which excite in us the ideas of beauty seem to be those in which there is *uniformity amidst variety*' (1995, p. 15). He goes on to say that, when we have uniformity, an increase in variety increases the beauty of the object; he gives mathematical examples to illustrate his point. 'The beauty of an equilateral triangle is less than that of a square, which is less than that of a pentagon, and this again is surpassed by the hexagon.'

4. Was Hutcheson right?
   (i) Is uniformity a necessary attribute of beauty? Using Hutcheson's exam-example, is a square always more beautiful than a non-square rectangle?

We can justify rejecting Hutcheson's hypothesis by citing the 'golden section' as a counter-example: rectangular objects whose sides are in the proportion of the 'golden section' have been used in architecture for millennia because they have always been considered to be more beautiful than square objects. This suggests that harmony gives us a better basis for judging whether something is beautiful than uniformity.

[Note: The ratio of the diagonal of a regular pentagon to one of its sides is the proportion known as the 'golden section'; its value is approximately 1.618 to one.]

Comment

(ii)   Does an increase in variety increase beauty? Using Hutcheson's example, is an octagon always less beautiful than a twenty-sided polygon?

If we reject Hutcheson's claim that beauty is found in uniformity, we are not necessarily obliged to reject its corollary (a proposition tagged onto the end of another and which follows obviously from it): it is possible that variety increases beauty for some other reason, such as maintaining the interest of the experience generated by the object.

Comment

_____

_____

At the turn of the nineteenth century Johann Gottlieb Fichte argued that beauty could be discerned by intuition. Beauty does not exist in the world in the way that yellowness does, ready for our senses to discern it; on the contrary, it exists in the beautiful soul. The soul operates in three realms: the 'sensible' realm of sense experience, the moral realm of spiritual experience and the aesthetic realm, which provides the means for the other two realms to interconnect. Beauty is not just in the eye of the beholder, but also in his soul.

In the story of Snow White and the Seven Dwarves, the wicked queen asks the mirror to tell her who is the most beautiful woman of them all. This question only makes sense if beauty is a universal property which anyone can judge.

5. Is the intelligibility of the wicked queen's question enough for us to justify a claim that beauty is not just in the eye or the soul of the beholder?

The fact that beauty may be in the eye or the soul of the beholder does not mean it must be subjective: if our souls were such that they all had the same characteristic when they experienced beauty, then we would all recognise that Snow White, and not the wicked queen, was the most beautiful of them all.

Comment

_____

_____

_____

Hegel developed Fichte's theory that beauty belonged to the spiritual, rather than the physical realm. According to him only the soul is truly beautiful, which means that nature can only be beautiful if it reflects the natural beauty of the spirit.

6. Is the beauty of nature only the reflection of the natural beauty of the spirit?

Beauty is unlike solidity or whiteness; it cannot exist without the presence of conceptualisations. This is sufficient for one to say that beauty is a characteristic which must have a spiritual component; but the spiritual component does not have to be the only one.

Comment

_____

_____

[Note: the question of the independence of qualities like solidity from conceptualisations will be addressed when we discuss the philosophy of science in Part IV, Chapter 13.]

Hutcheson's theory falls into the group of theories in which beauty is considered to be a quality which affects the senses, while Fichte's and Hegel's belong to the group which finds beauty in the charmed state of an intellectual or moral faculty.

One 'instrument' we could use to measure one theory against the other is seeing how well it fits in with our own ideas; this would be a subjective instrument.

7. What objective instruments could you employ to help you to decide between these two opposing types of theory?

We could use a purely empirical instrument, and ask ourselves whether each theory corresponds with actual experience. In other words, to what extent do people ascribe beauty to things in the way that the theories say they do? A second instrument we could use is the test of 'explanatory richness'. Using this test we would ask two questions: firstly, does each theory give the most extensive and convincing explanations of its domain, in this particular case everything associated with the concept of beauty; secondly, does each theory enrich our understanding of those aspects of the human condition which are not explicitly specified in its domain of inquiry. This second instrument merges theory construction with its application, so it is partly empirical and partly analytical.

[Note: These two instruments are not the only ones which can be used for comparing theories. It is possible to compare them without referring to experience at all by examining them for any logical inconsistencies or for equivocations in their use of concepts.]

Comment

_____

_____

8. Using the instruments you have set out in Question 7, assess the relative merits of the brief sketches of Hutcheson's and Fichte's theories of aesthetics.

According to the first criterion, Fichte's theory fares better: we indicated in the answer to Question 4(i) that uniformity is not, in practice, always used as a criterion of beauty; Fichte's notion that beauty is found in the beautiful soul must be consistent with experience because a beautiful soul could do nothing but identify beauty in experience. These same reasons lead us to assess Fichte's theory ahead of Hutcheson's when it comes to explanatory richness.

Comment

_____

_____

Exercise 10.2 (p. 139)

1. Consider art as a pursuit or occupation. Give two characteristics without which an activity could not be considered to be art.

We are looking for two necessary conditions, that is, the possession of certain characteristics, without which an activity cannot be called art. Possession of these characteristics does not guarantee that something is art: the conditions are necessary but not sufficient. The first is that the pursuit or occupation should have some purpose: it should not be a random activity – an activity which is carried out without purpose and knowledge of the purpose cannot be art. The second is that the pursuit of the activity should have some positive aspect to it: an activity which has no prospect of enhancing the human condition cannot be art. The positive aspect does not have to give pleasure; it can disturb people. We do not have to specify the nature of the positive aspect, but merely feel or sense that it is present.

[Note: This answer is likely to be disputed by someone who has a rival theory of the nature of art.]

Comment

---

2. Give three possible different aims of art as a pursuit.

One aim of art is to create beautiful things; another is to make people feel better, to give them pleasure; another is to reveal something about the nature of the human condition which is normally hidden from us.

These are not the only three aims. Philosophers of the past have come up with a wide variety of aims of art; many of these are listed in Leo Tolstoy's little gem (1930, Part VII, Chap. III). Here is part of his list with some additions. The types of aim can be put into three categories: representational, creative and restorative.

[Note: The subdivisions are not in Tolstoy's book; neither are they standard subdivisions of theories of art. The reason for placing them into these categories is to show that the theories have some common themes running through them, which is what is done when analysing a concept.]

Representational: as the reproduction of the beautiful and the good.
    Plato and Aristotle: the aim of art is to imitate or represent beautiful things.
    Plotinius: the aim of art is to reveal the form of an object more clearly than ordinary experience does – by using sense experience, it reaches the parts of the human condition that sense experience cannot reach.
Creative: as the development of the beautiful.
    Immanuel Kant: the aim of art is to create that which is sublime, which gives disinterested pleasure as natural beauty does.
    Benedetto Croce: the aim of art is to give people an immediate awareness of an object's form, to facilitate the faculty of intuition.
    Karl Marx: the aim of art is to raise people's consciousness and sharpen their understanding of the human condition.

Anthony Shaftesbury: the aim of art is to create proportionality and harmony.

Restorative: as overcoming the inadequacies of normal human experience.

Friedrich Nietzsche: the aim of art is to help us accept the tragedy of life with joy.

Jean-Paul Sartre: the aim of art is to liberate individuals from the constraints of everyday living and to enable them to accept their freedom to choose.

John Dewey: human experience is fragmented – the aim of art is to provide people with unified self-contained, complete experience which is enjoyed for its own sake.

Comment

---

3. Which of these views most closely encapsulates what you believe to be the aim of art?

A personal answer: Plotinius' and Sartre's capture the essence of art. There are three reasons for choosing them, which together indicate that the preponderance of evidence points towards accepting Plotinius' and Sartre's answers. Firstly, Plotinius' answer incorporates many of the other aims. The aims of art described by Kant, Croce and Sartre assume that ordinary experience fails to encapsulate something about the form of objects and events: something which is sublime, intuitive or unconstrained will not be revealed in ordinary experience. Secondly, Plotinius' and Sartre's answers make the practice of art, and debate about art, intelligible: the practice of taking ordinary materials in order to create aesthetic experience makes sense only if ordinary experience does not produce aesthetic experience and art is a free, creative activity. Thirdly, Plotinius' and Sartre's answers help to explain the endurance of the use of the word 'art' despite the disagreement about whether it is more than purely representational.

The first and the third reasons use 'explanatory richness' as the basis for accepting the claim that their answers capture the essence of art. The second reason uses a weak 'transcendental argument'; it is weak because we do not of necessity have to accept the premise that art, as a pursuit, is an intelligible activity.

Comment

Exercise 11.1 (p. 143)

> What are the material, formal, efficient and final causes of the following objects? Which ones are substances?
>
> 1. an automobile
> 2. a cherry tree
> 3. a cloud

1.   The material cause of an automobile is the metal, plastic and all the other component materials of the car; its formal cause is a means of self-propelling transport; its efficient cause is the manufacturing process on the production line; its final cause is the transportation of people in the direction chosen by the driver. The automobile is not a substance.

2.   The material cause of a cherry tree is the wood of its trunk and branches, its leaves, its roots, its flowers and its fruit; its formal cause is a plant which reproduces itself by producing fruit; its efficient cause is the seed from which it grew; its final cause is the production of fruit. The cherry tree incorporates its final cause, so it is a substance.

3.   The material cause of a cloud is the water vapour out of which it is made; the formal cause is an entity which carries water in the sky; the efficient cause is the wind which picked up its water up from the sea; the final cause is the production of rain. The cloud incorporates its final cause, so it is a substance.

Comment

Exercise 11.2 (p. 144)

See quote on p. 144.

> 1.   What reason does Aristotle give for claiming that each moral virtue does not form part of human nature?

Moral virtue needs to be formed by habit, whereas natural forms of behaviour cannot be changed by habits. Therefore moral virtue cannot be part of human nature.

Comment

_____

_____

2. Is Aristotle right when he says, 'nor can anything else that by nature behaves in one way be trained to behave in another'?

It can be argued that circus animals are trained to do things which are contrary to their nature, but the trainers refute this by saying that you cannot train an animal to do what it does not want to do. Ivan Pavlov's experiments to condition dogs to salivate even when they were not going to eat are famous. Pavlov conditioned dogs to salivate when a bell was rung by associating the ringing of the bell with the arrival of food. These experiments, however, involved invoking one natural response to overcome another. (Pavlov received the Nobel Prize for medicine in 1904 and described his experiments on the physiology of digestion in his Nobel Lecture). It is possible that, as far as Aristotle was concerned, any trait or quality which could be trained would, ipso facto, not be natural. His claim would then be based on a definition of what is natural: as such, the claim would be irrefutable.

Comment

_____

_____

_____

3. According to Aristotle, which part of our moral make-up comes from nature?

We are 'adapted by nature to receive them', so our natures are such that we have the potential to perfect the moral virtues.

Comment

_____

_____

_____

Exercise 11.3 (p. 146)

See quote on p. 146.

Aristotle gives two different reasons why we should accept that virtue aims at the intermediate. One of these is based on empirical observation of what people do and the other is based on an analysis of the concepts of success, failure, excess, deficit and the intermediate.

> 1. Do you think the two reasons Aristotle gives are valid ones? Assess both of them by giving them a grade A to F, with A being excellent and F being a failure.

The first reason he gives is an empirical one. 'The intermediate **is praised** and is a form of success; and being praised and being successful are both characteristics of virtue.' Aristotle is invoking the empirical fact that people actually praise the intermediate, to support his claim.

This reason accurately describes the way most people assess human characteristics, but does not take into account the many people who praise excesses. The word 'lucullan', which refers to an extremely extravagant life style, is derived from the very rich Roman General Lucinius Lucullus (c. 110–c. 56 BC); there are many people who aspire after such extravagance. The existence of a not insignificant minority of people who praise excesses lowers the grade to a C.

Comment

_____

_____

The second reason is independent of experience: it depends only upon an analysis of the five notions of success, failure, excess, deficit and the intermediate. Aristotle points out that success and the intermediate are both unique, whereas there are many ways of failing and many ways of achieving excesses and deficits.

His reasoning is not thoroughly rigorous in this instance. He is using the similarity of relationships between two sets of related phenomena in order to pair one set with the other: success and the intermediate moral characteristic are both unique while failure and the extreme moral characteristics both manifest themselves in multiple forms. When he pairs off the unique with the unique he needs to explain why they should be paired together. The argument is incomplete as it stands. The reason is only just above a failure; it deserves a grade E.

Comment

[Note: Firstly, these are not the only reasons Aristotle gives to support his theory that virtue aims at the intermediate, so a full assessment of the theory cannot be based on these two reasons. Secondly, the reason based on the analysis of concepts is weak because it employs an argument based on a similarity. Such arguments are not rigorous because it is the absence of a similarity which convinces people that something is not the case: the fact that the witness describes the person committing a crime as being dark haired tells us that X, who is fair haired, was not the criminal, but it does not mean that Y, who is dark haired committed the crime. The purpose of a reason based on a similarity is normally to make a claim more acceptable rather than to convince others beyond reasonable doubt.]

Aristotle states that the state of character concerned with choice is relative; it is not the same for everyone.

2. Does this principle allow me to claim that your virtue generates different moral imperatives from mine? If so, does this make Aristotle's theory of moral virtue unacceptable?

Rather than make the theory unacceptable, it makes it more acceptable. The principle that varying moral value can be associated with the same behaviour in different people is incorporated into the practice of many legal systems. It also accounts for the negative attitude we have towards people who waste their talent.

Comment

Exercise 11.4 (p. 148)

1. Describe a **maxim** and an **imperative** which regulate how or when you drive a car.

[Note: Naturally these are not the only possible answers.]

A maxim: I must avoid the rush hours.
An imperative: Drivers must stop when the traffic signal instructs them to do so.

Comment

_____

_____

2. Explain whether it is possible for the **maxim** to become a universal law.

It is logically impossible for the above maxim to become a universal law. For example, if the maxim 'I must avoid the rush hours' became the universal law 'Everyone must avoid the rush hours' there would be no rush hours to avoid!

Comment

_____

_____

3. Suppose you are an elementary school teacher. Describe a **maxim** and an **imperative** which regulate your behaviour towards your pupils.

A maxim: Keep an hourly record of what you have taught every child.
An imperative: Ensure that toxic substances are kept out of the pupils' reach.

Comment

_____

_____

4. Explain whether it is possible for the **maxim** to be turned into an **imperative**.

It is possible for the advice to maintain an hourly record to become an imperative, and in some places, it is; in fact, there is no contradiction involved in making this maxim a law. Teaching and keeping hourly records are not mutually contradictory, although teaching and keeping minute-by-minute records are mutually exclusive activities.

Comment

_____

_____

5. Is either the **maxim** or the **imperative** in your answer to Question 3 a moral rule?

The answer to this question depends on the basis upon which moral rules have been formulated, so it would be better to postpone answering it until after the discussions of the other moral systems.

Comment

_____

_____

Exercise 11.5 (p. 152)

1. Is duty any the less valuable if carried out for selfish motives?

Taken as an empirical question, the answer is 'Yes': people do tend to value a dutiful action less if it is undertaken for personal gain. The dictionary definitions of duty do not, however, mention value: they merely refer to the obligation under a rule.

Comment

_____

_____

2. Can any cognitive action be carried out with no regard for the consequences?

The answer is 'No'. If an action is cognitive then the agent understands what is happening. In order to do this the agent must, at minimum, have some understanding of the progress of the action, that is, of the immediate consequences of each part of the action.

Comment

___

___

Kant stated that 'the moral law should directly determine the will'.

3. Does this mean that he believed that worthy actions are non-reflective?

Kant's dictum cannot be used to support the assertion that worthy actions are non-reflective. From the fact that the moral law 'directly determines the will', we cannot conclude that an act of will is non-reflective. Any reflection which influences action must, however, be on the moral law and not on incidental consequences such as the benefit accrued to anyone by the action. In Kant's system, not only do the means not justify the ends, they are irrelevant to them.

Comment

___

___

(Advanced question)

Suppose I have a maxim of behaviour that I should act in accordance with my duty regardless of any advantages or disadvantages which might result from my actions.

4. (i) Can my maxim 'hold good as a principle of universal legislation' and become a 'Categorical Imperative'?

There appears to be no contradiction involved in everyone acting in accordance with their duty without regard for any advantages or disadvantages which might result from the actions. Therefore my maxim can hold good as a principle of universal legislation.

Comment

___

___

(ii) If it does become a 'Categorical Imperative', and I obey it because it makes me feel better, does my obedience have any Kantian moral value?

The question assumes that I can obey such a law with the good consequences of the action in mind. This assumption is self-contradictory because the compliance with the law requires me not to have these consequences in mind.

Comment

_____

_____

[Note: The technique of testing a theory by seeing if the theory can apply to its own assumptions is one which is used frequently by philosophers. We shall call it a 'theory self-application test'.]

Exercise 11.6 (p. 155)

See quote on p. 155.

Let us assume, for the sake of our argument on utilitarianism, that there are no grounds for disputing the feasibility of Nozick's experience machine.

1. (i) Nozick's question, 'Should you plug into this machine for life?' tests the validity of utilitarian moral value. In what way does it do this?

Utilitarianism is based on the assumption that the ultimate aim of human action is pleasure. If someone turns down an opportunity which guarantees permanent pleasure then we have a prima facie case for claiming that the utilitarian assumption is false.

Comment

_____

_____

(ii) Formulate a question using Nozick's machine which tests the validity of utilitarian moral values embodied in the Greatest Happiness Principle.

Should you plug as many people as possible into the experience machine for life? If you were to do so, you would certainly be promoting the greatest happiness.

Comment

_____

_____

2. (i) Is the duty to build an experience machine contained in utilitarian principles?

Duty consists of doing what is right and avoiding what is wrong. The action of building an experience machine would promote the greatest happiness, so it would be a right action and therefore a duty within a utilitarian system.

Comment

_____

_____

(ii) What appears to be the pressure which a person feels to act as a utilitarian?

Mill answers this question with the following words:

> Something far superior to this is sufficiently common even now, to give ample earnest of what the human species may be made. Genuine private affections and a sincere interest in the public good, are possible, though in unequal degrees, to every rightly brought up human being. (1962, p. 265)

This means that it is not our desire for pleasure, the *Summum Bonum*, which drives us to follow the Greatest Happiness Principle, but 'a sincere interest in the public good'.

Comment

_____

_____

In an open world where laboratory conditions do not hold, it is not possible to calculate the extent to which actions promote happiness and unhappiness.

3. Does our inability to calculate what promotes happiness and unhappiness mean that the Greatest Happiness Principle cannot serve as a proper moral principle?

The answer is 'No'. The difficulty of knowing whether a moral principle applies does not prevent it from serving as a proper moral principle. For example, the fact that I might find it impossible to discover my 'Aristotelian mean' does not signify that there is no moral mean. One could compare a moral principle with a watch which can never be absolutely accurate because it always either gains or loses a few seconds per day; the watch is nonetheless a very good indicator of the time.

Comment

_____

_____

[Note: The watch analogy belongs to Dr Samuel Johnson: 'Dictionaries are like watches, the worst is better than none, and the best cannot be expected to go quite true.' (James Boswell, 1791, p. 293n.)]

In the story about Elwood Dowd and Harvey, his six foot three-and-a-half inch (1.94m) white rabbit (p. 94), Elwood is portrayed as an extremely kind person who helps everyone in need and never knowingly harms anyone. The author, Mary Chase, creates great sympathy in her audience for Elwood and invites them to conclude that it would be unjust to commit him to an asylum.

4. Should the kind, harmless, affable Elwood Dowd be committed to an asylum?

If one accepts the assumption that the action tends to promote happiness, the utilitarian answer is 'Yes'. The fact that Mary Chase has written a play which successfully poses the question indicates that there is evidence to suggest that not everyone adheres to the Greatest Happiness Principle.

Comment

_____

_____

5. Does utilitarianism adequately account for people's reactions to the questions about the experience machine and Elwood Dowd?

The answer is unclear. Utilitarians would find the evidence from Nozick's experience machine difficult to refute. It makes us question the utilitarian claim that happiness is the ultimate aim of human existence, and that it is intrinsically good. The thought experiment sows this doubt without reference to the practicalities of building an experience machine. The evidence from Mary Chase's play is even more difficult for utilitarians to refute as no thought experiment is being conducted. People actually do feel that it might be wrong to commit Elwood to an asylum even though it may be contravening a rule of behaviour which promotes happiness.

Comment

_____

_____

6. (i) How well does the utilitarian theory of moral value correspond with what people actually value and use in practice to guide their actions? Give it a grade A to F, for empirical content, with A being excellent and F being a failure.

The suggested answer to the last question justifies an F: utilitarianism fails the test when it comes to empirical evidence – people tend to value things other than pleasure.

Comment

_____

_____

(ii) How well does utilitarianism account for all aspects of the human condition related to moral behaviour? Give it a grade A to F for explanatory richness, with A being excellent and F being a failure.

The existence of non-utilitarian reactions to Elwood Dowd's demise indicates that the Greatest Happiness Principle might not reflect human psychology very accurately. However, a full answer requires knowledge of the studies of human motivation, such as is carried out by psychologists. The grade should be withheld until such a study is carried out.

Comment

_____

_____

Exercise 11.7 (p. 159)

Consider the suggested answer to Exercise 11.6, Question 1(ii).

1. Are there any circumstances in which an ethical egoist would plug as many people as possible into the experience machine?

If the pleasure of other people gives the moral agent pleasure, then plugging other people into the experience machine would be consistent with the moral values of the ethical egoist. An unsavoury consequence of following this line of argument is that a sadistic ethical egoist would behave in such a way as to make other people feel pain.

Comment

_____

_____

2. Explain why an ethical egoist is not necessarily an egotist.

The explanation can be found in human motivation: if the moral agent experienced an element of human sympathy and this sentiment generated pleasure in him then his actions would be right if they promoted the happiness of others. A concern for the welfare of others is inconsistent with the notion of egotism, which is concerned solely, and exclusively, with the welfare of the self.

The existence of the sentiment of sympathy would also counteract any criticism of ethical egoism based on the actions of a sadist: the ethical egoist's reply to such criticism would be based on the notion that the sadist was somehow deficient as a human being.

Comment

_____

_____

3. According to the ethical egoist what is the nature of the pressure which pushes a person to act in a moral manner?

According to the ethical egoist the ultimate good is the pleasure of the individual. The pressure on the moral agent to seek her own ultimate good is, therefore, the pressure which pushes her to act in a moral manner. In the case of ethical egoism there is no need for separate arguments to validate the claim about moral value and moral values – the validations are the same.

Comment

_____

_____

Exercise 11.8 (p. 161)

1. Is there empirical evidence to support the claim that the ultimate goal of all behaviour is freedom rather than happiness or pleasure?

The fact that the Aristotelian, Kantian and utilitarian claims regarding the nature of the ultimate goal of all behaviour are not based on freedom shows that there is empirical evidence which does not support the claim that the ultimate goal of all behaviour is freedom. The thought experiment involving Robert Nozick's 'experience machine' (p. 155) gives some support to the notion that freedom is more valued than happiness or pleasure: if we refuse to plug in, it is probably because we value freedom above human happiness.

Comment

_____

_____

_____

In Exercise 11.6, Question 4 (p. 156) we asked ourselves whether a utilitarian would have committed the mild-mannered, harmless Elwood Dowd to an asylum.

> 2. If we accept that freedom is the foundation of value, do we commit Elwood Dowd to the asylum or refrain from doing so?

Sartre's statement that in 'willing freedom, we discover that it depends entirely upon the freedom of others' means that he would be highly unlikely to commit Elwood, since Sartre's freedom also depends upon Elwood's.

Nietzsche's rejection of moral rules makes his response less clear, but it is likely that he would have come to the same conclusion as Sartre, for similar reasons: by acknowledging Elwood's freedom, I am asserting my own.

Comment

_____

_____

(Advanced question)

> 3. To what extent are moral rules incompatible with the individual's freedom?

Rules are not incompatible with freedom. A rule that states what **must** be done is incompatible with freedom whereas one which states what **cannot** be done permits other actions to occur. If the legislator also happens to be the agent than the situation is a little more involved.

The full answer to the question depends, therefore, upon who makes the rules and what drives the individual to obey them. In order to address these issues we need to consider two points. The first is a general point about the relationship between rule-following and freedom: since rules specify which behaviour is or is not permitted, their operation constrains freedom. The second is a specific point about purposeful human behaviour: any action which is carried out for a reason can be described as complying with a rule.

In such circumstances, we must ask who formulates the rule and who enforces it. If the moral agent formulates the law and his will enforces it, as occurs in Kantian ethics, then he is free. The Kantian moral agent takes his own maxim of behaviour and turns it into a law using the 'Categorical Imperative'; he subsequently decides to comply with the law without regard for its consequences.

If, on the other hand, the law is formulated by an independent agency or is a law of nature, and the drive to obey the law is a natural impulse, then the individual is not free. In these circumstances the individual's behaviour is similar to the behaviour of an electron moving through an electro-magnetic field: the circular path along which it moves is determined by its initial velocity, the existence of the field, and its own property of possessing a fixed negative electro-magnetic charge. From the point of view of the moral agent, the Greatest Happiness Principle (an electro-magnetic field) drives his desire (a negative electro-magnetic charge) to produce specific moral behaviour (movement along a circular path).

Comment

[Note: In Aristotelian ethics there is no discussion of the freedom of the moral agent. The question is, however, central to all virtue ethics as moral value can only be ascribed to virtuous behaviour if the individual is free. In Kantian deontology, the 'Categorical Imperative' specifies that the moral agent should turn his own maxim of behaviour into a law of behaviour, which means that the moral agent formulates the rule of behaviour and is therefore free. In utilitarian ethics and ethical egoism the force that drives people to comply with the moral rule is derived from the operation of natural characteristics of human beings: in the case of utilitarian ethics the force is a feeling of sympathy for others; in the case of ethical egoism it is the natural drive to achieve pleasure. Neither of these two natural characteristics can be controlled by moral agents so their freedom is constrained by the moral rule.]

Exercise 11.9 (Advanced exercise) (p. 163)

See p. 163.
Aristotle's *Ethics* starts by claiming that virtue **is** the pursuit of excellence.

1. (i) What justification is given on p. 147 above that we **ought** to pursue excellence? How can we determine whether the justification is valid?

The reason Aristotle gives for suggesting that we ought to pursue excellence is that our need to feel in harmony with our essential selves as rational beings drives us to nurture intellectual and moral virtue.

We need to do two things in order to assess the validity of the Aristotelian claim. Firstly, we need to carry out an analysis of the concepts involved in the claim, considering whether being in harmony with one's essential self is necessarily linked to meeting the requirements of the rational side of our nature. Secondly, we need to examine the empirical evidence provided by the behaviour of people and to consider to what extent people strive to be in harmony with their rational selves. If they are not in harmony, we should ascertain whether it is possible to explain why this is the case – whether this is because they are prevented from being so by circumstances over which they have little or no control, or because of some other reason. Both these issues must be addressed before we can determine whether the Aristotelian claim is valid.

Comment

_____

_____

Hume criticises those theories which glide from statements of fact to statements of value. He uses the 'is/ought' dichotomy as an instrument of analysis to assess whether theories measure up to a standard of acceptability.

> (ii) According to which of these standards does Hume's 'is/ought instrument' assess theories: (a) **logical possibility**, (b) the **preponderance of evidence**, (c) **reasonable doubt** or (d) **incontrovertibility?**

Hume's 'is/ought instrument' criticises theories on the basis of inadequate logic. As Hume himself points out, his 'is/ought instrument' places a requirement on anyone who formulates a theory in ethics to explain the move from 'is' to 'ought'. 'For as this *ought*, or *ought not*, expresses some new relation or affirmation, it is necessary that it should be observed and explained.' The instrument is one which tests, but does not determine, whether a theory is incontrovertible: a theory which glides from 'is' to 'ought' is not ipso facto incontrovertible, but any conclusion based on the glide cannot be relied upon as being incontrovertible.

This means that the instrument does not test whether the theory is logically possible – the fact that a theory might have been put together with inadequate logic does not mean that the claims it makes are themselves logically impossible! The instrument cannot be used to clarify any question of empirical evidence, so it does not help us to find out whether the preponderance of evidence might lead someone to accept a theory. For the same reason, it cannot help us to find out whether a theory's claims are acceptable beyond reasonable doubt.

Comment

_____

_____

The hypothesis of Exercise 11.5, Question 3 (p. 152) questioned Kant's concept of moral worth. It did not cite any empirical evidence.

2. According to which of the four standards was this question measuring Kant's theory?

Logical possibility: in order to test a theory which makes claims about what happens in the world at a level greater than logical possibility one has to include some sort of empirical test. In this particular case Kant's theory would fail at the first hurdle of logical possibility if it is found that moral value is not associated with the non-reflective obedience of the 'Categorical Imperative'. The reason for this is that an alternative source of moral value would mean that it was this other source, rather than the 'Categorical Imperative', which determined an individual's duty.

Comment

In Exercise 11.6, Question 3 we discussed the efficacy of the Greatest Happiness Principle by pointing out that, in an open world where laboratory conditions do not hold, it is not possible to calculate the extent to which actions promote happiness.

3. According to which of the four standards was this question assessing utilitarianism?

The question does not assess the Greatest Happiness Principle according to any of the four standards we have been discussing here.

Logical possibility: The fact that a given result of an action is impossible to calculate tells us that we cannot be sure about the nature of the result. In particular the impossibility of the calculation cannot tell us whether it is logically impossible for the action to generate any type of result.

The **preponderance of evidence** and **beyond reasonable doubt**: These are criteria that enable one to judge whether something is more likely to have happened than not. In this particular case we wish to know whether empirical evidence indicates that the Greatest Happiness Principle should be accepted or rejected. The fact that we cannot know the outcome of events means we cannot gather empirical evidence for or against utilitarianism in order to decide whether it should be accepted or rejected.

Incontrovertibility: The claim, that it is impossible to measure the efficacy of the Greatest Happiness Principle, even if it is established as true, also tells us nothing about whether it is incontrovertible as a principle of ethics. At best it can only tell us that it is impossible to prove that the principle forms a valid basis upon which to build a system of ethics.

When answering the question we learn little or nothing about the validity of the Greatest Happiness Principle. What we obtain, however, is a good indication of its usefulness in practice – if we cannot calculate the outcome of events, a principle based on these calculations is of little practical use.

Comment

_____

_____

In one of the most influential books on ethics in the twentieth century, G.E. Moore argued that utilitarianism and ethical egoism committed the 'naturalistic fallacy': they both identified goodness with the natural phenomenon of pleasure (1903, pp. 6–17). The fact that the question, 'Is pleasure good?' is not tautological tells us that pleasure is not equivalent to goodness.

4. Did the use of the 'naturalistic fallacy' to criticise utilitarianism involve the use of empirical evidence? According to which of the four standards was Moore measuring utilitarianism and ethical egoism?

The criticism involves no use of empirical evidence. This means that Moore was criticising utilitarianism on the grounds of logical possibility: that is, he disputed the basis upon which utilitarian and ethical egoist theories were constructed – that pleasure is the *Summum Bonum* of human existence. If Moore was right, then the moral rules contained in the Greatest Happiness Principle collapse along with its moral value. If, on the other hand, pleasure is not the *Summum Bonum*, then pursuing it cannot be the criterion we use to determine whether something is right or wrong.

Comment

_____

_____

Existentialist moral value is based on the claim that the ultimate goal of all behaviour is freedom rather than happiness or pleasure. Exercise 11.8, Question 1 asked for empirical evidence to support this claim.

5. According to which of the four standards does this request measure existentialist moral value?

The question is about the nature of the evidence which supports the claim that people consider moral value to consist of the freedom to choose. This means that it essentially tests whether **preponderance of evidence** supports a claim, or whether a claim is acceptable **beyond reasonable doubt**.

[Note: Asking the question assumes that the will of an individual could be free to act. A philosopher would also wish to test this assumption (see Part V).]

Comment

Kant's theory of moral philosophy used a single notion (duty) to construct a theory of moral value and moral rules, whereas Mill's utilitarianism used two (pleasure as the *Summum Bonum* and a sentiment of sympathy to sustain the greatest Happiness Principle).

6. Does the fact that Kant used fewer concepts to build his theory give us a criterion for preferring it over the rival theory of utilitarianism?

The criterion of greater efficiency of a theory is a variant of William of Ockham's principle that 'Entities are not to be multiplied without necessity', known as 'Ockham's razor' (see Glossary of Terms). If a theory is able to explain a phenomenon by postulating the existence of, say, two entities rather than three, then it ought to discard the hypothesis that the third entity exists. Ockham's razor is, however, an instrument designed to cut out irrelevant concepts from a single theory; it does not give us a measure for the relative efficiency of theories which explain things differently.

Ockham's razor might be used as a criterion for comparing theories of morals which use the same concepts. For example, if utilitarianism were to discard the human sentiment of sympathy it would be reduced to ethical egoism. Thus, with all other things being equal, which they are not, conceptual efficiency would provide us with a criterion for preferring ethical egoism to utilitarianism.

Comment

Revision Exercises

Revision Exercise 9.1 (p. 169)

> 1. (i) Make a list of five things, actions or characteristics which are of value to some human beings.

Happiness, beauty, social status, wealth and friendship are all considered to be of value.

Comment

_____

_____

> (ii) Give the reason why each one is valued.

Happiness is valued for its own sake. Beauty is valued because it is a quality, or combination of qualities, which produces particular pleasure when something possessing it affects the human senses. Social status is valued because it enhances an individual's sense of self. Wealth is valued because it can generate social status or the power to obtain some of the things which give happiness and/or pleasure. Friendship is valued because it enhances an individual's sense of self.

Comment

_____

_____

> (iii) Explain how the value of one of them might change (or why it cannot change).

Wealth can change in two ways: firstly, if an individual loses the ownership of whatever produces the wealth; secondly, if the objects of value which represent the wealth lose their value, for example, during times of inflation, the value of money falls.

Comment

_____

_____

2. Describe a rule of behaviour which is not linked to something which is of value.

There are none. Only a rule without a purpose would qualify because the purpose of a rule of human behaviour is to link the behaviour to something of value. A rule without a purpose is an oxymoron (self-contradictory concept).

Comment

_____

_____

Revision Exercise 10.1 (p. 170)

Anthony Shaftesbury believed that beauty was a characteristic of things in the world discernible by a human sense in a similar way to the way size, shape or colour are discerned: humans have a beauty-detecting sense similar to the eye which detects colour. He considered the aim of art to be the creation of this natural characteristic and thereby the creation of beautiful things.

Jean-Paul Sartre considered the aim of art to be the liberation of individuals from the constraints of everyday living, and thereby developing their freedom to choose.

1. Describe an empirical method of evaluating the relative merits of these rival claims.

An empirical method could seek information from two sources in order to compare the claims: the artists who create works of art and the people who experience the created works. The method would involve asking both sets of people whether they considered art to be the creation of things which possessed a characteristic recognisable as beauty or whether they considered art to be a vehicle for liberating individuals from the constraints of everyday living. The results of the survey would give an indication of which of the two theories corresponded most closely to what people believed art to be.

Comment

_____

_____

2. Is it reasonable to use an empirical method to compare these claims?

The method would not be a reasonable one to use as would be unable to detect the possibility that Sartre's theory was indeed correct, but that art had not yet been able to liberate individuals from the constraints of everyday living.

For similar reasons the method might not be able to establish the validity of Shaftesbury's theory if an insufficient number of people had developed the skill to detect the natural characteristic which made things beautiful – the general level of knowledge about the nature of art might be similar to the level of knowledge about relativity physics in the years immediately after the publication of Einstein's theory.

Comment

Revision Exercise 11.1 (p. 170)

The rule 'Do not commit murder' is a law which is found in most ethical systems.

1. Would this be a moral law in the following ethical systems:
   (i)   Aristotle's virtue ethics;
   (ii)   Kant's deontological system;
   (iii) Mill's utilitarianism;
   (iv)   Sidgwick's ethical egoism;
   (v)   Sartre's theory of freedom as moral value.
2. In the cases in which it is a moral law explain why it has to be one.

   (i) The rule is a law because committing murder constitutes an excess of violence or an unrestrained extreme – in other words, it does not conform to the principle that virtue is to be found in the 'intermediate' course of action.
   (ii) The rule is a law because the rule can conform to the 'Categorical Imperative' – in other words, it is a maxim of one's will which 'can always at the same time hold good as a principle of universal legislation'. It is possible for 'Do not commit murder' to become a universal law so it is a Kantian moral law.

(iii) The rule is a law because the following of the rule 'Do not commit murder' obeys the Greatest Happiness Principle – in other words, it results in an increase in the total production of pleasure and/or a diminution of the total production of pain.

(iv) The rule is a law because the killing of another individual diminishes the human pleasure of the moral agent – in other words, it results in an increase of the production of the agent's pleasure and/or a diminution of production of her pain.

(v) The rule is a law because it obliterates the victim's ability to act freely: Sartre argued that a necessary condition of my ability to act freely was that I should promote the freedom of others – by committing murder I am acting in opposition to the basis of my own freedom.

Comment

Suggested Answers – Part IV

Exercise 12.1 (p. 178)

See quotes on p. 178.

> 1. According to Reid how do we know that there are first principles?

The existence of first principles is what makes it possible for people to reason with each other. In view of the fact that people reason with each other, the conditions needed for this to be possible must hold – in other words, there are first principles.

Comment

_____

_____

[Note: Reid's is a variation of the argument in the 'Transcendental Analytic' (a section of the _Critique of Pure Reason_), where Kant argued that 'categories' (in some ways analogous to Reid's principles) were necessary conditions in order for the human faculty of judgement (more accurately a 'capacity to make judgements' – _Vermögen zu urtheilen_) to activate itself. This faculty was a capacity to think (_Vermögen zu denken_) and 'Thought is knowledge by means of concepts' (_CPR_, B94). So concepts provide us with a possible source of knowledge.]

> 2. How do we know that qualities such as colour and motion have to be in a body which is coloured or moving?

According to Reid, the principle that the existence of qualities such as colour and motion cannot be distinct from a body is a first principle, because it makes it possible for people to reason with each other. If a man supposed that colour and motion were distinct from a body then he would be a man with whom one could not reason. This principle is a precondition of rational discussion. He deduced that these qualities are present in a body because people actually do reason with each other.

Comment

_____

_____

[Note: Reid's argument also implicitly challenges Plato's 'Theory of Forms' which states that qualities exist separately from the bodies which manifest the qualities.]

Exercise 12.2 (p. 179)

See list on p. 179.

1. Make a list of other possible sources of knowledge to supplement (i) to (vii).

Through the exploitation of imaginative capacities:
- (viii) using the imagination (metaphysical speculation and thought experiments);
- (ix) responding to revelation or religious experience (outer or exogenous impulses);
- (x) reacting to an intuition or inspiration (an inner or endogenous impulse).

Comment

_____

_____

[Note: The word' intuition' is being used here with its non-technical meaning to signify a direct or immediate insight' (*OED*). This is similar to the meaning given to the word by scholastic philosophy of the Middle Ages where the intuition was a 'spiritual perception or immediate knowledge, ascribed to angelic and spiritual beings, with whom vision and knowledge were identical'. (*OED*)

The present widespread use of the single English word 'intuition' to translate two distinct Kantian notions, both related to sense experience, could cause confusion. For example, Kemp-Smith always translated the German word *Anschauung* as 'intuition'. But, according to the context, Kant used it to refer either to the content of sense experience or to the faculty which absorbs that content.]

2. Specify which of these sources can, and which cannot, lead to incontrovertible knowledge.

(vii) Mathematical and logical reasoning can produce incontrovertible knowledge such as Pythagoras' Theorem. It is also feasible that logical reasoning, unfettered by empirical inputs, can produce knowledge; some 'proofs' of the existence of God constitute claims to knowledge based entirely on logical reasoning.

(viii) The imagination can produce knowledge, but great care should be taken over the changes involved in postulating new circumstances.

[Note: In Roberts (1993), I analysed the limitations of, as well as the possible uses of, thought experiments in producing knowledge. (FCR)]

Metaphysical speculation often involves postulates of the existence of entities whose behaviour cannot be detected by the senses. Such speculations were heavily criticised by Kant in the 'Transcendental Dialectic' of his *Critique of Pure Reason*.

[Note: Walsh (1975) gives an analysis of Kant's argument against speculative metaphysics.]

(ix) If a revelation conforms to an understandable pattern which can be manipulated, it becomes indistinguishable from an experience absorbed via a sense organ. But even if the revelation is inaccessible to scientific investigation, its reliability is certainly not greater than the reliability of a sense organ as a source of knowledge: the revelation and the information from the sense organ can both be contradicted by future experiences; therefore they are not incontrovertible.

(x) The argument in (ix) applies to an intuition as well as to a revelation.

Comment

_____

_____

Exercise 12.3 (p. 180)

1. Which of the following claims constitute knowledge, and which only belief?
   (i) There are three angles in a triangle.
   (ii) Michelangelo was the best sculptor of the last millennium.
   (iii) The atom was first split in 1932 by John Cockroft and Ernest Walton.
   (iv) When I am thinking, I exist.

(i) and (iv) constitute knowledge.
(ii) and (iii) constitute beliefs.

Comment

_____

_____

2. For each of the claims give the reasons why it is to be counted as knowledge or as only belief. Indicate whether the reasons are independent of experience.

(i) The knowledge is based on an understanding of the definition of a triangle as a mathematical figure with three angles, which is independent of experience.

(ii) There are two reasons why the claim should count as belief rather than knowledge: firstly, it describes an historical event, and as such is based on evidence which may be unreliable; secondly, the claim made is based on an unstated norm of aesthetic value which could be challenged.

(iii) There are also two reasons which make this claim a belief: firstly, it also describes an historical event and could, as such, be supported by unreliable evidence; secondly, the possibility remains that someone unknown to us split the atom before Cockroft and Walton. If, however, the evidence that they split a lithium atom in 1932 is reliable and there is reliable evidence that no-one else could have split any other atoms before they did, then normal use of English requires us to state that the claim constitutes knowledge.

(iv) This statement encapsulates René Descartes' famous affirmation _cogito ergo sum_ ('I think therefore I am'), which he claimed could not be refuted (_Discourse_, Part IV). Any attempt to refute the statement by the person who is thinking is self-refuting: I cannot think that I do not exist without falling into contradiction.

Comment

_____

_____

3. Does a claim have to be incontrovertible for it to count as knowledge?

A claim which is incontrovertible would certainly count as knowledge, but the converse does not hold: knowledge does not have to be incontrovertible.

If a true statement about a matter of fact can count as knowledge, then knowledge does not have to be incontrovertible since matters of fact are all, in principle, controvertible. This would mean that the burden of proving that a claim constituted knowledge would not lie in determining that it was incontrovertible, but in determining that it was true.

If we require a claim to be acceptable beyond reasonable doubt in order for it to be true, then knowledge does not have to be incontrovertible. If, on the other hand, we accept as true only statements that are incontrovertible, then incontrovertibility and knowledge become inexorably linked. This second, stricter interpretation of the meaning of the term 'true' would confine knowledge to all claims which made no reference to empirical facts, as none of these is incontrovertible. Since we claim that natural science produces knowledge we can reject this stricter interpretation of what we mean by knowledge.

Comment

_____

_____

4. Is the fact that I perceive something 'clearly and distinctly' to be true sufficient for me to count it as knowledge?

In normal circumstances we would say that this is not a sufficient condition because I might be mistaken despite my conviction to the contrary. René Descartes, however, used this psychological criterion to distinguish belief from knowledge, but it was not an arbitrary criterion dependent upon whim, and he was aware of the fact that the application of his criterion was problematic.

> And as I observed that in the words I think, therefore I am, there is nothing at all which gives me assurance of their truth beyond this, that I see very clearly that in order to think it is necessary to exist, I concluded that I might take, as a general rule, the principle, that all the things which we very clearly and distinctly conceive are true, only observing, however, that there is some difficulty in rightly determining the objects which we distinctly conceive. (*Discourse on Method*, Part IV)

Descartes took as his benchmark the state of mind he felt when he considered the proposition *cogito ergo sum*. As long as his psychological state when considering another proposition was the same, he felt confident about declaring it to be true, and also about knowing that it was true.

Comment

_____

_____

[Note: (i) The last sentence in the quotation indicates that Descartes' criterion for knowledge had an element of our criterion of **beyond reasonable doubt** – in practice his criterion was **free from all** my **doubt**. (ii) This meant that his criterion was a subjective one – the principles determining whether something counted as knowledge were subjective.]

Exercise 12.4 (Advanced exercise) (p. 182)

1. These judgements are the ones Kant used when discussing the distinction between analytic and synthetic judgements. Which ones are **analytic** and which **synthetic**?
   (i)   'All bodies are heavy.'
   (ii) 'All bodies are extended.'
   (iii) 'Everything which happens has its cause.'
   (iv) 'The world must have a first beginning.'

   (i), (iii) and (iv) are synthetic and (ii) is analytic. Being extended is a defining characteristic of a body, while being heavy is not since bodies do not have to be affected by gravity. It is also logically possible for things to happen which are uncaused, so both (iii) and (iv) are synthetic statements as they claim that events have causes.

Comment

_____

_____

2. Which of the following judgements are **analytic** and which **synthetic**?
   (i)   The President of the United States is less than 50 years old.
   (ii) God is omniscient.
   (iii) The President of the United States is less than 30 years old.
   (iv) God exists.

   (i) is synthetic, (ii) and (iii) are analytic and (iv) is neither. The constitution of the United States specifies that only people above the age of 35 can become President, so the concept of President excludes the possibility of being less than 30 years old but not of being less than 50 years old. The concept of God includes the notion of knowing everything, so (ii) is analytic. Judgement (iv) has caused some dispute among philosophers, some of whom argue that existence is not a predicate, that is, it is not a property or quality to be ascribed to a thing. If this is the case, then Kant's distinction between analytic and synthetic judgements does not apply.

Comment

_____

_____

Exercise 12.5 (Advanced exercise) (p. 183)

Consider the following two *a posteriori* judgements:
   (i)   The President of the United States is less than 50 years old.
   (ii) There are two apples and three pears on the table, so there are five pieces of fruit on the table.

1. Under which circumstances would each of them be false?

We could show (i) to be false if we could find evidence that the President was born 50 or more years ago. Judgement (ii) could only be false if its premise, that there are two apples and three pears on the table, were false.

Comment

_____

_____

Consider the following two *a priori* judgements:
   (iii) The President of the United States is less than 30 years old.
   (iv) $7+5=12$

2. Under what conditions would each of these be false?

(iii) could only be false if the constitution of the United States were to change and a new President were elected who was less than 30 years old. The very notion of what it is to be the President of the United States would therefore have to change, as well as the age of the particular President under consideration. In other words, (iii) would have to become an *a posteriori* judgement.

There are no conditions under which the statement 7+5=12 could be false. Given the axioms of mathematics, the definitions of the concepts of addition and equality and of the numbers seven, five and twelve, the statement 7+5=12 cannot be false.

Comment

_____

_____

3. By considering (iii) and the ichthyologist's claim that 'no sea-creature is less than two inches long', determine under what circumstances, if any, a synthetic judgement can be incontrovertible.

The truth value of both the statements is independent of experience only as long as experience is determined by certain rules. If it is possible for these rules to change, then what determines their truth value can change, and these synthetic judgements would become 'conditionally incontrovertible'! By contrast, the rules of mathematics cannot be changed, therefore the statement 7+5=12 is unconditionally incontrovertible.

In answering the question, therefore, we need to consider the possibility that rules that govern experience might change. Kant, for example, believed that the rules determining the three-dimensionality of the world we experience could not be altered because our sense organs could not interpret anything but three-dimensional signals. This meant that he believed that the statement 'The world we are able to experience is three-dimensional' would be synthetic *a priori* and incontrovertible (*CPR*, 'Transcendental Aesthetic').

We can therefore give the following answer: a synthetic *a priori* statement would be incontrovertible if the rules which determine any gathering of information (which was relevant to the statement) could not alter.

[Note: In his analysis of muscular sense and the development of a concept of space, Henri Poincaré argued that the information-gathering capabilities human beings have (using their sense organs and 'muscular sense' – see p. 65 above) permit them to develop concepts of multi-dimensional spaces which are limited only by the number of different muscles: each provides a separate muscular sensation which permits the processing of information for a separate dimension. Therefore five hundred muscles would permit a human being to interpret signals from a five hundred-dimensional space!]

Comment

_____

_____

4. What is the difference between the way the ichthyologist attained his knowledge that 'no sea-creature is less than two inches long' and the way he justified it?

Eddington's description of the ichthyologist's methods states: 'Surveying his catch, he proceeds in the usual manner of a scientist to systematise what it reveals. He arrives at two generalisations:

1. No sea-creature is less than two inches long.
2. All sea-creatures have gills.'

The ichthyologist makes a generalisation from experience to reach the conclusion that 'no sea-creature is less than two inches long', but justifies the truth of this conclusion using reasoning based on the nature of his net. The reasoning he uses is independent of any particular sense experience and based on the proposition 'A net with a mesh designed to catch sea-creatures which are more than two inches long cannot catch any sea-creatures which are less than two inches long.'

Comment

_____

_____

Exercise 13.1 (p. 189)

1. What sort of event or phenomenon is not investigated by natural science?

There is none: natural science seeks explanations for all events. What distinguishes natural scientists from other scientists are the characteristics of the events which they investigate: they attempt to explain only those aspects which they consider to operate independently of the particular scientific investigation and so apply in all places and at all times.

Comment

_____

_____

2. Which of the following could be the source of an explanation of the way things react to gravity, and which could be a method of validating an explanation?
   (i)   Being hit on the head by an apple.
   (ii) Observing lots of apples hit lots of people on the head.
   (iii) Thinking about lots of apples hitting lots of people on the head.
   (iv) Dropping a bag of feathers and different sized cannonballs from the top of the Leaning Tower of Pisa and observing which reached the ground first.
   (v)   Speculating about the existence of 'bosons' (Higgs particles) which 'give' particles their detectable mass.
   (vi) Consulting the Oracle at Delphi.

All of these can provide a scientist with information and so can be sources which could lead to a deeper understanding of gravity. However, because (ii) and (iv) involve the use of empirical evidence, they provide different means of contributing towards the validation of a theory of gravity than the other four. The evidence from (iv) is qualitatively better than that from (ii), being a deliberately constructed experiment designed to test a particular property of gravity. Examples (iii) and (v) can serve as validation procedures only to the extent that they can be used to check whether a given theory of gravity does not contradict either itself or some other accepted theory. A consultation with the Oracle at Delphi could serve as either a source of knowledge or as a validation procedure if the Oracle had itself developed and validated a theory of gravity.

Comment

_____

_____

3. Modern science uses laboratory methods to validate its claims. Describe a non-scientific method of validating a claim.

If the claim is that objects of different weights drop to the ground at the same speed, then Question 2 (iv) provides us with a scientific way of helping to validate the claim. Alice in Wonderland provides us with a non-scientific method. We discussed her method of validating her claim that it was safe to drink from a bottle which was 'not marked poison' in the suggested answers to Exercise 5.1 (p. 261). Her method was unscientific, being based on 'what her friends had taught her'.

Comment

Exercise 13.2 (p. 191)

1. Assess the Popper–Hempel theory of explanation when it is applied to explain a single event by giving it a grade A to F, with A being excellent and F being a failure.

The author's personal assessment is a B+. When it is possible to describe the circumstances which precede the occurrence of an event, the theory more than adequately describes the way explanations are offered for single events. There is, however, a practical problem which the theory faces: it might not always be feasible to describe all the circumstances under which an event occurs. This problem is faced by any explanation, so the mark remains high.

[Note: At a conceptual level we have to consider the possibility that the explanation predetermines which features of the circumstances are thought to be relevant and which irrelevant. The explanation could blind us to a relevant factor which we should be including. In his analysis of the conservative nature of 'normal science', Thomas Kuhn points out that this is a problem which every type of explanation faces.]

Comment

2. Assess the Popper–Hempel theory of explanation when it is applied to explain a universal law by giving a grade A to F, with A being excellent and F being a failure.

The author's personal assessment is an F. When it comes to offering expla-nations of why a universal law should hold, the deductive model becomes inadequate because it cannot describe all the possible particular circum-stances needed for the deduction to be universally valid.

Comment

Discussion Exercise 13.3 (p. 192)

> Is a deductive model appropriate for an explanation of why a general law is valid? Could it be used to explain why free-moving magnets always point towards the north?

The answer is no, because such an explanation would lead to an infinite regress of explanations: in view of the fact that the deductive model invokes a general law to deduce what is to be explained, this new general law would itself need to be explained, and so on ad infinitum. This would be useless rather than ridiculous; therefore the regress of explanations of general laws would be **benign** rather than **vicious** (see Exercise 9.3, Question 3, p. 128 above).

If we tried to explain why free-moving magnets always point towards the north we would need a deduction of the following type:

1. 'the association of ideas' permits us to formulate a general law (In the entry for David Hume (see Glossary of Names) there is a description of how, according to Hume, the principle of the association of ideas allows us to produce general laws.);
2. ideas have always been associated with free-moving magnets pointing north;
3. use 1 and 2 to deduce that free-moving magnets always point towards the north.

If we now ask for an explanation of why the general law contained in Statement 1 is valid, we find ourselves in a benign infinite regress.

A more appropriate explanation of a general law would be the sort that modern scientists offer in terms of the mechanisms which generate the behaviour of physical objects: the composition of the type of metal which can be magnetised, the existence of a magnetic field generated by the geophysical structure of the earth with the presence of certain material concentrated near the magnetic North Pole, and so forth. This also leads to a benign regress, as there is a requirement that we explain 'the composition of the type of metal which can be magnetised'. This regress is, however, of more practical use than the Humean one involving the association of ideas because each explanation helps us to understand more about why free-moving magnets always point towards the north – the validation of the association of ideas, on the other hand, moves us away from natural science and into psychology.

[Note: The aim of this discussion exercise was to further our understanding of the nature of scientific explanation and not to pinpoint any weaknesses in the deductive model, which its authors claim explains only single facts.]

Comment

_____

_____

Exercise 13.4 (p. 193)

1. (i) Give an example of a falsifiable claim which is an **analytic** judgement.

This is impossible: if a judgement is analytic and true, it is non-falsifiable by definition.

(ii) Give an example of a non-falsifiable claim which is a **synthetic** judgement.

God created the world in seven days.

Comment

_____

_____

2. (i) Having measured a cannonball dropping with an acceleration of 9.5m/s^2 have I falsified the theory that the acceleration due to gravity is 9.81m/s^2?

No. My measurements or methodology might have been faulty.

> (ii) If this does not falsify the theory, how will I know when it has been falsified?

The answer to Question (i) shows that the falsification of a theory does not just depend upon evidence which contradicts it; it also depends upon the reliability of that evidence. For criteria to determine the reliability of evidence, we can turn to those we discussed in Chapter 5 above (p. 59): incontrovertibility, beyond reasonable doubt, the preponderance of evidence and logical possibility. Empirical evidence can never be incontrovertible so the highest degree of confidence available to the scientist is that the falsifying evidence is convincing beyond reasonable doubt.

Comment

_____

_____

(**Advanced question**) If there were no known methods for detecting the presence of a particle, the theory postulating its existence would not be falsifiable.

> 3. Would such a theory be unscientific?

If the search for a method of detecting 'bosons' (Higgs particles) were declared to be outside the realm of science, then we would have to conclude that a great deal of the research which attempts to expand the boundary of science is unscientific.

In order for such research to count as science we need to be cautious about the use of falsifiability as a criterion for demarcating science from non-science. We can still use it as a criterion to identify a scientific claim: if it is falsifiable, then it is scientific; but if it is not falsifiable, it is not necessarily unscientific.

Comment

_____

_____

Discussion Exercise 13.5 (p. 196)

The common saying 'you cannot teach an old dog new tricks' appears to be stating that, once people have absorbed a way of looking at the world, it is difficult for them to change.

1. **Was Kuhn just turning commonsense into a complicated sounding theory?**

This is an unlikely scenario. What is more probable is that the common expression that 'you cannot teach an old dog new tricks' reflects a characteristic of humans as a result of which they tend to see things in the same way as they originally learnt them.

The one sense in which this expression with regard to Kuhn serves as a possible criticism of his position is that it highlights the fact that his theory does not fully take into account the human ability to learn. In one respect it considers humans to have the limitations which dogs have: if we tell a dog that it cannot be taught new tricks, its attitude towards learning new tricks does not change so its ability to learn them remains unaltered. However, telling human beings that they are too old to learn new tricks can change their attitude towards learning them, thereby altering their ability to learn. It is likely that, by describing the conservative characteristics of normal science, Kuhn has changed those very characteristics.

[Note: This last point is an illustration of the quality philosophy has of being self-referential. We noted above (p. 22) that, unlike physics, it forms part of its own subject-matter.]

Comment

_____

_____

Two things are said to be incommensurable if they cannot be measured against each other. Kuhn claimed that successive paradigms were incommensurable, and that one could not say that one was better than the other.

2. **Is this true? Do we have no way of comparing the medieval theory that the earth is at the centre of the universe with the Copernican theory that the sun is at the centre of a solar system?**

We can state with confidence that the vast majority of modern scientists accept the Copernican theory and reject its medieval predecessor. Their preference for one over the other indicates that they have criteria which enable them to compare the two theories.

A Kuhnian philosopher of science would now ask what these criteria are. If one happens to be that the Copernican theory ties in with modern scientific methods of assessment, then the response would strengthen the Kuhnian claim that the standards inherent in present-day 'normal science' determine which theory is acceptable.

This Kuhnian response applies even if we invoke the criterion of 'explanatory richness' to decide between the theories. We noted in our answer to Exercise 7.1, Question 7 (p. 301) that explanatory richness is a psychological criterion which requires an explanation both to be convincing and to enrich our understanding of the human condition. It is not a criterion which involves measurement, and as such does not directly affect the incommensurability of theories – Kuhn's claim that theories set in different paradigms are incommensurable is not compromised by the claim that explanatory richness enables us to measure the relative worth of two theories.

The absence of a compromise is, however, also a weakness, because we wish to explain why it is that scientists in fact do choose between rival incommensurable theories and we assume that the choice is rational, and therefore can be explained. We do expect to be able to compare the relative merits of scientific theories, and Kuhn claims that there are circumstances in which we cannot.

Comment

___

Exercise 14.1 (p. 200)

α (*alpha*)   No greater being than God can be conceived.

β (*beta*)   There are two possibilities:
1. such a being exists in my imagination;
2. such a being exists in reality.

γ (*gamma*)   A being which exists both in reality and in my imagination is greater than one which exists only in the imagination.

δ (*delta*)   It is impossible that a being, greater than which none can be conceived, is less than of maximum greatness.

ε (*epsilon*)   Therefore a being, greater than which none can be conceived, exists.

1. Is the notion of God as a being, greater than which none can be conceived, the same as the notion of God as a superhuman person who has power over nature?

No. This does not, however, weaken St Anselm's argument because the notion of a being, greater than which none can be conceived, includes the notion of a superhuman person who has power over nature. Conversely, a superhuman being without the power over nature would not be a superhuman person greater than which none can be conceived.

Comment

_____

_____

2. At what point does St Anselm's argument bridge the gap between experience and what is beyond possible experience?

St Anselm bridges the gap at Statement γ where he presupposes that existing things are just imaginary things with an extra quality which can be added to them.

Comment

_____

_____

3. Does an island, greater than which none can be conceived, exist? If it does, can we say that St Anselm's argument fails?

This question contains an implicit criticism of St Anselm's theory. Alvin Plantinga points out (*Routledge Encyclopaedia of Philosophy*) that it was levied by Anselm's 'contemporary and fellow monk Gaunilo in his *On Behalf of the Fool*', and that Anselm replied by stating that there was a difference between notions of things and notions of qualities.

His reply is based on the notion of maximisation. Maximising something involves making it reach the greatest quantity that it is possible for it to reach. The notion of a thing cannot be maximised while the notion of a thing's quality can be: the notion of a maximised island does not make sense; the notions of maximum goodness or knowledge do, however, make sense. This reply leaves Anselm open to the rejoinder that his argument indicates that a being with perfect whiteness also exists.

These criticisms are, however, ones which do not affect the logical validity of Anselm's arguments. The fact that a similar argument might be used to establish the existence of other entities which we know do not exist does not mean that the argument fails to prove the existence of God. All these criticisms do is make us suspect that there might be something wrong with the type of argument Anselm employed.

Comment

_____

_____

Exercise 14.2 (p. 202)

1. Is Paley's first premise true? Does a well-ordered mechanism have to have been designed for a purpose?

The answer is 'Yes'. Aristotle's illustration of the cart which was not a substance because it did not include its own final cause (p. 142) shows us how it is possible for a designer to design a mechanism without a purpose. The cart's final cause (*telos*) was in the mind of the artisan who made it. If we suppose that an artisan makes something without having anything at all in mind, and that the thing just happens by chance to be well-ordered, then it would be something without a final cause. However, the fact that the designer was not aware of the purpose does not mean that it is absent; it merely means that the artisan is the means through which the purpose has been transferred to the well-ordered object.

[Note: Using Duns Scotus' terminology, we would say that the artisan is a 'dependent causal agent' (see the Suggested Answers to Exercise 14.3).]

Comment

_____

_____

2. Is Paley's third premise true? Is the universe well-ordered?

This premise is not proven. Unexpected things happen so there does seem to be a certain amount of disorder in the universe. The existence of disorder does not mean that scientific laws are not universally valid (gravitational forces, for example, operate in the same way throughout the universe, which is detectable by astronomers). It just means that scientific laws might not account for some events – just as the law of gravitation does not account for the reproduction of amoebas.

[Note: Paley was aware of the existence of a certain degree of disorder and used it to sustain a secondary argument for the existence of God based on the necessary conditions for a rational being to be able to recognise the Deity (1802, Chap. V) – it is a sort of inverted cosmological argument.]

Comment

_____

_____

3. Does the designer of the universe have to have power over nature and the fortunes of mankind?

The answer is 'No'. A designer merely has to have the power to harness the forces within which the designed object has to operate. It is logically possible that a designer of the universe could set it up in such a way as to have different degrees of order, just as some watches are better-ordered than others. Paley's argument might be convincing beyond reasonable doubt, but it is not incontrovertible.

Comment

_____

_____

Exercise 14.3 (Advanced exercise) (p. 203)

β Each effected change must be caused by something other than itself because:
(i) no effect can be produced by itself;
(ii) a loop of causes bringing about an effect is impossible.

1. Are Statements β (i) and (ii) **analytic** or **synthetic**? Explain your answer.

Statement (i) is analytic because the notion of an effect separates itself from the agency which produces the effect. To effect something is to bring **it** about, the use of the pronoun 'it' in these circumstances indicates that what is doing the bringing about is distinct from the 'it'.

Statement (ii) is also analytic because any section of the loop could be considered as a caused effect. In particular, the whole loop could be considered as a single effect, in which circumstance we would have a case in which an effect produced itself, which we have just declared to be impossible.

Comment

_____

_____

δ If S is a series of randomly occurring causes then there is an ordered, non-random, series of causes OS. We accept this statement because:
1. a caused event in series S occurs because of the operation of a certain procedure P.
2. procedures do not operate randomly.
From 1 and 2 we can conclude that:
3. the procedure P must be part of an ordered series of causes, call it OS, which is different from the random series S.
(This ordered series OS **must exist** if S exists.)
(Therefore an ordered series, either S or OS, **must exist** if X exists.)

2. Why does Duns Scotus need to go through step δ and show that random sequences can only exist if there are non-random ones backing them up?

He does this to avoid the sceptic's counter-argument that it is possible for all sequences of events to be random. If all sequences were random, there would be no need for a causal agent, thus invalidating the final step of the proof in which the necessity of a first causal agent is invoked.

Comment

_____

_____

ε An infinite series of ordered, non-random, causes is impossible because:
1. it is logically possible for causal agent Y to possess its own causal power in a perfect way;
2. an agent possessing its causal power because it has received it from another causal agent further back in the chain is dependent upon this other agent;
3. dependence is an imperfection;
4. if it is not possible for any causal agent such as Y to possess the transmittable

causal power without dependence then every Y possesses its causal power in an imperfect way;

Duns Scotus deduces that ϵ (1) must be true and ϵ (4) false.

3. Assess the value of the deduction by giving it a Grade A to F, with A being excellent and F being a failure.

As a personal assessment of the deduction I would give it two marks: a grade A for subtlety and ingenuity and a D for logical rigour. The A is awarded because of the great difficulty in pinpointing the point at which Duns Scotus bridges the gap between the actual world and the world beyond possible experience; he appears to glide smoothly from one to the other. His glide is one which depends upon a similar analysis to the one used in the ontological proof: ϵ (1) states the possibility that something exists, and we move from this possibility to the actuality of existence, giving as the reason the impossibility of the existence of universal imperfection.

The D for logical rigour is awarded because the proof does not establish that it is not possible for all causal agents to be dependent upon a prior one. This is a point made by Philo, the sceptical character in Hume's *Dialogues on Natural Religion*. In his highly informative essay on the *Dialogues*, David Weddle (2001) describes Philo's rejoinder to the orthodox believer Demea: Philo comments that we need

> several prior cases of the cause-effect relationship in order to establish a customary connection, such that effect B always presupposes cause A. But the origin of the universe is unique; thus, we have no prior cases on which to base the analogy.

By its nature, the independent, perfect, causal process needs to be evaluated in a different way from the dependent one; Duns Scotus' proof lacks this different evaluation.

Comment

_____

_____

_____

Revision Exercises

Revision Exercise 12.1 (p. 207)

See quote on p. 207.

1. (i) What was the basis of Wendy's knowledge?

The basis of her knowledge was her conviction that she had the knowledge.

(ii) What was the source of Wendy's knowledge?

The source of her knowledge is likely to have been her imagination. It was neither experience nor reason.

(iii) Was Wendy justified in her claim to know that Peter Pan visited the nursery?

Of course she was justified! All readers of Peter Pan just know she was justified.

Comment

_____

_____

2. (i) Does the fact that Wendy did not know how she knew that Peter came into the nursery in the night affect the status of her claim that she knew?

Yes. If we accept that knowledge involves having the ability to assert and support a theory or claim, then Wendy's ability to support her claim is limited. She found it difficult to convince her mother, who only began to consider the possibility that Wendy might be right because the leaves on the nursery floor did not belong to the nearby trees; this extra fact, not quoted in the extract, gave Wendy some reasons to support her theory.

(ii) In what way, if any, was Wendy's knowledge different from Descartes', which was based on his 'clear and distinct ideas'?

There are some similarities between Wendy just knowing that she knew and Descartes knowing because he had 'clear and distinct ideas': neither of them is appealing to experience, or to an accepted theory. The difference lies in the fact that Descartes was appealing to his powers of reason, which had convinced him that his 'clear and distinct ideas' were sufficient grounds for justifying his claim that he knew something, whereas Wendy had no criterion to support her claim.

Comment

Revision Exercise 12.2 and 13.2 (Advanced exercise) (p. 209)

Consider Sir Arthur Eddington's fishy story of the ichthyologist whom we first met on p. 85.

In the suggested answer to Exercise 7.1, Question 1 it was stated that the ichthyologist's second generalisation was *a posteriori* knowledge (as a result of experience), while the first was *a priori* (independent of experience) because it depended upon the nature of his net.

1. How do **we** know that the nature of the ichthyologist's net affects the truth of the statements?

   Our knowledge is based on an awareness of other methods for examining sea creatures: these range from the ability to make nets with a finer mesh to using submersible craft which enable us to observe sea creatures without having to catch them in a net.

Comment

---

2. Assuming the ichthyologist is not aware of our alternative methods of examining sea creatures, should it be important to him to know that the nature of his catch is determined by the type of equipment he uses?

   Yes. He should be aware of the fact that his methods may limit the nature of his catch and the knowledge that results from interpreting the information his methods enable him to gather. This is the sort of awareness scientists need to have about the limitations of their own methods. Indeed, a desire to make scientists aware of these limitations prompted Eddington, an eminent scientist himself, to tell the story of the ichthyologist.

Comment

_____

_____

Revision Exercise 13.1 (p. 209)

Theories formulated in different scientific 'paradigms' are 'incommensurable.' (Claim TK)

1. (i) Is Claim TK an **analytic** or a **synthetic** proposition?

Kuhn gives the word 'paradigm' a technical meaning to signify 'an achievement – a collection of shared beliefs held by a group of scientists about what the basic problems and methods of scientific inquiry are'. He argues that this definition precludes the possibility that scientific theories can be measured against each other; therefore, 'incommensurability' is incorporated in the concept of a 'paradigm'. The proposition is an analytic one.

Comment

_____

_____

(ii) According to Karl Popper's criterion of falsifiability, is Claim TK a scientific claim?

Analytic propositions cannot be falsified so Claim TK is not a scientific claim in the sense described by Popper. It has the same status as propositions in logic or mathematics which are true in virtue of the meanings of the terms they use.

Comment

_____

_____

_____

2. Is the knowledge that, in the nineteenth century, science moved from one 'paradigm' to another *a priori* or *a posteriori* knowledge?

This is *a posteriori* knowledge because its truth is not determined solely by the truth of Claim TK; it is also determined by historical information gathered about what happened in the past.

Comment

_____

_____

Revision Exercise 14.1 (p. 210)

Consider the following paraphrase of René Descartes proof of the existence of God:

α I know I am an imperfect being because I am able to doubt.
β I have a concept of perfection and of a perfect being.
γ Since I am imperfect I cannot have generated this concept of perfection.
δ The concept of perfection must have been generated by a perfect being.
ε Therefore, a perfect being exists.

1. Is Descartes' proof an **ontological**, **teleological** or a **cosmological** proof?

It is ontological. An ontological proof is one which starts with a concept of a perfect being or of perfection and deduces the existence of a perfect being.

2. Identify the premises in the argument and state whether they are necessarily true.

Statements α, β and γ are the premises of the argument. Statement α is necessarily true because a perfect being would have no need to doubt anything.

Statement β needs clarification: in order to determine whether Statement β is true, we need to know the nature of the concept of perfection and compare it with Descartes' version of it. However, being imperfect beings, we can never be sure that we have truly grasped the concept of perfection, so we cannot determine the truth or falsity of Statement β. Statement γ is not necessarily true. If we take the concept of perfection to involve the absence of faults then such a concept could be generated by anyone who understood the notions of absence and fault. There is no contradiction involved in supposing that an imperfect being could generate these two notions and then put them together.

Comment

_____

_____

3. At what point does Descartes bridge the gap between experience and what is beyond possible experience?

It is at Statement δ. A being which is beyond possible experience is invoked as the cause of something in the world we experience.

Comment

_____

_____

Revision Exercise 14.2 (p. 211)

We now return to the question asked in Discussion Exercise 3.2.

1. What is the relationship between **wisdom** and **knowledge**?

By accepting that knowledge involves having the ability to assert and support a theory or claim we also accept that the ability to apply a theory is not strictly speaking included in the definition of knowledge: a person with knowledge need only be able to communicate how a theory or claim is supported; the ability to apply the knowledge is not required.

Wisdom, by contrast, involves more than knowing how to support a claim or theory; it involves the ability to choose between theories and between different means of achieving specified ends. Wisdom involves soundness of judgement in practical matters, which is not required of someone who has knowledge.

Comment

_____

_____

2. Does having infinite **wisdom** necessarily involve having infinite **knowledge?**

Since wisdom involves the ability to decide what to do when the outcome is uncertain, it is clearly not the case that infinite wisdom necessarily involves infinite knowledge; indeed, in order for wisdom to operate there must be an absence of perfect knowledge.

Comment

_____

_____

Suggested Answers – Part V

Exercise 15.1 (p. 218)

1. Being taller than someone else and being a good conversationalist are **extrinsic** qualities of a person, both being relations which are dependent upon other people. List four other properties of persons which are **extrinsic**.

A person's weight depends upon the gravitational pull of the planet: on the moon we would all be lighter; a person's social status depends upon other people's status; a person's hair colour depends upon whether it has been tinted and on whether it is seen in daylight, candle light or ultraviolet light; a person's wealth depends upon other people's acceptance of the notion of property. There are other answers: nationality, membership of a club, etc . . .

Comment

David Armstrong (1968) argued that **all** properties of persons are extrinsic whereas Descartes argued (*Meditations*) that some properties are intrinsic.

2. List four properties of persons which could be said to be **intrinsic**.

Happiness, intelligence, a sense of taste, and goodness – there are many other answers.

Comment

3. Are there any characteristics which differentiate the possible **intrinsic** properties from the **extrinsic** ones?

All the intrinsic properties are mental or spiritual and all the extrinsic ones are related to the experiences of others. This indicates that if the property is not mental or spiritual then it has no chance of being considered intrinsic, and if it cannot be related to the experiences of others it has no chance of being considered extrinsic.

Comment

_____

_____

Exercise 15.2 (p. 219)

α (*alpha*) 'I have a clear and distinct idea of myself, in as far as I am only a thinking and unextended thing'
(By 'unextended' he means 'cannot be measures in space')

β (*beta*) 'and as, on the other hand, I possess a distinct idea of body, in as far as it is only an extended and unthinking thing'

γ (*gamma*) 'it is certain that I, that is, my mind, by which I am what I am, is entirely and truly distinct from my body, and may exist without it.'

1. Does the fact that Descartes had a clear and distinct idea of himself as a thinking and 'unextended' (with no length, area or volume) thing mean that we all must have similar clear and distinct ideas of ourselves? If not, is Descartes' argument only valid for people who have such clear and distinct ideas of themselves?

The notion of a thinking thing is not, of necessity, linked to the notion of lack of extension: stating that a thinking thing is measurable in space is not self-contradictory. Therefore there is no contradiction involved in claiming that the subject of thought is located in the whole of a person's brain, which occupies a portion of three-dimensional space; in such circumstances the subject of thought would be 'extended', and so measurable in space.

The possibility that someone might not be an 'unextended' thing does not, however, invalidate Descartes' argument that the subject of thought is separable from the body: being 'unextended' is not the only quality

Descartes cites, and it is possible that the quality of being a thinking thing is sufficient to establish a separation of body from mind.

Comment

_____

_____

2. Does the fact that a mind might be analysed separately from the body with which it interacts mean that the body and the mind can exist separately?

The separability of two notions in an analysis does not necessarily imply the separate existence of the two entities that the notions refer to: an analysis can consider the surface area of a brain to be distinguishable from the volume of the brain, but this does not mean that the surface area of the brain can exist without the volume or vice versa.

Comment

_____

_____

3. In Statement γ Descartes suggests that his mind is that by which he is what he is. Does this claim assume the conclusion that his body may exist without his mind?

In suggesting that his mind was what he was, Descartes was assuming the possibility that the mind **could** exist independently, but he was not assuming that his mind **actually did** exist independently of his body. Statement γ does not assume Descartes' conclusion.

Comment

_____

_____

Exercise 15.3* (Advanced exercise) (p. 221)

In Questions 1 and 2 assume that Parfit's thought experiment is valid.

1. Is it logically possible for a single Cartesian thinking and 'unextended' subject to split into two versions of itself?

   No. The notion that something with no length, area or volume can split is self-contradictory.

Comment

_____

_____

2. Is it logically possible for my 'unextended' Cartesian subject to be transferred into one of my brothers' bodies and for another different 'unextended' subject to enter the body of my other brother when the brain transplants are being carried out?

   Yes. There is no logical contradiction in the idea that the brain transplant operation could succeed only if, at the same time, it consisted of the birth of a new person through the entry of an 'unextended' thinking thing into one of Parfit's brothers. Any argument basing itself on a thought experiment such as Parfit's ought to permit a refutation based on another thought experiment.

Comment

_____

_____

3. Do the arguments based on the person-splitting thought experiment repudiate the validity of Cartesian dualism?

   No. The answers to Questions 1 and 2 show that the arguments claiming to refute Cartesian dualism by invoking person-splitting thought experiments are not incontrovertible: equally fantastic thought experiments can be invoked to maintain the logical possibility of dualism.

Comment

_____

_____

4. If Cartesian dualism were true, what would the outcome of Parfit's experiment be? Would such an outcome be logically impossible?

If a Cartesian 'unextended' thinking thing were the subject which was essential for the existence of a person, then Parfit's thought experiment could not work: at some point in the transplant operation the Cartesian soul would locate itself in only one of the two receiving bodies and only that body could survive. This outcome is logically possible.

Comment

[Note: The logical possibility of this outcome demonstrates that the successful outcome of Parfit's thought experiment presupposes that Cartesian dualism is false. This means that the experiment cannot be used to **demonstrate** the falsity of Cartesian dualism.]

Exercise 15.4 (p. 224)

1. In Questions 1 and 2 assume that Parfit's thought experiment is valid. Does the division of Parfit's consciousness mean that Locke's definition of a person as 'a thinking intelligent being, that has reason and reflection, and can consider itself as itself, the same thinking thing, in different times and places' was mistaken?

No. Parfit's thought experiment is designed to test the criteria which we use to identify a person as being the same one on different occasions: each of the surviving Parfit replicas would still be a thinking intelligent being with all the other Lockean qualities.

Comment

---

2. Does the division of Parfit's consciousness mean that we cannot use the continuity of consciousness to identify him as the same person on different occasions?

Given that he can be divided, the continuity of consciousness of the person would not provide incontrovertible reasons for supporting a claim that anyone was Parfit: the person could be either Parfit-Lefty or Parfit-Righty. (Although under the current state of medical knowledge it can be assumed that the characteristics of the left and right sides of the brain are sufficiently different for someone to tell which one they were talking to: Parfit-Lefty would be likely to be mostly rational while Parfit-Righty would be mostly imaginative!)

Comment

_____

_____

(Advanced question)
A thought experiment which postulates no change of energy while an atom divides into two identical atoms would violate the principle of the conservation of mass and energy.

3. (i) Is it legitimate to conclude from such a thought experiment that we cannot use the continuity of an atom's history to identify it as the same atom on different occasions?

No, we could reject the validity of the thought experiment – we are faced with a choice between accepting its validity and the validity of the scientific principle that it violates.

Comment

_____

_____

(ii) Does Parfit's person-splitting thought experiment violate any principles?

The common-sense answer to this question is 'Yes', as the general use of the concept of a person excludes the possibility that one could split in two; the more considered answer, however, is 'Maybe'. The stability of the mass of an atom (when no changes in energy levels occur) is a necessary condition for the maintenance of the laws of physics. The stability of the identity of a person **could** also be a necessary condition for the maintenance of the procedures by which we retain the meanings of terms such as 'person', 'brain', 'mind', 'I', 'you', and so on. It seems reasonable to assume that where a person's consciousness could bifurcate into two identical conscious unities, the concept of identity itself would be different from ours: by questioning the stability of the concept of personal identity we are questioning the stability of the concept of identity in general.

Questioning the stability of the concept of identity is fundamentally different from investigating the nature of the identity of an object or person. This is because the concept of identity plays as important a role in sustaining our explanations of human interactions with the physical world as the concepts of mass and energy play in physicists' explanations of the interactions between physical objects.

Comment

Exercise 15.5 (p. 225)

α The body is made of matter and the brain is part of the body.
β The behaviour of matter complies with the laws of nature therefore the behaviour of the brain complies with the laws of nature.
γ The mind functions through the operations of the brain.

From these premises we draw the following conclusions:

δ The mind's functions have to comply with the laws of nature.
ε The mind's functions can be explained by explaining the brain's functions.
ζ A person is nothing but a physical object.

A driver has to comply with the laws governing motoring.

1. Does this mean that the driver's behaviour can be explained by using the laws governing motoring?

It is clear that a driver's decision to obey a traffic signal cannot be explained in terms of the laws governing motoring any more than they can explain his decision to exceed the speed limit. There are other factors affecting the behaviour of the driver.

Comment

2. Does the brain's compliance with the laws of nature mean that the behaviour of the mind can be explained by using the laws of nature?

In a similar way to the driver, the laws of nature do not necessarily determine the behaviour of everything which has to comply with their provisions. The mind, in its interactions with the brain, has to comply with the laws which govern the behaviour of the brain, but, as in the case of the driver, there could be other factors affecting its behaviour.

Comment

_____

_____

(Advanced questions)

3. The argument α to ζ may have been formulated in a manner prejudicial to the materialist case. How might a materialist amend it?

We could substitute 'obeys only' for 'complies with' in β and δ. This would make it more difficult to challenge the validity of the deduction of δ as no other regulations could govern the mind's behaviour which would be completely determined by the laws of nature.

Comment

_____

_____

4. Questions 1 and 2 may have been formulated in a manner prejudicial to the materialist case. How might a materialist amend them?

The changes suggested in Question 3 necessitate similar changes to Questions 1 and 2. If the only laws governing the behaviour of the driver were the laws governing motoring then the truth of the materialist theory would be assumed in the question. In order to eliminate this assumption we would have to formulate a prior question asking whether the laws governing motoring were indeed the only laws governing the behaviour of the driver.

Comment

_____

_____

Exercise 16.1 (p. 232)

'Freedom is the source from which all significations and all values spring. It is the original condition of all justification of existence. The person who seeks to justify his life must want freedom itself absolutely and above everything else.'

1. (i) In allocating meaning to words could I be merely processing data in the same way as a computer does?

Yes. From the point of view of an individual, there is no logical contradiction in supposing that any particular episode of an allocation of meaning is determined by a process which follows the instructions set out in a program.

Comment

(ii) Do I have to be free to allocate meaning?

No, for the reasons given in (i). De Beauvoir's argument is not, however, one which is directly affected by the answer to (i) since she is referring to giving meaning to existence rather than to the allocation of meaning to a particular word, symbol or occurrence. In order to be applicable to her argument the computer analogy would need to be amended to refer to the writing of the program which controls the processing of data, rather than to the process involved in running the program. The only way of avoiding de Beauvoir's conclusion that the writer of the program is free would be to enter into a (benign) regress of programs where each process of writing a program was determined by another process of writing a program.

In these circumstances we would be faced with a simple choice: either, we could accept de Beauvoir's claim that the individual is the writer of the program and is free; or, we could accept the infinite regress of writing programs, each of which was determined by how the previous program had been written; or, we could reject the notion that we can give meaning to existence (the condition which gave rise to de Beauvoir's argument).

Comment

'Man cannot decide between the negation and assumption of his freedom, for as soon as he decides, he assumes it. He cannot positively will not to be free for such a willing would be self destructive.'

2. Does the fact that I cannot will my freedom away mean that I must be free?

No. It just means that any attempt you made to convince yourself that you were not free would be logically incoherent. De Beauvoir's point is that anyone attempting to establish that they are not free becomes logically incoherent.

Comment

_____

_____

'However, man does not create the world. He succeeds in disclosing it only through the resistance which the world opposes to him. The will is defined only by raising obstacles, and because the facts in the world are open to different outcomes certain obstacles let themselves be conquered, and others not.'

3. (i) Does the world have to resist me in order for me to obtain knowledge of it (disclose it)?

Yes. Two sets of discussions in earlier chapters have indicated that it is 'only through the resistance which the world opposes' that we gain an understanding of our environment: the first set consisted of Henri Poincarés arguments on the formation of the concept of space (such as on p. 65) and the second the discussions on the nature of laboratory activity (such as the one which distinguished scientific demonstrations from the demonstrations of the existence of God on p. 199). Poincaré argued that we need to be able to move our bodies in order to formulate a concept of dimensions in space (1952, pp. 58–9), but he went on to argue in the succeeding pages that we also need to feel the resistance of solid objects in order to formulate such a concept. The discussions about the nature of laboratory activity make very similar points about the need to interfere with the patterns of events which occur in the world in order to develop scientific understanding of what causes the patterns. De Beauvoir is making a similar point about the requirement for a resistant response from the world in order for the individual to understand what 'the world is doing' (not de Beauvoir's phrase).

(ii) If so, does this mean that I must exercise some freedom when I act?

Yes. The resistance of a causal agent (the world) to another (the individual) only makes sense if the two causal agents are independent of each other.

Comment

_____

_____

In the last quotation de Beauvoir argues that freedom is situated in a world in which other things behave independently of it – freedom always functions in a particular context and it is said to be 'situated'. This means that an individual's freedom is dependent upon her ability to interact not only with a resistant world but also with other individuals who, like her, are free. De Beauvoir argues that in order to realise our own freedom we **must** recognise the freedom of others.

4. If in order to be free I do not have to recognise that the world which resists me is free, am I obliged to recognise that other cognitive individuals are free?

No. In order to perceive myself as free, I do not have to attribute freedom to anything other than myself, and this includes other individuals who consider themselves to be free. I can consider other individuals to be of the same category as the physical objects of the world which strictly adhere to natural laws. There appears to be no logical reason why I cannot 'disclose' the world of cognitive individuals 'through the resistance which that world opposes to me'.

Comment

_____

_____

[Note: It is probable that de Beauvoir would have rejected the simplistic formulation of the question. She is likely to have responded by claiming that in order for me to formulate any sort of concept, all cognitive individuals must be free; I, as one of these individuals, could fail to recognise their freedom because I fail to recognise that their freedom is a precondition of my being able to give meaning to the concepts I hold in consciousness (the inner, or 'intensional', aspect of a concept). The freedom of others is not a precondition of my being able to apply a concept (the outer, or 'extensional', aspect of a concept).]

Exercise 16.2 (p. 234)

> Is it logically possible for God to be the source from which all 'significations' and all values spring?

Yes, and the question of freedom would not necessarily be compromised by God being the source of all 'significations' and all values. There are some existentialist philosophers, notably Søren Kierkegaard, who would argue that God is that source. For philosophers like Kierkegaard discussions about the freedom of the individual would become closely linked with discussions about the nature of God.

Comment

Exercise 16.3 (p. 235)

> 1. Is the claim that people are responsible for their actions only if they are able to act otherwise an **analytic** or **synthetic** claim?

To be responsible is to be morally accountable for one's actions. It is logically possible to make people accountable for their actions even if they are unable to act otherwise. The meaning of the term 'responsibility' is derived from an externally imposed duty, and so does not include the notion of an ability to act otherwise. Thus the claim is not an analytic one.

Someone wishing to maintain that the claim is an analytic one would have to show that the moral aspect of accountability necessarily involved the ability to act otherwise, which would move the argument onto the question of what moral value consists of. The consequentialist theories of moral value would tend to separate the concept of responsibility from the ability to act otherwise while the essentialist theories would tend to link them. Unless the notions of responsibility and the ability to act otherwise were clearly interdependent, one would have to decide that they were not, so the claim would remain a synthetic one.

Comment

2. Are people responsible for their actions when they break the law only if they are able to act otherwise?

No. This is because a legal system can decide this issue either one way or the other, so responsibility is not ascribed **only** when someone can act otherwise. This answer adds further support to the argument in Answer 1 that the claim is a synthetic one.

Comment

_____

_____

3. Describe an activity which you cannot do without assuming the responsibility for your actions.

The learning of concepts is an activity which requires learners to assume the responsibility for their actions. People who refuse to accept the responsibility for their own learning process cannot trigger that process and learn: learning a concept involves focusing the mind on an idea, a process which requires a mental commitment, and therefore the assumption of the responsibility for focusing the mind on the idea. It is, nonetheless, theoretically possible to learn a skill through being conditioned to respond like a Pavlovian dog (see Exercise 11.2, p. 306), but this cannot be done in the case of learning concepts.

For similar reasons, teaching abstract concepts requires teachers to assume the responsibility for their actions, as this involves the teacher in inviting the learner to focus the mind on an idea. The teacher's invitation itself requires a mental commitment and therefore the assumption of the responsibility for focusing the teacher's own mind on the invitation. This responsibility has cost some philosophers dearly: in the eighteenth century David Hume was refused the professorship of philosophy at Glasgow University because of the corrupting influence of his teaching and Socrates was put to death for the same reason two thousand years earlier.

Comment

_____

_____

[Note: It is likely that a philosopher who accepts the materialist theory that all mental occurrences can be expressed as physical ones (see Chap. 15 p. 225) would argue that even abstract concepts can be taught and learned without the learner assuming responsibility for his learning.]

Revision Exercises

Revision Exercise 15.1 and 16.1 (p. 238)

When an animal is cloned, the clone is genetically indistinguishable from the original.

1. Does this mean that a cloned human being would be the same person as the one from whom he was cloned?

No. The clone can be distinguished from the original using criteria which are independent of genetic characteristics. These criteria include the use of physical and mental characteristics to distinguish the two people: only one of the two people would have had the same physical body with the same history as the original and that one would have had the same mental history and memories as well. Two clones would be distinguishable using the same criteria as non-scientists use to distinguish identical twins.

[Note: Parfit's division described above (p. 220) avoids these counter-arguments because, in his thought experiment, bodily and psychological continuity are the same for two distinct individuals.]

Comment

_____

_____

Descartes claimed that he had 'a clear and distinct idea of myself, in as far as I am only a thinking and unextended thing'.

2. Can a 'thing' be unextended (non-measurable in space)?

No. A 'thing' is necessarily extended. A 'thing' which interacts with another extended (measurable) 'thing' must itself also be extended. This can be seen by considering a mathematical point in space which has no dimensions; the fact that it has no dimensions means that it is unextended. A mathematical point with no dimensions is not a 'thing'. It is possible that the translations from the original Latin through French and then to English might have altered the meaning of Descartes original 'unextended thinking thing'.

Comment

_____

_____

Kant's deontology required a person to choose freely to obey any of the person's own maxims of behaviour which could be made into universal laws. David Armstrong claimed that a person is fully definable as a material object.

3. (i) Can a material object freely choose to obey universal laws?

No. Material objects are defined as those which obey the laws of nature, so they cannot choose to obey any law, they just obey them.

(ii) Given the answer to (i), do we reject Kant's theory, Armstrong's or neither?

The answer to this question does not depend solely upon the answer to (i). We also need to know whether it is possible to formulate a complete description in physical terms of the processes a person goes through when making a choice.

If the formulation of a complete physical description of the functioning of the mind is not possible, then the Armstrong theory should be rejected. But this does not mean that we are thereby obliged to accept Kant's theory, the fact that physicalism should fail does not mean then Kantianism succeeds.

If, however, the formulation of a complete physical description of the functioning of the mind were possible, then a 'choice' would be describable in terms which made no reference to the person doing the choosing. In these circumstances the word 'choose' would have a significantly different meaning from the one we give it at present. A theory, like the Kantian one, could not remain unchanged.

Comment

_____

_____

_____

Revision Discussion Exercise 16.2 (Advanced question) (p. 239)

When we see the symbols 10 and 100 we normally interpret them as the numbers 'ten' and 'one hundred'. However, if we were mathematicians working in a different number base, for example with binary numbers, we would interpret them as the numbers 'two and four'.

The symbols written as 10+10=100 would form the same image on the eye but would be interpreted with one meaning in one set of circumstances and a different meaning in another – the different meanings would make the symbols represent falsehood in one case and truth in the other.

Working in the standard number base non-mathematicians use, the set of symbols would catch the eye as being out of place; we would focus on them and look for an explanation as to why a false statement were there. Working in binary numbers we might not even notice them.

Cognitive beings have the ability to interpret the images they gather from their environment in different ways. They also have the ability to focus the mind on the different interpretations and meanings of these images.

1. Does the fact that cognitive beings have the ability to ascribe different meanings to the same physical images mean that they have a free will which is able to alter the content of consciousness?

It means that they have a will which is able to alter the content of consciousness; whether it is free or not depends upon the answer to Question 3(ii) of the previous exercise.

Comment

_____

_____

2. Does an individual's ability to give different meanings to the same images she gathers from her environment depend upon the existence of other individuals who have the same ability?

Yes. The ability to allocate meaning is dependent upon the existence of a cultural context in which a concept can be given meaning. In the absence of other individuals who have the ability to allocate different meanings to different physical images, an individual would be unable to learn how to allocate meaning at all.

[Note: This is a one-sentence synopsis of one of the arguments in the author's as yet unpublished doctoral thesis. There are other philosophers who have put forward arguments supporting the same conclusion as was stated in Chapter 16 above. (FCR)]

Comment

Bibliography

Adair, R. K., Astumian, R. D. and Weaver, J. C.: 'Detection of weak electric fields by sharks, rays, and skates', *Chaos* 8: 576–87 (1998).

Allen, Deborah and Duch, Barbara: *Thinking toward Solutions: Problem Based Learning Activities for General Biology* (Harcourt, 1998).

Arendt, Hannah: *The Human Condition* (University of Chicago Press, 1958, and 1998 introduction by Margaret Canovan).

Aristotle: *Physics* (*P*); *Nicomachean Ethics* (*NE*); *Posterior Analytics* (*PA*).

Armstrong, David: *A Materialist Theory of the Mind* (Routledge and Kegan Paul, 1968).

Bell, Linda: 'Existential Ethics' in Simon Bell (ed.) *The Edinburgh Encyclopedia of Continental Philosophy*, pp. 163–73 (Edinburgh University Pres, 1999).

Berkeley, George: *A Treatise Concerning the Principles of Human Knowledge* (Collins, 1710) (http://eserver.org/18th/berkeley.txt)

—: *A New Theory of Vision* (Collins, 1710) (http://onlinebooks.library.upenn.edu/ authors.html)

Bhaskar, Roy: *A Realist Theory of Science* (Harvester Press, 1978).

Boswell, James: *Life of Samuel Johnson* (Book 3 originally published in 1791) (http://digital.library. upenn.edu/webbin/gutbook/lookup?num=1564)

Broad, C. D.: *The Mind and its Place in Nature* (Routledge & Sons, 1925).

Brodie, Alexander (ed.): *The Scottish Enlightenment – An Anthology* (Canongate, 1997).

—: *Why Scottish Philosophy Matters* (The Saltire Society, 2000).

Burnet, John: *Early Greek Philosophy* (Oxford, 1920).

Burwood, S., Gilbert, P. and Lennon, K.: *Philosophy of Mind* (UCL Press, 1999).

Carroll, Lewis: *Alice's Adventures in Wonderland* (1865) (http://www.cs.indiana.edu/ metastuff/wonder/wonderdir.html)

Cranston, Maurice: *Sartre* (Oliver and Boyd, 1962).

Descartes, René: *Discourse on Method*, and *Meditations on First Philosophy*, both included in *Descartes – Key Philosophical Writings* (Wordsworth Classics of World Literature, 1997).

Dews, Peter: *Habermas – A Critical Reader* (Blackwell Publishers, 1999).

Eccles, John (with K. Popper): *The Self and its Brain: An Argument for Interactionism* (Springer International, 1977).

Eco, Umberto: *Art and Beauty in the Middle Ages* (Yale University Press, 1986).

Eddington, Sir Arthur: 'The Philosophy of Physical Science' [Tarner Lectures, 1938] (Cambridge University Press, 1939).

Freud, Sigmund: *An Outline of Psycho-Analysis* (Hogarth Press, 1949).

Gleick, James: *Genius: The Life and Science of Richard Feynman* (Little, Brown and Co, 1992).

Hall, Stuart and Gieben (eds): *Formations of Modernity* (Polity Press, 1992).

Hankinson, Jim: *Bluff your Way in Philosophy* (Ravette Books, 1985).

Hare, R. M.: *The Language of Morals* (The Clarendon Press, 1952).

Harvey, David: *The Conditions of Postmodernity* (Blackwell, 1990).

Hempel, Carl Gustav: *Aspects of Scientific Explanation and Other Essays in the Philosophy of Science* (Free Press, 1965).

Hume, David: *A Treatise of Human Nature* (Oxford, 1888, Selby-Bigge edition).

—: *An Inquiry Concerning Human Understanding* (1748) (http://www.eserver.org/18th/hume-inquiry.html)

—: *Dialogues on Natural Religion* (Baron David Hume (Hume's nephew) posthumously, 1777) (http://www.anselm.edu/homepage/dbanach/dnr.htm).

Hutcheson, Francis: *An Inquiry into the Original of our Ideas of Beauty and Virtue* (1725; Everyman, 1994).

Kant, Immanuel: *The Critique of Pure Reason* (C1) (1781 and 1787); *The Critique of Practical Reason* (C2) (1788); *The Critique of Judgement* (C3) (1790); *Fundamental Principles of the Metaphysic of Morals* (*FPMM*) (1785) (http://eserver.org/philosophy/).

Kierkegaard, Søren Aabye: *On my Work as an Author* (trans. Walter Lowrie) (P. C. Kierkegaard (Kierkegaard's brother), posthumously, 1859).

Kuehn, Manfred: *Kant: A Biography* (Cambridge University Press, 2000).

Kuhn, Thomas: *The Structure of Scientific Revolutions* (University of Chicago Press, 1970).

Locke, John: *An Essay Concerning Human Understanding* (Thomas Ballet, London: 1690) (eds Gary Fuller, Robert Stecker and John P. Wright) (London; New York: Routledge, 2000).

MacDonald, Paul (ed.): *The Existentialist Reader: An Anthology of Key Texts* (Edinburgh University Press, 2000)

Makkreel, Rudolf: *Imagination and Interpretation in Kant* (University of Chicago Press, 1990).

Mill, John Stuart: *On Liberty* (Parker, Son and Bourn, 1859) reprinted in *Utilitarianism* (Collins, 1962).

—: *Utilitarianism* (Parker, Son and Bourn, 1863) reprinted in *Utilitarianism* (Collins, 1962).

Moore, George Edward: *Principia Ethica* (Cambridge University Press, 1903; reprinted by Prometheus, 1988).

Nietzche, Friederich: 'The Birth Tragedy' (*TBT*) in *The Birth of Tragedy and The Case of Wagner* (trans. Walter Kaufmann) (Vintage Books, 1967).

Nozick, Robert: *Anarchy, State, and Utopia* (Basic Books, 1974).

Paley, William: *Natural Theology: Or, Evidences of the Existence and Attributes of the Deity Collected from the Appearances of Nature* (Faulder, 1802) (Digital version available from the Pacific Data Conversion Corporation).

Parfit, Derek: *Reasons and Persons* (Clarendon Press, 1974).

Plato: *The Republic*; *The Phaedo*; *The Laws* (http://onlinebooks.library.upenn.edu/authors.html)

Poincaré, Henri: *Science and Hypothesis* (Flammarion, 1902) (Dover Publications, 1952).

Popper, Karl: *The Logic of Scientific Discovery* (Hutchinson, 1959).

—: *Conjectures and Refutations: The Growth of Scientific Knowledge* (Routledge and Kegan Paul, 1963)

—: *The Poverty of Historicism* (2nd edn) (Routledge and Kegan Paul, 1961).

—: *Objective Knowledge: An Evolutionary Approach* (Clarendon Press, 1972).

— (with J. C. Eccles): *The Self and its Brain: An Argument for Interactionism* (Springer International, 1977).

Putnam, Hilary: *Realism with a Human Face* (Harvard University Press, 1990).

Quine, W. V.: *On What There Is* (Review of Metaphysics, 1948) reprinted in *From a Logical Point of View* (Harper & Row, 1953).

Radcliffe-Richards, Janet: *Human Nature after Darwin* (Routledge, 2000).

Reid, Thomas: *Inquiry into the Human mind on the Principles of Common Sense* (1764) and *Essays on the Intellectual Powers of Man* (1785). Extracts reprinted in Brodie (1997).

—: *Essays on the Active Powers of Man* (1788).

Roberts, Francis: 'Thought experiments and Social Transformation', *Journal for the Theory of Social Behaviour* (December, 1993).

Russell, Bertrand: *History of Western Philosophy* (George Allen & Unwin, 1946).

Ryle, Gilbert: *The Concept of Mind* (Hutchinson, 1949).

Shaftesbury, Anthony: *Characteristics of Men, Manners, Opinions, Times* (originally published in three volumes 1711 by Shaftesbury himself but the names of neither the printer nor the publisher are given in any of the volumes) (Liberty Fund, 2001).

Sidgwick, Henry: *Methods of Ethics* (7th edn, Macmillan & Co., Ltd, 1907; Oxford University Press, 2001). (http://www.la.utexas.edu/research/poltheory/sidgwick/me/)

Tolstoy, Leo: *What is Art? and Essays on Art* (trans. Aylmer Maude) (Oxford University Press, 1930).

Strawson, P. F.: *The Bounds of Sense* (Methuen, 1966).

Vinci, Leonardo da: 'Paragone: A Comparison of the Arts' in *Trattato della Pittura. (c.* 1510). (trans. Irma Richter) (Oxford University Press, 1944).

Walsh, W. H.: *Kant's Criticism of Metaphysics* (Edinburgh University Press, 1975).

Weddle, David: *Outline of David Hume's Dialogues Concerning Natural Religion* (2001) Only available on the internet (http://www2.coloradocollege.edu/dept/RE/religionweb/courses/re102/hume.htm).

Reference texts and dictionaries

Craig, Edward (ed.): *The Routledge Encyclopedia of Philosophy* (Routledge, 2000).

Glendinning, Simon (ed.): *The Edinburgh Encyclopedia of Continental Philosophy* (Edinburgh University Press, 1999).

Liddell, H. G. and Scott, R.: *The Oxford Abridged Greek–English Lexicon* (Clarendon, 1863).

Maunter, Thomas (ed.) *The Penguin Dictionary of Philosophy* (Penguin Books, 2000).

The Oxford English Dictionary (Clarendon).

Runes, Dagobert D. (ed.): *The Dictionary of Philosophy* (Routledge & Sons, 1944).

Speake, Jennifer (ed.): *A Dictionary of Philosophy* (Macmillan, 1979).

Glossary of Names

Entries marked with [P] are based on primary sources, those with [PT] on primary sources in translation and those with [S] on secondary sources.

Anaximander: (6th century BC) The second major philosopher of the 'Milesian School' in ancient Greece. Like Thales before him and Anaximenes after him, he claimed that the cosmos consisted of an infinite, eternal, ageless 'primary substance': this primary substance could not be one of the known substances because each one of these was competing with others to establish itself as the dominant substance. According to Anaximander the manifest failure of the attempts by known substances to become dominant enables us to conclude that there is something, the 'primary substance', which thwarts dominance. The absence of the dominance of one of the existing substances justified his claim that the primary substance must operate according to a principle of harmony or 'justice' among the other substances in the cosmos. Both of his arguments are forms of 'transcendental proof' that some things or some properties exist beyond what we can perceive. [S]

Anaximenes: (6th century BC) The third major philosopher of the 'Milesian School'. Like Thales and Anaximander before him, he believed that the cosmos consisted of an infinite, eternal, ageless 'primary substance' that continually changed form. He argued that the primary substance was air, the reason being that air had the attribute of infinity and so could give a better account for the variety we see in the world than water could (which had been Thales' choice of primary substance). In doing this he was using 'explanatory richness' as a criterion for deciding between rival theories. [S]

Aristotle: (c. 384 BC–323 BC) A Greek polymath who has become one of the most influential philosophers in the history of European culture. Although he was Plato's pupil, he went on to equal his master in philosophy and to surpass him in many other fields. Unlike Plato, Aristotle believed that ultimate reality was what we perceive, rather than in some other separate realm which was independent of our senses.

He divided knowledge (επιστημαι: *epistêmai*, literally 'knowledges') of reality into three spheres: the theoretical sciences, which included what we call the natural sciences as well as mathematics, and aimed at truth; the practical sciences, which incorporated politics and ethics, and aimed at the goodness of human behaviour; and the productive sciences, which aimed at making things.

He laid the foundations of the deductive model of explanation in science. In the *Posterior Analytics* (Bk I–6) he argued that a science needs to be set out as an axiomatic system with first principles which are necessarily true, and a set of deductive inferences which lead to all of the true statements about the subject matter of the science (*PA* (Bk I–6). Scientific knowledge is therefore demonstrative: the knowledge we obtain in science is what we can derive from first principles, which themselves do not require to be proved.

According to Aristotle each branch of science studies a particular part of reality and tries to explain the changes that occur in it. Like Plato, Aristotle went deeper than this and sought an understanding of the nature of being or existence. He distinguished between things which have independent existence, calling them 'substances, and those whose existence was not independent. For example, a horse is a substance but its whiteness is not, and neither is the cart the horse is pulling: the whiteness and the cart do not have independent existence.

To determine whether something has independent existence, Aristotle invoked his 'Doctrine of the Four "Causes"'. The first three explained why something is what it is, and the fourth, the thing's final cause or purpose, explained why it changed. Aristotle provided examples of each of the four types of cause: (i) A 'material cause' was the material or physical stuff, from which something was made. The bronze of a statue was its material cause; (ii) a 'formal cause' was the essence or nature of something: it is what it is. The formal cause of a particular statue of Athena was the representation of the Goddess Athena; (iii) an 'efficient cause' was that by which something comes into existence. The parents were the efficient cause of the child: they were the source of the child's origins; (iv) a 'final cause' of a thing or process, its τελος (*telos*), was the purpose for which it existed or was done. Health was the final cause of physical exercise.

A substance contained its own final cause; this meant that the cart being pulled by the horse was not a substance because the purpose for which it was built was in the mind of the artisan who made it. The horse, by contrast, had an essence which contained the purpose for which it existed.

The notion of a final cause, or *telos*, the purpose for which something existed, provided the basis of Aristotle's analysis of moral issues. The purpose for which humans existed was the achievement of ευδαιμονια (*eudaimonia*), which means happiness. *Eudaimonia* was not sensual pleasure, but a happiness which consisted of properly fulfilling our function as human beings. Humans shared certain functions with all animals which centred around their survival as individuals and as a species: they used their senses to help feed themselves and reproduce. Humans, however, had a function of the soul, rationality, which distinguished them from animals. Their happiness, therefore, consisted of nurturing the faculty of reason.

The business of ethics was to discover how humans achieve their purpose of nurturing the faculty of reason. Aristotle argued that they did this by developing virtue, a quality of excellence (αρετη: *aretê*) (*NE* (I)7). There were two types of virtue, or excellence: moral and intellectual. Moral virtue consisted in avoiding the negative aspects of excesses and deficiencies by developing a balance to maintain harmony between the self and its *telos* (purpose). Intellectual virtue was needed in order for individuals to know how to obtain moral virtue: they needed it in order to understand that by achieving the mean between excess and deficiency they achieved human happiness. Intellectual virtue also had a value of its own, as it achieved *eudaimonia* directly: by developing intellectual virtue, humans were attaining the purpose of being human. The highest form of intellectual virtue was theoretical contemplation. Aristotle's ethical system is one of the oldest known systems of virtue ethics. [PT]

Bacon, Francis: (1561–1626) An English philosopher who is remembered for suggesting that there was an 'inductive method' for discovering scientific truth. The method relied on the primacy of observation and experiment as means of gaining knowledge of nature. His major published works included the four *Idols* (of the *Tribe*, the *Cave*, the *Market Place* and the *Theatre*) where he criticised the forces which made the use of the inductive method more difficult. [S]

Bacon, Roger: (c. 1214–c. 1294) A Franciscan scholar who was born in the West of England and died in Oxford. He was one of the six scholastic philosophers to be given the epithet 'Doctor' in the thirteenth century – he was known as 'Doctor Mirabilis', which has been interpreted as meaning either 'wonderful teacher' or 'miraculous doctor'. His interest in science tends to lend more credence to the latter: he stressed the need for experimental evidence, developing ideas for optic lenses, automobiles, aeroplanes and submarines. His inventions aroused the suspicions of the church authorities and he was imprisoned for a short period. Along with William of Ockham, he was one of the founders of English empiricism. As a good empiricist, he was strongly critical of the claim of his contemporary John Duns Scotus that things have essences which are incommunicable. His major published work was the *Opus Majus*, which was virtually a scientific encyclopaedia of the time. [S]

Baumgarten, Alexander Gottlieb: (1714–62) A German philosopher who was the first person to have used the term 'aesthetics' to refer to the branch of philosophy which inquires into art and the nature of beauty. His system contrasted the aim of logical knowledge with sensuous, or aesthetic, knowledge: logic sought truth and aesthetics sought beauty. [S]

Berkeley, George: (1685–1753) An Irish 'idealist' philosopher who challenged the Cartesian dualism of mind and matter by denying that matter could exist without mind. In *The Principles of Human Knowledge* (sections 15–24) he argued that the notion that matter exists without being perceived was nonsensical. [P] (Dr Johnson famously 'refuted' his theory by kicking a large stone.)

Brentano, Franz: (1838–1913) Was born in Marienberg, Germany and became a Catholic priest in 1864. He taught at the universities of Würzburg and Vienna. He is remembered for his 'Intentionality Thesis' in which he claimed that every mental event, be it a perception, thought or judgement, is intentionally directed towards some object. According to this thesis consciousness is fundamental to philosophy: this contrasts with the empiricism of the English-speaking world which claims that experience is fundamental to philosophy. [S]

De Beauvoir, Simone: (1908–86) A French philosopher, novelist and political theorist who, along with her life-long companion Jean-Paul Sartre, was the first to be described as an 'existentialist'. Like Sartre, she brought together two strands of philosophical thought: the phenomenology of Franz Brentano and Edmund Husserl; and the freedom and subjectivity found in the work of Søren Kierkegaard. She agreed with Sartre on three points: that individuals created themselves as conscious beings through their own free actions; that it was in these freely chosen actions that ultimate moral value (*Summum Bonum*) was to be found; and that the freedom of the individual could only be sustained through the promotion of the freedom of 'the other', that is, another person. It was in analysing the relationship between the freedom of the individual and that of 'the other' that she diverged from Sartre: unlike him, she focused on the positive aspects of the complementarity of one individual's freedom and that of other individuals – that is, on the recognition that the freedom of 'the other' enhanced the freedom of the subject of consciousness.

She developed this notion in two major philosophical works. In 1947 she published *Pour une morale de l'ambiguïté* (The Ethics of Ambiguity) followed two years later by *Le deuxième sexe* (The Second Sex). In *Pour une morale de l'ambiguïté* she reaffirmed the notion that an individual was a free agent, but contrasted this unstructured freedom with the structured social context in which the free agent acted. According to this analysis, social structures which promoted freedom were to be built on the firm foundations of a free individual, considered as a subject rather than an object. In *Le deuxième sexe*, she argued that women's secondary and subjugated social role throughout history stemmed from their being portrayed as 'the other' rather than the subject. Social structures and practices had developed reproducing the values which treated women as objects and so institutionalising their subjugation. It would be through treating 'the other' as a free agent, as a subject rather than an object, that women would become free. This would also necessitate the development of social structures and practices which did not turn women into objects. De Beauvoir was one of the first political activists to produce a philosophical, rather than purely social, analysis of the role of women; as such, she gave birth to the feminist critique of those social values which have led to the subjugation of women. It would therefore not be unreasonable to consider her to be the founder of modern feminism. [PT] [S]

Descartes, René: (1596–1650) The French scientist, mathematician and philosopher who has been one of the most influential writers of the last four hundred years. His influence in epistemology and the philosophy of mind has been immense. His major philosophical works, *Discourse on Method* and the *Meditations on the First Philosophy* are standard texts in university philosophy courses in many countries around the world.

In the field of epistemology he developed a 'method of doubt', consisting of a test which any claim had to pass if it were to be accepted as knowledge – nothing could be recognised as knowledge if it could be doubted in any way. This led him to conclude that, when restricted to trusting his own powers, the only thing free from doubt was his own existence. His conclusion, *cogito ergo sum* (I think, therefore I am), has become one of the most famous statements made by a European philosopher. The *cogito*, as it has come to be known, served as the foundations for his system which enabled him to deduce all the principles of knowledge. Starting with the *cogito*, he used an 'ontological proof' to deduce the existence of God. Having established the existence of an infinitely benevolent God, Descartes deduced that God would not deceive him, so he was able to overcome the doubt cast by his 'method of doubt' and rely on his powers of reasoning; this gave him a basis from which to attempt his deduction of all the principles of knowledge.

He is also remembered for his theory of the person. From the certainty of the existence of his mind and the uncertainty of the existence of matter, including his own body, he concluded that body and soul were distinct; in other words, there is a 'dualism' of soul and body. From a historical perspective, the dualist theory had positive effects, releasing medical science from the grip of the seventeenth-century Church in France. Similarly, the separation of body and soul allowed scientists to argue that they were justified in carrying out autopsies on bodies, as they were not affecting the already departed eternal soul of the deceased. [P]

Duns Scotus, John: (1270–1308) A Franciscan scholar who studied in Dumfries and then Oxford. He also taught in Paris and Cologne. His major work, *Opera Omnia*, was republished in Paris (1891–5). Alexander Brodie (2000, p. 13) argues that Scotus' ideas form part of the central vein of Scottish philosophy and culture, in which the independence and integrity of the individual are central. The principle is found in other traditions in European philosophy: Scotus was 'a medieval precursor to the phenomenological concept of intentionality' (see p. 283 above).

Scotus argued that the will and the intellect formed part of a unified mind; in spite of this they were distinct and had different powers. The intellect could do nothing other than seek truth; it was 'constrained to a single effect'. By contrast, the will had various options from which it could choose; it was 'open to contraries' and so was free. He resolved the apparent contradiction between these two positions by arguing that the intellect proposed while the will disposed. The will was able to do something which went against the principles set out by another faculty of a unified mind: it could go against the intellect and act irrationally.

Allied to this theory of a unified mind was a principle of individuation of an object based on an incommunicable nature of the object as well as its communicable essence. The will corresponded to the incommunicable nature of individuals and the intellect to their communicable essence. [S]

Hume, David: (1711–76) The Scottish philosopher whose ideas were more in tune with the

English empiricism of Thomas Hobbes and John Locke than with the Scottish philosophy exemplified by his contemporary Thomas Reid and the medieval Franciscan friar, John Duns Scotus. Reid overshadowed him in his home country for over a century. Hume failed to obtain Glasgow University's chair of logic and rhetoric in 1745 and Edinburgh's chair of moral philosophy in 1751. However, he was, and still is, considered to be one of the greatest figures of empiricism in the English-speaking world.

His philosophical heritage comes partly from Descartes and partly from Hobbes and Locke. Following in the footsteps of Hobbes and Locke, he based his theory of knowledge on the assumption that all knowledge springs from what he called 'impressions'. Following Descartes, he adopted a method of doubt with regard to all knowledge. According to Hume, the only knowledge which is certain is the content of the mind when perceiving an impression; this process consists of a vivid image that strikes the mind when our senses send signals to it. The mind, by using the faculty of the 'imagination', can then produce 'ideas', which are less vivid copies of the impressions. From these 'ideas' we can obtain an understanding of the way the world operates by using the principle of the 'Association of Ideas', in which sequences of impressions are reproduced which enable us to develop rules to describe the behaviour of things. For example, we notice that people tend to link similar ideas together; we also observe that hot objects regularly cool down in cold environments, thereby establishing a rule which states that heat transfers itself from hot objects to a colder environment.

According to Hume, we use these two processes of association to explain how something is caused: we associate 'ideas' with each other based on resemblance and contiguity (proximity).

This principle also extends to the determination of the rules which govern human behaviour. If we see that people generally approve of being kind to others, we can conclude that being kind is morally valuable. This meant that Hume's moral philosophy was also based on principles which are typical of the empiricism of the English-speaking world. As Alexander Brodie (2000, p. 59) points out, it is interesting to note that *Being an Attempt to Introduce the Experimental Method of Reasoning into Moral Subjects* is Hume's subtitle to his major philosophical work *The Treatise of Human Nature*.

The 'Association of Ideas' is a principle which applies only to the realm of ideas – there is no basis on which to claim it applies to the world of things or events. This means that, according to Hume, we must remain sceptical about our understanding of any world which operates separately from our sensations. There are no compelling arguments which apply to the relationships between events in the world beyond our perceptions. This 'scepticism' inspired responses, first from Reid, then from Kant.

Hume's ethics and aesthetics, which were also based on empirical principles, were strongly influenced by the Irish philosopher Francis Hutcheson. Hume accepted Hutcheson's claim that humans had a moral sense and an aesthetic sense, analogous to sight, touch, smell, taste and hearing. He argued that we find moral and aesthetic principles by observing how our moral and aesthetic senses operate and how people, in practice, ascribe moral and aesthetic value. The moral principles discovered by using this procedure are 'utilitarian'. The aesthetic values which we discover are those of classical antiquity, not because they are classical but because they have stood the test of time.

Hume's major work in philosophy, *A Treatise of Human Nature*, was published in 1739–40. He commented that it fell 'dead born from the press', probably because the language is not easy to follow. He responded by rewriting it in the form of two more accessible texts, *An Inquiry Concerning Human Understanding* (1748) and *An Inquiry Concerning the Principle of Morals* (1751). These, along with the *Dialogues Concerning Natural Religion*, are still widely used as university texts. [P]

Hutcheson, Francis: (1694–1746) An Irish philosopher who made a significant contribution to the Scottish Enlightenment. He became Professor of Moral Philosophy at Glasgow

University in 1729. His major work in philosophy, *Philosophical Writings*, was influenced by Anthony Shaftesbury's notion that humans have senses akin to the five senses, which detect moral goodness and beauty. As a result of this, theories of beauty and morals had to concern themselves with the operations of these senses. This opened the door to Hume's empirical analysis of a sense of taste and sense of moral values. [P]

Kant, Immanuel: (1712–1804) A colossus among philosophers who lived out his entire life in Königsberg, a small university town in East Prussia, but now in Russia. He is remembered for having developed a 'critical philosophy', written in his famous three critiques: *The Critique of Pure Reason*, *The Critique of Practical Reason* and *The Critique of Judgement*. These evolved, in part, from a reaction to Hume's scepticism, which Kant stated had awakened him from his 'dogmatic slumbers'. The awakening led him to undertake a double task: firstly, he wanted to answer Hume's extreme 'scepticism'; secondly, he wanted to question the assumption, common among metaphysicians of his time, that an understanding of reality could be obtained through the faculty of reason's analysis of concepts – that thought, unaided by the senses, could give us knowledge of what exists. He responded to Hume by arguing that the faculty of reason could give us knowledge which was not limited to making judgements about the content of our inner experience. He responded to the speculations of the metaphysicians by arguing that the faculty of reason had limits beyond which it cannot justifiably stray. In his 'critical' philosophy he sought to establish both these sets of limits.

His response to the speculations of the metaphysicians was similar to Hume's. He argued that, as far as reason was concerned, what actually happens in the world could always be other than what we experience. Any claim that the world conformed to a particular description could be met with a perfectly reasonable claim that it conformed to another particular description which contradicts the first one. In attempting to tell us what actually happened in a world which is beyond what we experienced, reason was exceeding its powers. This applied to every claim about what existed beyond the content of our minds, including God. Kant's refutation of speculative metaphysics extended to their proofs of the existence of God. He produced his own proof which restricted its starting point to the individual's own experience, and so was only valid for the individual (see p. 205).

In responding to Hume, Kant argued that we could know the rules by which the senses and reason operate. Unlike mathematical knowledge, this knowledge could not be acquired by analysing the meanings of the terms we use. In mathematics we know that two plus two equals four by understanding the meanings of the terms 'two', 'four, 'plus' and 'equals'. The statement 'two plus two equals four' is true by virtue of the meanings of the terms it contains – this characteristic defines it as an 'analytic proposition'. According to Kant no amount of sense experience, or of analysis of concepts independently of sense experience, could tell us that the senses can only absorb three-dimensional information set in a temporal context. Reason could, however, examine the rules, which the senses have to obey in order for them to function. Kant argued that this examination told us that the world, which provided our senses with information, had to be three-dimensional and time-dependent, and events in it had to be caused.

Reason could also examine the rules which reason itself has to obey in order for it to function. Kant argued that this further examination gave us two types of knowledge. The first type of knowledge concerned the rules governing the physical world which provides our senses with information – reason then has to interpret the information. In order for us to be able to interpret sense information, the world from which it comes must be ordered, and events in that world must be caused. This is one of the necessary conditions for reason to be able to interpret sense information about the world.

The second type of knowledge, obtained by further examination of the rules which reason itself has to obey, concerns the rules that govern our moral lives. Reason is the faculty which provides the justification for accepting, as a moral law, a particular rule governing human behaviour. In providing this justification, reason has to obey its own rules of operation: it could not accept a rule governing any sort of behaviour as a law unless that rule had these properties characteristic of a law. One of the properties which characterises a law is that it be universally applicable. Therefore, to be a moral law, a rule of human behaviour had to be universally applicable. Kant went on to argue that this condition was not only necessary in order for a rule of human behaviour to be a moral law, it was also a sufficient condition: that is, if a rule of behaviour could be generalised into a universal law governing human behaviour, then reason would accept that rule as a moral law.

Kant's three arguments in response to Hume's scepticism involved finding the conditions which had to hold in order for a human faculty to function. These types of argument utilise what are known as 'transcendental proofs'. They also lead to conclusions which are not 'analytic propositions'.

The three statements 'the world which provides our senses with information is three-dimensional and time-dependent', 'causal mechanisms operate in the world from which our sense information comes' and 'moral laws tell us to act in such a way as the rule which governs our actions can be a general rule governing all behaviour' are all 'synthetic'. Kant argued that these were true statements whose truth could not be determined from the meanings of the terms they contain – they are 'synthetic statements'. He also argued that the analyses which determine them as being true were also independent of experience, thereby being *a priori* analyses. He therefore claimed that it was possible for there to be 'synthetic' *a priori* statements, a claim which has not remained unchallenged.

Despite the highly abstract nature of Kant's philosophy, there was a very practical side to his nature. In his biography of Kant, Manfred Kuehn (2000, p. 64) quoted Christopher Friedrich Heilsberg's declaration that he, Kant and another fellow student earned money by gambling on their prowess at the billiard and card tables – it seems Kant was a hustler – and in a section in his *Critique of Pure Reason* (A824/B853) there are indications that he was fully acquainted with gambling. [PT]

Kierkegaard, Søren Aabye: (1813–55) Danish philosopher and theologian who is said to have influenced the development of twentieth-century 'existentialism'. The philosophical themes he pursued included: freedom, subjectivity, the sterility of pure intellect, and the primacy of individual independence over any system. His approach to philosophical study is encapsulated in the following quotation, 'What would be the use of discovering so-called objective truth . . . if it had no deeper significance for me and for my life; what good would it do me if truth stood before me, cold and naked, not caring whether I recognised her or not, and produced in me a shudder of fear rather than a trusting devotion?' (1939, p. 15.) These words put him out of phase with mainstream Continental philosophy of the time, which was dominated by Hegelian idealism. Kierkegaard felt that the Hegelian mainstream was misguided in two respects. Firstly, it valued the system above the free and responsible individual; secondly, by making reality dependent upon thought, it had reversed the natural relationship between thought and reality.

His analysis of moral issues is famed for the contrast he draws in his two-volume work *Either–Or* between the aesthete and the ethicist: the aesthete has a passion for sensuous beauty, pleasure and amusement, while the ethicist is drawn towards ideals of fidelity, integrity and the moral life. The choice between the two depended upon one's goal in life and could not be a question of intellectual assessment. This goal was determined by faith because, at root, ethics was based on a personal commitment. [S] [PT]

Kuhn, Thomas: (1922–96) An American philosopher concerned, like Karl Popper, with the question of explaining how science makes progress. He argued that science did not advance by making small steady strides; rather, it was 'a series of peaceful interludes punctuated by intellectually violent revolutions'. He described the violent revolutions as 'the tradition-shattering complements to the tradition-bound activity of normal science'. The terms 'scientific revolution' and 'normal science' have become standard terms of reference in discussions in the philosophy of science. They are used to describe two different phases in the progress of science and are characterised by the ways in which scientists formulate their explanations and conceptualise their activities. During the 'normal science' phases scientists deepen their understanding of nature using the accepted theories and practices of the day. Research in science is 'firmly based upon one or more past scientific achievements, achievements that some particular scientific community acknowledges for a time as supplying the foundation for its further practice' (1970, p. 10). Kuhn called these achievements 'paradigms' (p. 10). 'The successive transition from one paradigm to another via revolution is the usual developmental pattern of mature science' (p. 12). [P]

Locke, John: (1632–1714) A philosopher who made significant contributions to the English empiricist tradition. He rejected the notion that there are any innate ideas, all knowledge being derived from experience. He believed that, at birth, a person's mind is a *tabula rasa* (blank table) on which experience would make impressions which then formed the basis of knowledge. He distinguished 'primary qualities' of things (consisting of shape, extension motion and unity) from 'secondary qualities' (consisting of colour, taste and sound). The secondary qualities would be the ones which are subjective, and the primary ones would somehow inhere in things in a world independent of our experiences.

He believed that the continued identity of a person is based on the continuity of an individual's consciousness, linked together by the person's memory.

He was also a political theorist, developing a theory of government based on a social contract between citizens and the sovereign authority. [P]

Mill, John Stuart: (1806–73) Educated by Jeremy Bentham and his father James Mill so as to develop the English 'utilitarianism' which they had started. He differed from Bentham in believing that happiness, the generation of which is the aim of moral action, could vary in quality – a difference which has laid Mill open to the criticism that his moral value had moved away from the 'principle of utility'. Like Bentham and his father before him, he was also involved in political reform based on the principle of utility; his *Principles of Political Economy* (1851) and essay *On Liberty* (1859) were influential in bringing about political reform in Britain. Mill also made significant contributions in philosophy, in particular in logic and the philosophy of science: in his *System of Logic* (1843) he argued that inference is fundamentally a process of 'induction'.

Nietzsche, Friedrich: (1844–1900) A German philosopher and psychologist who, like Søren Kierkegaard, considered philosophy to be more a vehicle for developing **a** philosophy of life than an academic discipline – which makes a summary of his thought virtually impossible. At the heart of his system was the belief that the individual was free, and that human value was to be found in the expression of this freedom. This made him highly critical of all systems of values (principles) which were prescriptive, and therefore conflicted with human value (worth). This led him to develop the notion of the 'will to power' through which the individuals attained the self-development needed to express their freedom.

Ockham, William of: (c. 1287–1347) Was an English Franciscan scholar famous for his dictum which has come to be known as 'Ockham's razor'. Along with his fellow Franciscan, Roger Bacon, he laid the foundations of English empiricism. [S]

Plato: (c. 428 BC–347 BC) The Greek philosopher who, along with his pupil Aristotle, was one of the most influential figures in the history of European philosophy. He founded the 'Academy' in Athens in about 387 BC. It was eventually closed in 529 AD, some 900 years later, by the jurist Emperor Justinian, by which time the word 'academic' was firmly synonymous with 'learned'. It is believed that Plato called his institution of learning the 'Academy', naming it after the Greek epic hero Academus: 'In 387 BC, Plato returned to Athens and founded a school of philosophy and science that became known as the Academy. The school stood in a grove of trees that, according to legend, was once owned by a Greek hero named Academus . . . ' (*World Book Encyclopaedia*). The *Oxford English Dictionary* casts doubt on this version. It states that, according to John Robinson (1807): 'Academy . . . was a large enclosure of ground which was once the property of a citizen of Athens named Academus. Some however say that it received its name from an ancient hero.'

Plato wrote many books in the form of dialogues, with his teacher Socrates as the main speaker. Perhaps the most famous dialogue is *The Republic* in which Socrates used a question and answer technique to discuss the nature of 'Justice'. In *The Republic* as well as in *The Phaedo*, Plato developed his 'Theory of Forms' (or 'ideas') as well as outlining the perfect form of government for a society: the ultimately good moral values in such a society emanated from its rulers who were philosophers, and the philosophers, who became the 'guardians' of the perfect society, were people who sought wisdom.

Philosophers achieved a state of wisdom through long training in abstract reasoning which eventually gave them access to true knowledge of moral values by achieving a state of knowledge of the 'form', or 'idea', of 'the good'. According to Plato, this 'form', like all 'forms' or 'ideas', existed independently of any particular good thing or action. The 'form' of 'the good' was, in a sense, a primary form which somehow sustained the essence of each of the other 'forms', similar to the way in which the 'primary substance' sustained the other substances. Every phenomenon we experience, every one of our actions and every abstract idea we have, has been determined by the 'form' which inhabits it – or more accurately inheres in it. By understanding the 'form', we understand the experience, action or abstract idea. This means that Plato's 'Theory of Forms' claims to provide the philosopher with a deep understanding of all branches of knowledge. [PT]

Poincaré, Henri: (1854–1912) A French theoretical physicist, mathematician and philosopher and author of a major work on the philosophy of mathematics and the philosophy of science (1905). [P]

Popper, Karl: (1902–94) One of the foremost philosophers of the twentieth century. He was one of the leading philosophers of science, and made significant contributions to social and political philosophy. Like Kuhn, he wanted to explain how scientific progress was achieved. As an essential preliminary to this task, he set out to distinguish science from what he called 'non-science': according to Popper, a theory was scientific only if refutable by a conceivable event.

He then used this criterion of 'falsifiability' to explain scientific progress. Science made progress from one scientific, and so falsifiable, theory to another by taking a series of steps. It attempted to falsify the accepted falsifiable theory. If it succeeded in falsifying the theory, attempts would be made to develop a new scientific theory which was free from falsification. The new theory would itself be falsifiable, so the process of attempting to falsify the accepted theory would start again. By using the criterion of falsifiability, Popper avoided one of the main problems created by the use of the 'inductive method' in science.

His major works in English include: *The Open Society and its Enemies* (1945); *The Poverty of Historicism* (1957); *The Logic of Scientific Discovery* (1959); *Conjectures and Refutations: The Growth of Scientific Knowledge* (1962); *Objective Knowledge: An Evolutionary Approach* (1972); *The Self and Its Brain: An Argument for Interactionism* (with J. C. Eccles) (1977). [P]

Quine, W. V.: (1908–2000) An American logician and philosopher. He was an 'empiricist' but not a 'positivist'. He argued that concepts gained their meanings within a network or web of interconnected concepts. According to Quine, single sentences could not be said to have a meaning outwith the context of the interconnected network of concepts. This led to three results: firstly, no part of the network was immune to revision in the light of experience; secondly, no set of experiences could refute only part of a theory; and thirdly, a sentence could be thought of as meaning a large array of different things. Quine encapsulated this last result in a phrase for which he became famous: the 'indeterminacy of radical translation'. Roughly speaking, this meant that a sentence could always have meanings other than the one which it was given at a particular time – it was possible that it could mean something else.

The idea of an interconnected network of concepts led Quine to formulate another notion for which he became famous – 'ontological commitment'. In accepting a given interconnected network of concepts, we commit ourselves to accepting that reality consists of certain types of things; in other words, we commit ourselves to a particular ontology. [P]

Reid, Thomas: (1710–99) The founder of the Scottish 'School of the Philosophy of Common Sense'. In his first major book (1764) he offered a powerful critique of David Hume's theory of perception. His later books (1785) and (1788) set out, in reasonably simple and accessible language, many of the epistemological considerations that were later to appear in twentieth-century 'Continental' philosophy. [P]

Sartre, Jean-Paul: (1905–80) A French philosopher, novelist and political theorist who, along with his life-long companion Simone de Beauvoir, was the first to be described as an 'existentialist'. He brought together two strands of philosophical thought: the phenomenology of Franz Brentano and Edmund Husserl and the freedom and subjectivity found in the work of Søren Kierkegaard. He elaborated Kierkegaard's idea of freedom and the individual's independence over any system as well as Brentano's and Husserl's notion that consciousness involved intentionality, thus he developed a concept of individuals who create themselves as conscious beings through their own free actions. It was in these freely chosen actions that ultimate moral value (*Summum Bonum*) was to be found. According to Sartre, freedom was to be found in an individual's conscious act of distinguishing between herself as a subject of consciousness and everything else which was not that subject – thus establishing a distinction between the self and 'the other', with 'the other' complementing the existence of the self. The complementary nature of the relationship between the self and 'the other' meant that the freedom of the indivdual could only be sustained through the promotion of the freedom of 'the other'. This meant that the context in which an individual found herself conditioned, but did not determine, the individual's freedom. In contrast with de Beauvoir, Sartre focused on the negative aspect of the complementary relationship: a failure to recognise the freedom of 'the other' left the individual isolated and alienated from her true self as a free agent.

Sartre's political activity was closely related to the promotion of the freedom of all individuals; he embraced Marxist politics and reacted strongly to the oppressive regimes which emerged in Europe in the middle part of the twentieth century. This led him to write his major philosophical work, *Critique de la raison dialectique* (Critique of Dialectical Reason) (1960), which attempted to reconcile the principles of Marxism and existentialism. [PT] [S]

Socrates: (c. 470 BC–399 BC) A Greek philosopher and Plato's teacher. There is no written record of his philosophy and much of what we know about his ideas comes from the *Platonic Dialogues* in which Socrates is usually the main protagonist. It was probably he who developed the platonic 'Theory of Forms'.

Shaftesbury, Anthony: (1671–1713) An English philosopher who was one of John Locke's pupils. He is remembered for his theory that humans have a moral sense which detects moral goodness in a manner similar to way the eye detects colour and ear detects sound.

Thales of Miletus: (c. 620 BC–546 BC) The first known philosopher of the 'Milesian School'. He believed that the cosmos consisted of an infinite, eternal, ageless 'primary substance' that continually changed form. He claimed that the 'primary substance' was water. [S]

Glossary of Terms

Aesthetics: The branch of modern philosophy which inquires into the nature of beauty and art, and into theories about beauty and art. The term was first used in this sense by Alexander Baumgarten.

Analysis: The process by which we break down a complex thing into its simple elements.

Analytic philosophy: This is the type of philosophy in which the process of analysis is seen as determining the acceptability of any claim. It focuses on the analysis of concepts and language and it reached its zenith in the analytic philosophy of the second half of the twentieth century. In the English-speaking world analytic philosophy is often contrasted with Continental philosophy. European philosophers, labelled as 'Continental' by the analytic philosophers, do not draw a distinction between different types of philosophical tradition.

Analytic proposition: A proposition whose truth is determined by considering the meanings of the terms contained in it. For example, the truth of 'All circlers are round' can be determined by examining the meanings of the terms 'circle' and 'round'.

Apodosis: The concluding clause in a sentence following a protasis (conditional introductory clause). For example, 'If he is hungry, feed him.'

A posteriori: A Latin term for that which comes after. It is used to categorise specifically the knowledge of the truth of a claim, statement or argument that is attained as a result of experience. The term is also applied to an idea or a concept.

A priori: A Latin term for that which comes before. It is used to categorise specifically the knowledge of the truth of a claim, statement or argument that is attained independently of experience. The term is also applied to an idea or a concept.

Arguments, types of:
1. *Reductio ad absurdum*: An argument that sets out to prove that a claim is false by assuming that it is true, and then by proceeding to show that this assumption leads us to an absurd conclusion. Any claim which leads to an absurd conclusion must be false.
2. Inductive: An argument which uses the' inductive method in science' to show that a claim is true.
3. Transcendental: An argument which uses a 'transcendental proof' to show that a claim is true. See **Transcendental proof**.

Arguments, validity and acceptability: An argument is 'valid' if it obeys all of the laws of logic. An argument is 'invalid' if it goes against the laws of logic. It is possible either to accept an invalid argument or to refuse to accept a valid argument: in either case this will involve one in a logical contradiction.

A valid argument is not always an 'acceptable' argument. If a valid argument is based on premises which are false then the conclusions will not be acceptable – they could be either true or false.

An argument is 'acceptable' if it is both valid and if all its premises and reasoning can be accepted as reasonably likely to be true. If a valid argument is based on premises which are reasonably likely to be true then the conclusions will also be reasonably likely to be true. A valid argument transmits the acceptability of the premises to the conclusions.

Association of ideas: The term used by David Hume to describe the principle used to develop explanations of the behaviour of human beings as well as physical objects.

Consequentialist: The term used to describe those qualities of an action relating to events which result from the action. See **Consequentialism**.

Consequentialism: A term referring to those moral theories which claim that we decide on whether actions are good, bad, right or wrong by assessing the results produced by the actions. There are two types of consequentialism in theories about morality: one assesses the results of **each individual** action and the other assesses the results of **classes** of actions. See **Act Utilitarianism** and **Rule Utilitarianism**.

Continental philosophy: A term used in the English-speaking world to contrast the 'analytic' tradition in philosophy with the one predominant in continental Europe. The analytic tradition emphasises the analysis of the concepts used in philosophy, whereas Continental philosophy emphasises the analysis of the assumptions underlying human activities. Continental philosophy has three main strands to it: 'existentialism', 'structuralism', and 'critical theory'. Each one of these assumes that all forms of explanation, description and analysis are value-laden. This contrasts with the presumption by the analytic philosophers that their activities are, or can be, free from values.

Cosmology: In ancient Greece this was the study of the cosmos. Liddell and Scott (1863) give four definitions of the word 'cosmos'. The first is 'order, in order, duly' while the fourth is 'the world or universe, from its perfect arrangement'. The term is now used to mean the study of, or theory of, the universe as an ordered whole.

Efficient Cause: See **Aristotle**

Deontology: The branch of knowledge which is concerned with moral obligations or duty.

Dualism: See **Descartes**.

Egoism: See **Ethical egoism**.

Empiricism: There is more than one meaning of the term 'empiricism'. The different meanings often lead to confusion, but in all cases the meaning is linked to experience.

There are two broad categories of meaning:

1. Empiricism can be the adherence to the principle that experience is the only way to obtain either a valid or an acceptable understanding of the world. Interacting with the world in a laboratory is the best way to obtain such an understanding. In this case empiricism is a practice, a method or a methodology.

2. Empiricism can be the adherence to the principle that experience using the senses provides us with 'the only true building blocks of knowledge'. In this case empiricism is a doctrine or principle which specifies the source of all, or part of, our knowledge. Other sources such as religious revelation or even the faculty of reason are rejected as sources of knowledge – at best, reason can work on the data provided by the senses, but it cannot furnish us with new building blocks.

This is distinguished from 'empiricist practice', which is a procedure rather than an adherence to a principle. It involves the idea that learning is often best achieved through participating in activities.

(It is interesting to note that German has two distinct words for our word 'experience': *Erfahrung*, which represents a bank of experience, and *Erlebnis*, which represents the current experience of an individual.)

Empirical: This can be used as an adjective for the philosophical term 'empiricism'. It can also refer to a method or approach to problem solving and learning. Where the use of direct experience is the force which drives problem solving and/or learning, we say that the method is 'empirical'.

Epistemology: The branch of modern philosophy which inquires into the nature and scope of knowledge and into the reliability of claims to knowledge.

Essentialism: A term referring to those theories which explain the behaviour of an object on the basis of its 'essence' (essential property). Three essentialist theories portray the essence of things in different ways.

1. The 'Aristotelian theory' portrayed the essence of something as being an integral part of an object existing independently of any concept of it – the task of the philosopher was to discover what this essence was in order to understand the behaviour of the object. This is the type of theory which modern natural science uses.

2. A second form of essentialist theory rejects the Aristotelian notion that an essence exists in an object independently of how we define it. According to this theory, our definitions determine the essential characteristics needed for something to be what it is. A human being is a rational animal by virtue of the definition of the term 'human' and not necessarily because of some natural characteristics humans possess. This version of essentialism has close links with 'nominalism'.

3. The third theory of essentialism, the Platonic 'Theory of Forms', is the oldest. According to Plato the essence of a thing was to be found in its abstract qualities which existed independently of that specific thing. This abstract, independently-existing real 'form', or 'idea', was what gave a specific object (or action) its essential qualities. Plato elaborated this theory in his books *The Republic* and *The Phaedo*. An 'idea', or 'form', endowed an object (or action) with a particular quality. For example, the 'form' of circularity endowed a particular circle with its essential characteristic of being circular and the 'form' of goodness endowed a particular act of charity with its essential characteristic of being good. [See Exercise 8.3 p. 106 and **Plato**]

Essentialist: The term used to describe those qualities of an action relating to nature of the action and are independent of any resulting effects. See **Consequentialist**.

Ethical egoism: The theory which regards self-interest as the foundation of morality. It operates according to the principle that a moral agent's actions are right in proportion as they tend to promote the happiness of the agent; wrong as they tend to promote her or his unhappiness.

Ethics (moral philosophy): The branch of philosophy which inquires into the nature of theories about good and evil and into the nature of the duties and responsibilities of human beings.

Existence of God – proofs:

1. Ontological argument: A proof which starts with a concept of a perfect being or of perfection, and deduces the existence of a perfect being.

2. Teleological argument: A proof which starts with the experience of an ordered and purposeful universe and deduces that there has to be a designer who gave the universe its order and purpose (*telos*).

3. Cosmological argument: A proof which starts with the experience of causation in the universe and deduces the existence of a being which sustains the causation.

Existentialism: 'A doctrine that concentrates on the individual, who, being free and responsible, is held to be what he makes himself by the self development of his essence through acts of the will.' (*OED*) The four key themes of existentialism are: the individual and systems; being and absurdity; the nature of communication; and the nature and significance of choice.

Explanatory richness: A criterion for assessing the relative merits of explanations or theories. It generally employs two methods: firstly it asks which theory gives the most extensive and convincing explanation of the phenomena in its domain; secondly, it compares the ability of the rival theories to increase the understanding of aspects of the human condition which lie outside their domains.

Extrinsic property: A property a thing has which is dependent upon its relations with other things.

Falsifiability: A term coined by Karl Popper as a criterion which distinguishes scientific theories from those found in 'non-science'. A theory is falsifiable if it is possible to refute it.

Final cause: See **Aristotle**.

Formal cause: See **Aristotle**.

Fundamental entity: A term referring to something whose existence cannot be determined by referring to other entities. See **Primary substance**.

Idea: In everyday language, we use the word 'idea' to refer to either the subjective content of consciousness or even to an objective notion: for example, the ideas that guide the government are libertarian. In philosophy the word has been given several rather technical meanings; of the nine listed below, those associated with Plato and Descartes are the most widely discussed.

1. Plato (and Socrates): Ideas are **objective** timeless essences that endow particular things with their properties. The ideas enable us to explain why things possess their qualities.
2. Descartes identified ideas with **subjective**, logical concepts of the human mind. Locke also considered them to be subjective, and identified them with all objects of consciousness.
3. Berkeley: sense objects or perceptions, a type of mind-dependent being.
4. Pre-Platonic Greek: a form, semblance, nature, fashion, mode, class or species.
5. The Stoics: class concepts in the human mind.
6. Scholasticism: archetypes eternally subsistent in the mind of God.
7. Hume: a 'feint' memory copy of a sense 'impression'.
8. Kant: concepts or representations which are incapable of being adequately subsumed under the categories. They escape the limits of cognition.
9. Hegel: the 'Idea', or the 'Absolute', is the absolute truth of which all phenomenal existence is an expression.

Induction: See **Inductive method in science**. Induction in science is contrasted with **Mathematical induction**, which is a method for developing formal proofs of formulae that are valid for all natural numbers.

Inductive method in science: A method for discovering truth, proposed by Francis Bacon, based on the observation of events, the analysis of the observed data, and the development of a rule which links the observed data. The rule is then verified by repeated observations. Experiments provide the ideal setting for making the observations. A scientist using the inductive method in science would attempt to differentiate what is essential from what is not essential and try to discover the 'formal cause' of what is being investigated. This would be done by comparing particular observations, studying any variations between them and accounting for any negative instances. According to the inductive method, results can never be definitive – they can never rigorously establish the truth of a rule. The possibility that some negative instance may come along to refute the rule always exists.

Francis Bacon was trained as a lawyer in England. The inductive method has many features in common with English law, which relies more on precedent rather than principle for its criteria for the application of a specific law.

Inner sense experience, the primacy of: See **Primacy of inner sense experience, theory of**.

Intentionality Thesis: Franz Brentano's hypothesis that every mental event, be it a perception, thought or judgement, is intentionally directed towards some object.

Inter-subjective values: See **Values**.

Intrinsic property: A property which a thing has which is independent of its relations with other things.

'Justice' in ancient Greece: Francis Cornford (1941), in his translation of *The Republic* writes:

> The Greek word for 'just' has as many senses as the English 'right'. It can mean: observant of custom, righteous; fair, honest; legally right, lawful; what is due to or from a person, deserts, rights; what one ought to do. Thus it covers the whole field of the individual's conduct in so far as it affects others – all that they have a 'right' to expect from him or he has a right to expect from them, whatever is right as opposed to wrong. A proverbial saying declared that **justice is the sum of all virtue** (p. 1 – emphasis added).

The breadth of the meaning is also reflected in the fact that it was used by Anaximander to describe the behaviour of the 'primary substance' in maintaining harmony between all the substances.

Mathematical induction: A form of reasoning developing a proof of a mathematical theorem which uses formulae for numbers, and holds true for all natural numbers – for example, the theorem that if we square an odd number and then subtract one, we always get a multiple of eight. In the proof we start by showing that the formula is true for the number one. We then assume that it is true for a general number, say n, and we then show that the formula is also true for 'the number one greater than n'. These three steps allow us to conclude that the formula is true for n equals one, two, three and so on. Mathematical induction provides us with a very different form of reasoning from Francis Bacon's principle of induction.

Material cause: See **Aristotle**

Metaphysics (See Chapter 6) The field of study in which we make a link between how we see the world and what we believe exists in the world or beyond it. The *Shorter Oxford English Dictionary* definition 1 states that metaphysics is: 'that branch of **speculation** which deals with the first principles of things, including such concepts as being, substance, essence time, space, cause, identity, etc.' (emphasis added).

Milesian school: Term often given to a group of philosophers who lived in Miletus from the seventh to the fifth centuries BC. The first notable member of the school was Thales who was followed by Anaximander and Anaximenes.

Natural kind: A class of entities whose members have a common characteristic that differentiates them from non-members and whose properties are independent of cognitive interactions between individuals.

Naturalistic fallacy: A term coined by G.E. Moore to denote a logical fallacy made by any theory which claimed that goodness was a natural quality or phenomenon. Moore argued that if the answer 'Yes' to the question, 'Is X good?' needs to be justified, then X must be good because of something other than X. He said that, because the answer to the question 'Is X good?' always needs to be justified when X is a natural object or phenomenon, goodness must be something other than a natural object or phenomenon.

Nominalism: The term used in scholastic philosophy of the Middle Ages for the theory claiming that 'universals' had no objective existence and were merely names which had sense but did not refer to anything. See **Essentialism 2**

Normal science: A term coined by Thomas Kuhn denoting 'past scientific achievements that some particular scientific community acknowledges for a time as supplying the foundation for its further practice'.

Objective values: See **Values**.

Ockham's razor: A term referring to William of Ockham's principle that 'Entities are not to be multiplied without necessity'.

This is an 'ontological' principle that deals with what we claim to exist. Ockham suggested that, in our explanations, the things we imagine to exist should be kept to an absolute minimum. For example, we might postulate the existence of three things, object A, object B, and object C to explain something that we see. If the explanation still makes sense without reference to object C, then we should discard our supposition that object C exists. Ockham used this principle to argue against Plato's 'Theory of Forms' by claiming that, in order to explain why things are circular, we do not need to suggest that the 'idea', or 'form', of circularity exists independently of us and of circular things.

Ontological commitment: A belief in the existence of something, that an individual is obliged to hold due to his behaviour. If a person's behaviour cannot be intelligible without an assumption that some 'thing', let us call it X, exists, then the person is said to have made an implicit ontological commitment to the existence of X. For example, a person's use of a particle accelerator implicitly commits that person to accepting that a particular type of elementary particle exists, and a person's use of a money order implicitly commits that person to the belief that a banking system exists. See **Quine, W. V.**

Ontology: (See Part II) The branch of philosophy which inquires into the nature of what exists.

Paradigm: A term used by Thomas Kuhn to refer to 'an achievement – a collection of shared beliefs held by a group of scientists about what the basic problems and methods of scientific inquiry are'.

Particular: A term used to denote a specific thing and so can be applied to only one thing. This contrasts with a 'universal', which is a term that is used to denote an idea which can be applied throughout the universe. See **Universal**.

Phenomenology: In the eighteenth century it was used to denote the theory of appearances which form the basis of empirical knowledge. Edmund Husserl redefined it as the study of what makes psychology possible. It is now considered to be the attempt to describe our experiences directly without reference to causal explanations.

Philosophy:

1. The meaning of the ancient Greek word φιλοσοφια (*philosophia*) was: 'the love, study, or pursuit of wisdom, or knowledge of things and their causes, whether theoretical or practical'.
2. From this original definition we derive the everyday notion of 'a philosophy'. It is: 'the system which a person forms for the conduct of his or her life', that is, a system of beliefs.

   The modern definition of 'philosophy', as an academic activity, takes a slightly different form from that of the original Greek. This definition dates from the early part of the eighteenth century, and is given in the *OED* in the following two forms:
3. 'the study of the general principles of some particular branch of knowledge, experience or activity.'
4. 'that department of knowledge or study which deals with ultimate reality, or with the most general causes and principles of things.'

   Definitions (3) and (4) ignore the modern tendency in philosophy to **assess** principles as well as **study** them – definition (5) reflects it.
5. Finding and assessing the principles which sustain and govern the explanations of the phenomena we experience.

Philosophy of science: The branch of modern philosophy which inquires into the nature of explanations of natural phenomena, that is of the theories produced by natural scientists.

Philosophy of the social sciences: The branch of modern philosophy which inquires into the nature of explanations of social phenomena, that is of the theories produced by social scientists.

Platonic 'Theory of Forms' (or '**Ideas**'): See **Essentialism** 3.

Positivism: The name given to the view that every rationally justifiable assertion can be verified scientifically or proved using logic.

Practical reason: A human faculty which both establishes which aims are morally valuable for individuals to pursue and ascertains what means must be used in order to attain these aims.

Premise: A previous statement from which a conclusion is drawn. For example, 'All men are mortal' and 'Socrates is a man' are both premises which lead to the conclusion 'Socrates is mortal'.

Primary substance: (in Greek philosophy) The basic matter which manifests itself in different forms to produce all existing things.

Primacy of inner sense experience, theory of: A term coined in this book to describe the philosophical position which takes inner sense experience as the fundamental starting point of philosophical analysis.

Protasis: The introductory clause in a sentence expressing a condition which leads to an 'apodosis' (conclusion). For example, '**If he is hungry**, feed him.'

Rationalism: The adherence to the principle that the use of reason, rather than experience, provides the only way to obtain truth and knowledge.

Rationalist values: See **Values**.

Reductio ad absurdum: See **Arguments, types of**:

Reductionism: The term used to describe a claim that explanations of all phenomena in one subject can be provided by the explanations given in another subject. For example, the claim that all psychological phenomena can be explained by the operations of physical entities is a reductionist claim.

Scepticism: A term referring to an approach to philosophy which maintains that every claim to knowledge of matters of fact, except perhaps what is directly presented to us by our senses, is open to doubt. See David Hume (p. 378).

Scientific revolution: A term coined by Thomas Kuhn to denote 'the tradition-shattering complements to the tradition-bound activity of **normal science**' (emphasis added).

Signification: The designation of meaning, focusing on the qualities or properties of a concept as it is perceived in consciousness, rather than meaning seen in terms of the things which fall under the concept.

Social construct: Definitions of 'social construct' do not appear in dictionaries of sociology, yet it is an often-quoted expression, especially with reference to 'gender'. The Department of Fine Arts, Okanagan University College offers a definition of the term 'construct': 'CONSTRUCT Fashionable term indicating something constructed by mental effort or, more particularly, through political and social mechanisms.' (http://www.ouc.bc.ca/fina/glossary/c_list.html#construct)

Social kind: A class of entities whose members have a common characteristic that differentiates them from non-members and whose properties are manifested through cognitive interactions between individuals. See **Natural Kind**.

Subjective values: See **Values**.

Subsidiary substance: (in Greek philosophy) A substance whose nature is subordinate to, or determined by, the nature of the 'primary substance'. See **Primary substance**.

Substance: A thing that exists by itself, a separate or distinct thing. It has also been used to denote the stuff which underlies phenomena which change, but does not itself change. See **Primary substance**.

Summum Bonum (**Supreme Good**): The intrinsically good thing which is the ultimate goal of human action, conduct or behaviour. Different philosophers have considered it to be different things: according to Aristotle it was happiness; according to Kant, virtue; according to J.S. Mill, pleasure and the absence of pain; according to Sartre, freedom; while others have variously considered it to be the will of God, self-realisation, power, and even obedience.

Synthesis: The process by which we construct a complex thing from its simple elements (the opposite of 'analysis'). See **Analysis**.

Synthetic proposition: A proposition whose truth cannot be determined solely by considering the meanings of the terms contained in it. For example, the truth of 'It was raining yesterday' cannot be determined by examining the meanings of the terms 'raining' and yesterday'. See **Analytic proposition**.

Teleological theory of ethics: A theory which interprets an action as being right if its aim is the achievement of something which is valued, such as human happiness, virtue, pleasure or freedom.

Teleological theory of value: A theory which claims that value is to be found in the aims of an action, a person or even of a biological organism.

Teleology: The study of purposiveness. The original Greek τελος (*telos*) meant 'an end accomplished: the fulfilment or accomplishment of any thing' (Liddell and Scott, 1863).

Transcendental proof: A proof showing that what is proved is a necessary condition without which something else would not be possible or intelligible. It is most closely associated with Immanuel Kant. For example, Kant argued that the existence of Euclidean physical space was a condition without which human experience would be impossible – thus 'proving' the existence of Euclidean physical space.

Universal: A term that is used to denote an idea which can be applied throughout the universe. This contrasts with a 'particular', which is a term that is used to denote a specific thing and so can only be applied to that one thing. See **Particular**.

Unconscious mental processes: A term used by Sigmund Freud to identify mental processes which are not conscious but can be brought into consciousness: a 'conscious mental process' is one of which an individual is immediately aware; a 'preconscious mental process' is one which can become conscious without the individual's activity; and an unconscious mental process is one which can be made conscious as a result of the individual's efforts.

Utilitarianism: A term referring to the moral theory which claims that we decide whether an action is good, bad, right or wrong by considering the happiness produced by the action.

1. Act utilitarianism: A type of moral theory which claims that the goodness of each action depends upon the happiness generated by that particular action.
2. Rule utilitarianism: A type of moral theory which claims that the goodness of an action depends upon the results of the following of a general rule: where following the rule leads to the maximisation of the total happiness of all people, the rule is morally good; a good action is one which obeys a morally good rule. See **Ethical egoism**.

Value: This is the status of an object, event or process, or the esteem in which it is held, according to its worth, usefulness, or importance.

1. Extrinsic value: The value something has solely on account of its association with something else.
2. Intrinsic value: The value something has on account of its very nature, independently of its association with anything else.

Values: The principles or standards of a person or group of people.

1. Inter-subjective values: The principles or standards of behaviour of a group of people based upon standards set by criteria of mutual acceptability of the individuals in the group.
2. Objective values: The principles or standards of behaviour of an individual or group of individuals based upon standards set by criteria which are independent of the cognitive experiences of any one individual.
3. Rationalist values: The principles or standards of behaviour of a cognitive individual or a group of cognitive individuals based upon standards conforming to the rules set by their 'practical reason'. See **Practical reason**.
4. Subjective values: The principles or standards of behaviour of an individual based upon standards set by criteria which are dependent upon the cognitive experiences of the individual.

Virtues (the four cardinal): In *The Laws* (Bk. I, p. 631), Plato lists the four Greek virtues: '**Wisdom** is the chief and leader; next follows **temperance**; and from the union of these two with **courage** springs **justice**. These four virtues take precedence in the class of divine goods' (emphasis added).

Index